MW00830972

How BRITAIN Underdeveloped the CARIBBEAN

How BRITAIN Underdeveloped the CARIBBEAN

A Reparation Response to Europe's
Legacy of Plunder and Poverty

Hilary McD. Beckles

The University of the West Indies Press
Jamaica • Barbados • Trinidad and Tobago

The University of the West Indies Press
7A Gibraltar Hall Road, Mona
Kingston 7, Jamaica
www.uwipress.com

© 2021 by Hilary McD. Beckles
All rights reserved. Published 2021
A catalogue record of this book is available from
the National Library of Jamaica.

ISBN: 978-976-640-869-5 (print)
978-976-640-871-8 (ePub)

Cover concept by Hilary McD. Beckles; design by Cj Bonadie and Robert Harris.
Book design by Robert Harris
Set in Adobe Garamond Pro 11/14.5 x 24

The University of the West Indies Press has no responsibility for the persistence or
accuracy of URLs for external or third-party Internet websites referred to in this
publication and does not guarantee that any content on such websites is, or will
remain, accurate or appropriate.

Printed in the United States of America

For Tajani Rodney Beckles, my grandson

To the people, prime minister (Mia Mottley) and
Government of Barbados, for raising the republic

Contents

Acknowledgements

MANY SOURCES OF ENERGY GAVE LIFE TO THIS BOOK: three decades of researching, debating, and teaching Caribbean economic history at the University of the West Indies; brief but impactful discursive sessions with the late Walter Rodney, who encouraged the concept; and a lifetime of commitment to the global reparation movement.

My participation in UNESCO's Slave Route Project and its General History of Africa series, as vice president and co-editor respectively, facilitated opportunities for frequent conversations with many colleagues known and respected for their expertise in Atlantic economic history. These projects represented ongoing learning fora in which my understanding of underdevelopment was simultaneously focused and deepened.

As a member of UN Secretary-General Ban Ki-moon's Scientific Advisory Board on Sustainable Development, I came to appreciate more profoundly the structural and dialectical relationships between extractive colonization and its legacy of persistent poverty. I wish to thank all colleagues who engaged my initial perceptions of this process and facilitated its conceptual clarification.

At the University of the West Indies, I benefited from countless conversations with colleagues, some of the finest scholars, who defined regional research agendas and global perspectives on the practice and legacy of European extractive colonialism. I wish to mention in particular Sir Arthur Lewis, George Beckford, Norman Girvan, Douglas Hall, C.Y. Thomas, Compton Bourne, Lloyd Best, Mark Figueroa, Elsie Le Franc, Trevor Farrell and Winston Dookeran. They provided sound and compelling Caribbean perspectives, building upon the seminal work of Eric Williams and C.L.R. James in the field of capitalism and the globalization of slavery.

Finally, I thank my assistants Camileta Neblett, Shakira Maxwell, Marvette Thompson and Kimberly Maxam for their support in preparing early drafts of the manuscript. For two decades, Grace Jutan, my executive assistant, has been my committed manuscript curator, taking responsibility for delivering final pages to publishers. The debt I owe her cannot be repaid.

My wife, Mary, was encouraging and supportive, facilitating writing in a crippling Covid-19 environment, within which I often functioned in an antisocial manner. I am grateful for her generosity. Many other people, too numerous to mention here, supported my research and writing in multiple ways. I alone am responsible for any shortcomings identified. I thank you all most sincerely.

Origins of Caribbean Underdevelopment

We carry a grave responsibility for a colonial policy based on cheap labour and cheap raw materials. The facts are out, and we can no longer plead ignorance and indifference. Of course, there has been official irresponsibility and the dominance of narrow calculating colonial interests. We can point to years of criminal neglect when official ineptitude and sloth have permitted affairs to drift and the islands to sink into unpardonable misery. Now a point has been reached when action is desperately urgent and British concern must be *paid in hard cash*. The hopeless squalor of today is in a real way the measure of the shortcomings of our colonial policy and of our economic neglect.

—A. Creech Jones, member of Parliament, Colonial Office Advisory Committee on Education, 5 April 1939 (emphasis added)

While we may deride the claim that Britain owes a debt to the West Indies for the fortunes taken out of them in the plantation days, the fact remains that until quite recently nothing was done to put money back into these islands in order to expand their economy, and that the effects of this neglect are now being felt.

—Sir S.E. Luke, assistant undersecretary of state with superintending responsibility for the West Indies, CO 1031/760, minute on no. 8 and no. 9, January 1952

THE MODERN CARIBBEAN ECONOMY WAS INVENTED, structured and managed by European states for one purpose: to achieve maximum wealth extraction to fuel and sustain their national financial, commercial and industrial transformation. Therefore, for each European state, the Caribbean economy was primarily an external economic engine propelling and promoting national economic growth.

No other large and lucrative colonized economy in the five-hundred-year history of Western economic development has ever been created for such a singular purpose. No such economy has ever been as intensively exploited as that of the Caribbean by imperial entrepreneurs and nation states. In every respect, the European creation and integration of the Caribbean economy into the Western financial and commercial system was intended for the former group's exclusive economic benefit. This objective overshadowed any other considerations.

The hegemonic economic objective of Europe called into being a new, immoral entrepreneurial order that defined the Caribbean colonized economy as a frontier beyond the accountability of civilization, where crimes against humanity became a cultural norm. That is, the Caribbean was converted by Europe into a criminal ecosystem with full political and legal sanctions. The "offshore" economic engine completely set aside the common standards and expectations of Europe's civic cosmos to accumulate wealth without cultural or ethical constraints.

This primary objective led to the invention and deployment of techniques and tools of labour exploitation, some of them long purged from European legal and business practices. These included the displacement and enslavement of conquered natives, chattel enslavement of imported "others", the use of uninhibited violence as the main method of labour control and management, and the legal definition of racially defined "others" as non-human, property and real estate.

Such legal techniques, economic technologies and social systems framed and defined Europe's Caribbean economy. They reactivated and enabled the institutionalization of piracy and plunder, genocide and slavery, violent hostility and hatred, and notions of black subhumanity. These were the driving forces in Europe's wealth extraction as it rose to economic dominance.

All European nations deployed these strategies as they participated in the opportunity for enrichment in the colonial Caribbean economy. The conquest, enslavement and genocide of the indigenous people, the trade in enslaved Africans, the chattel commercialization of the enslaved, the investment in diverse navigations industries, the promotion of domestic manufacturing from the extracted raw materials and other primary commodities, and the prestige associated with owning people and places combined to contribute to their success.

Spain initiated the Caribbean colonized economic system, followed immediately by England, Scotland, France, the Netherlands, Portugal, Norway, Sweden and Denmark. In the margins of the jealously guarded system were Russia, Germany and Switzerland. These European nations collectively managed the economic order as a commercial network, production institutions, and entrepreneurial culture and consciousness.

The Columbus Economy

It all began with Christopher Columbus's arrival in the Caribbean. By the time he was ready to sail across the Atlantic in 1492, Spain was prepared politically for establishing economic control over peoples, resources and lands in the Caribbean. Its earlier colonization of the Canary Islands was the critical first step. These islands were Spain's learning ground.

The gold-mining mania, which dominated Spain's colonization before the Canary Islands, was a prelude. When Columbus arrived in the Caribbean on 12 October 1492, it was already a wealth-extracting imperial nation. The Caribbean islands were merely places further west. He noted of the native Tainos: "They ought to make good servants, and they have lively minds, for I believe they immediately repeated what I said to them. I think it would be easy to convert them, as they do not seem to me to belong to any religion."[1]

Despite their spirited resistance to Spain's military might, the Tainos were defeated and forced to pay tribute. This was the beginning of the wealth extraction system that defined the region for four hundred years. The indigenous agricultural economy, which produced a surplus, could not support the Spanish. It soon collapsed. The same experience was repeated in each island. By 1500, Cuba and Hispaniola had been reduced to famine. Spain had imposed an economic regime on the Caribbean, and human destruction was its most obvious feature.[2]

At this stage, the Spanish thought that trade in enslaved Tainos could reap greater rewards. They saw how the sale of enslaved Africans in Europe by Portugal had brought wealth to that nation. There was an attempt in the winter of 1545 to sponsor a trade in enslaved people from the region. On 24 February, a fleet of ships took a cargo of some six hundred enchained Tainos for sale in Spain. Between the mid-Atlantic and Cadiz, half died. The experiment was not repeated. By the end of the sixteenth century, the indigenous population of the northern Caribbean had been decimated: the genocide was complete. Their numbers were reduced from over one million in 1492 to a few thousand

---

1. F.R. Augier, S.C. Gordon, D.G. Hall and M. Reckord, *The Making of the West Indies* (London: Longman, 1960), 3.

2. C.H. Haring, *The Spanish Empire in America* (New York: Oxford University Press, 1947), 3–23.

in 1548, by 1560, there were fewer than five hundred indigenous people, and by 1600 there were not enough left to form a small village.

The sugar cane industry replaced mining by the mid-sixteenth century as the dominant economic activity. Columbus had introduced the sugar cane from the Canaries on his second voyage to the region. Hispaniola was the first centre of the Caribbean sugar industry; the first sugar mill had been set up there in 1516. Tobacco was also grown for export. In a short time it dominated the European market, and to this day, it is still rated among the best in the world.

During the 1520s and 1530s, the Roman Catholic Church, in support of the economic interest of colonists, proposed that enslaved African labour should be imported to shore up the economy. By 1540, some thirty thousand enslaved Africans had been imported into Hispaniola, and by the 1570s, they were being imported into the island at a rate of two thousand per year. By the end of the sixteenth century, the enslavement of Africans was a fully established institution. This was the beginning of the "sugar and black slavery" relationship that defined economic life in the Caribbean.[3]

The European Economic Engine

Spain was determined to have exclusive extracting rights to the Caribbean so that no other competing nation could tap its wealth. Other Europeans were not prepared to allow the Spanish exclusive rights to Caribbean wealth. From 1555 to about 1640, the British, French and Dutch launched a consistent attack upon the Spanish Caribbean economy. The earlier part of this period was dominated by pirates and buccaneers, but by organized merchant companies and competing states in the latter part. After the mid-seventeenth century, formal trade wars forced Spain to make considerable economic concessions. The Dutch, French and British formed military alliances against the Spanish.

But between the British capture of Jamaica in 1655 and the Seven Years' War from 1756, the four nations fought each other for economic dominance. War and trade went together. European nations jostled each other for advantage in the Caribbean economy. By the end of the eighteenth century, France had lost

---

3. Augier et al., *Making*, 15–26; R. Davis, *The Rise of the Atlantic Economies* (London: Weidenfield and Nicholson, 1973), 37–56; Eric Williams, *From Columbus to Castro: The History of the Caribbean, 1492–1969* (London: Andre Deutsch, 1970), 23–30, 46–58.

St Domingue (Haiti) – the largest slave-based colony – while Spain receded to the margins, leaving the British as the most successful wealth extractors in the Caribbean.

With the proliferation of French and English settlements in the Lesser Antilles and the rise of the Dutch trading network, the Caribbean economy assumed a new level of importance in the world economy. Sugar was the new gold, and it meant more enslaved Africans. By 1650, Barbados had only 5,680 enslaved people. In 1700, it had 42,000. Jamaica followed Barbados into "sugar and slavery". In 1656, the island had only 1,410 enslaved Africans, but in 1698 there were over 41,000.

Each European government wanted the full economic benefits of its exclusive trading rights with its colonies. They devised complicated commercial systems to ensure their economic monopoly. This trade structure became known as the mercantile system. Its principles and provisions were designed to maximize wealth extraction and produce revenue streams to fund national economic development. Its features were as follows:

1. Goods could only be imported into or exported from a colony in ships belonging to its metropole.
2. The export trade from a colony was confined to its metropolitan market.
3. The goods of the metropole obtained a monopoly of its colonial market.
4. Colonial goods received preferential treatment on their metropolitan market.
5. The colony could not establish any manufacturing industry to compete with the industries of its metropole.

This was the mercantilism that entrapped and exploited the Caribbean for four hundred years.

Without an active trade in enslaved people, the Caribbean economy would not have been as profitable as it was. During the eighteenth century, Europeans fought each other for the right and privilege of shipping enslaved Africans to the Caribbean. They fought on the West African coast and in the Caribbean. In 1763 the British occupied Spanish Havana for ten months. The interaction between English merchants and Cuban sugar and tobacco planters had a transformative impact on the Caribbean economy. The Spanish government observed this development and, over the second half of the century, used Cuba as a testing ground for restructuring its Caribbean economic policy. In the ten months of the occupation, over ten thousand enslaved Africans were imported. Between

1520 and 1760, no more than sixty thousand had been sold. Between 1760 and 1820, some four hundred thousand were imported, and Havana became one of the most active slave-trading ports in the Caribbean.

Spain did not have the capital to finance the colony's economic expansion. The English were invited to invest. Sugar production rose from a mere 2,000 tons per year in the 1740s to over 10,000 tons per year in the 1770s. In 1789, Havana and Santiago were declared free ports open to all European merchants. Similar arrangements were made in Puerto Rico and Santo Domingo, with expansive results. Havana became the boomtown of the Caribbean. The economic revolution in Cuba and Puerto Rico had begun. By the 1840s, Cuba was the largest supplier of cane sugar in the world – signalling the total triumph of European extractive capitalism in the Caribbean.[4]

The Caribbean in Western Globalization

The strategy of creating an external economy as a zone of exploitation was common to imperial nations, "but in the case of the Caribbean", noted David Eltis, "the economic motive seems particularly stark". It was imagined and developed for unrestrained, violent plunder and maximum wealth extraction. This, concluded Eltis, was the "economic system Europe imposed on the region".[5]

No part of the world economy in the seventeenth and eighteenth centuries generated as much wealth for Europe as the Caribbean. The economy was unique both in terms of its volume of capital accumulation and transfer of 80–90 per cent of its wealth to Europe. The 10–20 per cent wealth retention was intended to cover core functions such as sustaining the enslaved and promoting basic, rudimentary infrastructures and institutions such as roads and bridges, churches, domestic defence and political assemblies.

Mainland Europe was home to Caribbean-supported manufacturing. Hamburg, for example, emerged as a major sugar-refining and alcohol-distilling town, even though Germany possessed no sugar colonies in the Caribbean. The

---

4. Stuart Schwartz, ed., *Tropical Babylons: Sugar and the Making of the Atlantic World, 1450–1680* (Chapel Hill: University of North Carolina Press, 2004).

5. David Eltis, "The Slave Economies of the Caribbean: Structure, Performance, Evolution and Significance", in *General History of the Caribbean*, vol. 3, *The Slave Societies of the Caribbean*, ed. Franklin Knight (Paris: UNESCO, 1997), 105.

industrial benefits to Europe were extensive, while the Caribbean was stripped of backward and forward linkages in the economic supply chain.

Trading in enslaved Africans was the biggest business in the growing global economy, and its management was directly in the hands of Europeans. It was organized by large corporations and cartels and constituted a unique opportunity to accumulate massive returns on investment. Though there were high-risk factors, it was attractive to venture financiers and respected, established institutions. Banks and insurance companies, many well known today as high-street financiers and insurers, from London and Amsterdam to Paris and Geneva, drank from the well of slavery and replenished it from their super-profits.

Over five million enslaved Africans were sold by European traders into the Caribbean economy. The demand for enchained labour seemed insatiable. The British sold the majority, as Britain dominated sugar production in the seventeenth and eighteenth centuries. The British share of the trade in enslaved Africans was nearly 45 per cent. The Spanish accounted for 25 per cent, the French 20 per cent, and other traders, flying Dutch, Danish, Norwegian, Swedish, Russian and American flags, accounted for the remainder.

After the Civil War, in which slavery was abolished, the United States entered the Caribbean as a management part of the economy. The slave system of the mainland colonies and those in the Caribbean had been integrated commercially from the beginning. The slave-owning families considered themselves a business class, and the enslaved population could be traded between colonies within the plantation complex. This interaction had survived the War of Independence and was intensified in the aftermath of the Civil War.

American investors, empowered by national foreign policy, began the drive to annex, in an imperial fashion, significant segments of the northern Caribbean economy, particularly those with plantations and a legacy of slavery. Their enthusiasm for investing and owning the agricultural part of the Caribbean economy injected large sums of capital into the region.

The focus of American economic intervention was Cuba, followed by Haiti, and all Spanish-speaking parts of the region. There was an intense negotiation with Spain to purchase Cuba. The Dominican Republic, which had declared itself independent of Spain in 1821, was annexed by Haiti until 1844, and lobbied thereafter to become a part of the United States.

The British, meanwhile, who had abolished trading in enslaved people and slavery in their colonies, were actively investing in sugar plantations in Cuba –

the emerging heartland of the regional economy. In 1914, British investments in Cuba amounted to over £60 million. The Americans had investments of half of this amount. French and German business interests ran a close third.

The interface of imperial politics and economic interests led to the American invasion and occupation of the Dominican Republic in 1916, which lasted until 1924. Haiti was similarly occupied in 1915. Furthermore, in 1917 the Americans, pushing deeper into the Caribbean economy, bought the Virgin Islands from the retreating Danish for the paltry sum of US$25 million. During the decades leading up to these interventions, American investments in the Caribbean constituted the driving force in the sugar plantation sector.

It was the age of the corporate plantation. The American-led management and ownership came with the United Fruit Company, the region's first mega-corporation in the agricultural sector. Sugar production in Cuba, Puerto Rico and the Dominican Republic was reorganized and brought under the new corporate system. Alongside the United Fruit Company were the South Puerto Rico Sugar Company and the West Indies Sugar Corporation.

These companies invested heavily in railway networks that linked the plantation fields to ports, also enabling great production and productivity in the sugar factories. They also encouraged the concentration of power in the hands of corporate owners and their American political allies. Added to this powerful new linkage between capital and political power was the further expansion of the labour force, much of it made up of the formerly enslaved and landless peasants.

By 1930, the entire Caribbean economy, except for Haiti, was enveloped in labour exploitation associated with plantations and minimally paid gang workers. After four hundred years it could be said to have jumped from the European pan into the "American pot". Wealth extraction has remained the constant and most dynamic feature of the underdevelopment of the region.

Poverty stands unredressed as the most visible sign and enduring symbol of the economy, despite centuries of engagement with the global world order. It has been an experience of extraordinary exploitation by the richest and most developed economies of the Western market system. The European states taught the Americans the art of wealth extraction in the Caribbean, but they remain the principal producers of Caribbean poverty.

Toussaint L'Ouverture, who led the successful anti-slavery revolution that created the state of Haiti

Jean Jacques Dessalines, first ruler of independent Haiti

Thomas Buxton, British politician and anti-slavery leader

Adam Smith, British economist and critic of the dying slavery system

Thomas Clarkson, British anti-slavery leader

PART 1

British Emancipation as Wealth Extraction

Persistent Poverty

The British Legacy of Plunder

> Despite their colour, and aura of calypso, West Indians are a sophisticated western people, who take their standards from North America and Europe. The problems her leaders have to face are not so much those of absolute dire poverty (though there are certainly large patches of this especially in the small islands) but the economic and social expectations of a population long accustomed to semi-European standards and attitudes. The premature withdrawal of the United Kingdom aid will almost certainly make it impossible to retain the standards achieved with the help of our assistance, and the rate of development will certainly slacken. The present level of aid has indeed barely averted decline in some of the smaller islands, and their future would be in real hazard.
>
> —Colonial Office, note to Cabinet, 6 January 1960, CAB 134/1630, DP (60) 4

THE LABOUR MOVEMENT THAT SOUGHT TO end the British Empire in the West Indies, and to push for independence, was determined on the political front, but insufficiently insistent on the financial aspects. This exposed the vulnerability of the movement to the expected British backlash to its economic development agenda. The demand for development funding was effectively brushed aside by British governments.

Eric Williams, for example, reflecting on three hundred years of British economic exploitation of the region, stated at a gathering of students at the London School of Economics in November 1962: "The West Indies are in the position of an orange. The British have sucked it dry, and their sole concern today is that they should not slip and get damaged on the peel."[1] More than two decades earlier, in 1938, Alexander Bustamante, in a blunt exchange in

---

1. Cited in Colin Palmer, *Eric Williams and the Making of the Modern Caribbean* (Chapel Hill: University of North Carolina Press, 2009), 149.

Jamaica with members of the Moyne Commission, made a statement which more than any other rattled the commissioners:

> Mr Henderson: In answer to Lord Moyne you [Bustamante] said that you regarded Great Britain with this country [Jamaica] as a dumping ground for British goods? Dumping is rather a vague phrase. What do you mean?
>
> Mr Bustamante: I mean that they keep this country to dump their products and then we can starve.[2]

Comments such as these were often made and represented the acute West Indian political perspective on British colonial rule.

But at best such proclamations reflected a profound understanding in the region of the economics of underdevelopment. Williams and Bustamante went on to become the first prime ministers of Trinidad and Tobago and of Jamaica respectively, bringing with them a grasp of the colonial mess they had inherited and were expected to clean up in preparation for national economic development.

Williams's comment especially still resonates within the region as a starting point for a comprehensive discussion of underdevelopment. It was a discursive response to Britain's decision to punish the region for its 1930s revolt. Britain had refused to fund capital development as a contribution to nation-building. It took no official economic responsibility for what were described as the "slums of the empire". Williams's remark serves as a critical reminder to those who, in recent years, have promoted the self-blaming neoliberal notion that the region must take full responsibility for its persistent poverty.

It is not the intention here to designate the West Indian self-blaming discourse a travesty or to deny the empirical integrity of arguments from the other side. Rather, it is to draw attention to new official evidence from the imperial archive that supports conceptual conclusions drawn in decades of Caribbean scholarship. The three hundred years of Britain's wealth extraction referenced by Williams strengthens the evidentiary base of the case against Britain: that it did all it could to suppress regional economic development following the popular revolt in the 1930s, and thereby solidified relationships and institutions that kept the region poor and dependent.[3]

---

2. "Bustamante before the Royal Commission", *Daily Gleaner*, 17 November 1938, 18.

3. See Colin Palmer, ed., *The Legacy of Eric Williams: Caribbean Scholar and Statesman* (Kingston: University of the West Indies Press, 2015), 38–39.

The scholarly literature and recent archival documents support this proposition. They also show that the institutionalized system of poverty bred by colonialism can be identified in socio-economic measurements. Poverty, for example, can also be explained in terms of inflexible structures of social and racial resource differentiations and inequalities. This is the conceptual background to the argument made in the 2016 United Nations Development Programme's Caribbean Human Development Report, that "deep-seated" socio-economic factors account for economic underperformance in the region.[4]

The West Indian experience mirrors that found in the literature of Africa's postcolonial mobilization of Caribbean intellectual energy to promote and propel social change and economic transformation. Eurocentric doom-and-gloom opposition arguments were galvanized to destroy the continent's development. It was in this specific phase of Africa's eruption that Walter Rodney published the seminal book *How Europe Underdeveloped Africa*. It has since served as a manifesto for and clarion call to Africans to reject the neocolonial narrative of self-doubt.[5]

Rodney's book represents, furthermore, the backdrop to phase two of the global development discourse. It informs this text. I call for an end to intellectual timidity. I hope that as a discursive tool, this book will equally provide a reliable vehicle for the return journey to the progressive, anti-colonial side of the West Indian development narrative.

Pedagogically, I have straddled the disciplines of economic history, economics and political science that constitute the framework within which Caribbean economic development scholars – Arthur Lewis, Lloyd Best, Owen Jefferson, George Beckford, Compton Bourne, Elsie LeFranc, Michael Witter, Mark Figueroa, C.Y. Thomas and many others – have investigated the origins and operations of underdevelopment in the region.[6] Simultaneously, I have

4. UNDP, *Multidimensional Progress: Human Resilience beyond Income*, Caribbean Human Development Report (New York: UNDP, 2016), 25.

5. Walter Rodney, *How Europe Underdeveloped Africa* (1974; reprint, Baltimore: Black Classic Press, 2011), xi–xxiv.

6. George Beckford, *Persistent Poverty: Underdevelopment in Plantation Economies of the Third World* (Oxford: Oxford University Press, 1972); W. Arthur Lewis, "Economic Development with Unlimited Supplies of Labour", *Manchester School of Economic and Social Studies* 22, no. 2 (May 1954): 139–91; Lloyd Best, "Outlines of a Model of Pure Plantation Economy", *Social and Economic Studies* 17, no. 3 (September 1968): 283–326; William Demas, *Essays on Caribbean Integration and Development* (Kingston: Institute of Social and Economic

connected to global conversations in and beyond academia that map the transition from earlier UN millennium development thinking to current concerns around sustainable development goals.

The act of bringing forward the earlier views of Caribbean development scholars, as well as those of underdevelopment theorists such as Wallerstein, Prebisch, Amin and Frank, in order to interface with recent observations from Escobar, Bourne and Figueroa, helps create a clearer, more compelling understanding of persistent poverty, underdevelopment and "mal-development".[7]

Zondi and Mthembu, for example, in an edited collection of essays that conceptualizes for Africa the post-national experience of transitioning from underdevelopment to sustainable development, present a perspective that corresponds with post-plantation economic thinking in West Indian analysis. According to Zondi: "The liberation movements that would assume control of the state and its policymaking capacity displayed insufficient understanding of this racist, capitalist and ethnocentric legacy of super-exploitation and its evidence of underdevelopment. They allowed neo-colonial designs . . . in the

---

Research, University of the West Indies, 1976); Alister McIntyre, "Caribbean Economic Community", in *Readings in the Political Economy of the Caribbean*, ed. Norman Girvan and Owen Jefferson, 165–86 (Kingston: New World, 1971); Norman Girvan, *Foreign Capital and Economic Underdevelopment in Jamaica* (Kingston: Institute of Social and Economic Research, University of the West Indies, 1971); Havelock Brewster, "Planning Economic Development in Guyana", in *Readings in the Political Economy of the Caribbean*, ed. Norman Girvan and Owen Jefferson, 205–13 (Kingston: New World, 1971); Michael Witter, "Some Reflections on the Economic Development of Jamaica", in *Rethinking Development,* ed. Judith Wedderburn, 101–19 (Kingston: Department of Economics, University of the West Indies, 1991); Mark Figueroa, "Peasants, Plantations, and People: Continuities in the Analysis of George Beckford and W. Arthur Lewis", in *The Critical Tradition of Caribbean Political Economy: The Legacy of George Beckford*, ed. Kari Levitt and Michael Witter, 36–56 (Kingston: Ian Randle, 1996); C.Y. Thomas, "Monetary and Financial Arrangements in a Development Monetary Economy", *New World Quarterly* (Kingston: Institute of Social and Economic Research, University of the West Indies, 1965).

7. Immanuel Wallerstein, *The Politics of the World Economy* (New York: Cambridge University Press, 1984); Luis Eugenio Di Marco, ed., *International Economics and Development: Essays in Honor of Raul Prebisch* (New York: Academic Press, 1972); Samir Amin, *Imperialism and Unequal Development* (London: Monthly Review Press, 1976); Andre Frank, *On Capitalist Underdevelopment* (London: Oxford University Press, 1976); Arturo Escobar, *Encountering Development: The Making and Unmaking of the Third World* (Princeton, NJ: Princeton University Press, 1995); Niall Ferguson, *Civilization: The West and the Rest* (New York: Penguin, 2011).

false hope that imperial forces were, in fact, partners in (their) quest for full sovereignty, independence and freedom."[8]

Zondi also argued, like many earlier development theorists, that underdevelopment in the colonies was strategically pursued by Britain and other imperial nations at the height of their independence struggles. The evidence to support this perspective is palpable in the case of the West Indies. During the transition from the defeated federation to independent nation states in the early 1960s, the British government bluntly, at critical moments, withdrew its financial resources and foreign-policy support to ensure West Indian subservience by means of institutional weakness.[9]

The "Enterprise of the Indies", as colonialism was called by West Indian economist Lloyd Best, persisted for three centuries because Britain found it productive and profitable. To this, Trevor Farrell added that the West Indian economy was governed by one fundamental law: to be a "positive" force in the economic life of "the dominant elites in the colonizing country". Economic success was measured, therefore, in terms of the extent and efficiency of wealth extraction.[10]

There was no more prominent supporter of this truth than British prime minister Winston Churchill (1940–45, 1951–55). Reflecting on the role of the West Indian economy in Britain's economic development, he stated:

> Our possession of the West Indies . . . gave us the strength, the support, but especially the capital, the wealth, at a time when no other European nation possessed such a reserve, which enabled us to come through the great struggles of the Napoleonic Wars, the keen competition of commerce in the eighteenth and nineteenth centuries, and enabled us not only to acquire the appendages of possessions which we have, but also to lay the foundation of that commercial and financial leadership which, when the world was young, when everything outside of Europe was underdeveloped, enabled us to make our great position in the world.[11]

8. Siphamandla Zondi, "The UN, the Idea of Development: Between Dissensus and Consensus", in *From MDGs to Sustainable Development Goals: The Travails of International Development*, ed. Siphamandla Zondi and Philani Mthembu (Cape Town: Institute of Global Dialogue and UNISA, 2017), 27.

9. Ibid.

10. Trevor Farrell, "Decolonization in the English-Speaking Caribbean: Myth or Reality", in *The Newer Caribbean: Decolonization, Democracy, and Development,* ed. Paget Henry and Carl Stone (Philadelphia: Institute for the Study of Human Issues, 1983), 3.

11. Cited in A.N.R. Robinson, *The Mechanics of Independence: Patterns of Political and*

Such descriptions of the West Indies from Lloyd George (slums of Empire) to Churchill (saviour of Empire) framed the relationship between the economic extraction model and its legacy of poverty and decay.

Fast-forward seventy years beyond Churchill's admission, and we find another Conservative British prime minister, David Cameron, arriving in Jamaica at the end of September 2015, addressing the nation on the same view of this historical relationship. No British prime minister had officially visited these oldest parts of the empire for over a decade. Cameron was given the honour of addressing a joint sitting of the national parliament, a gathering mostly of descendants of those enslaved by the British. Like many prior British prime ministers, he too was a descendant beneficiary of an elite slave owner. Sir James Duff, his ancestor, received in 1834 the handsome financial reparation of £4,101 when the state forfeited his 202 enslaved Africans on the Grange Plantation in Jamaica – over £3 million in today's value.[12]

With his personal history scattered across the Caribbean and British press, Cameron spoke of the need to celebrate the "extraordinary ties" between Britain and the West Indies. After commenting for ten minutes in a sanitized official speech, he delved into the legacy of British enslavement of Africans in the Caribbean: "That the Caribbean has emerged from the long, dark shadow it [slavery] cast is testament to the resilience and spirit of its people. I acknowledge that these wounds run very deep indeed. But I do hope that, as friends who have gone through so much together since those darkest times, we can move on from this painful legacy and continue to build for the future."[13] This was immediately labelled the "Let's Move On" speech. The Caribbean community was outraged and defined him as insensitive and racist. He further inflamed local passions with another comment in which he called upon West Indians to "get over it". September is a month that often sees hurricanes in the region. The "hurricane" that released these statements was named David. Cameron's remarks provided further context for understanding British persistence in punishing the West Indies.

Economic Transformation in Trinidad and Tobago (1971; reprint, Kingston: University of the West Indies Press, 2001), 16.

12. Hilary Beckles, "An Open Letter to the Honourable David Cameron, Prime Minister of the UK and Northern Ireland", *Gleaner*, 27 September 2015.

13. David Cameron's speech to the Jamaican Parliament, 30 September 2015, https://www.gov.uk/government/speeches/pms-speech-to-the-jamaican-parliament.

Cameron's speech did not use the word "slavery", nor was there a hint of a possible official apology. No support for reparation was mentioned or offered. He did say, however, that the reparatory justice approach to reading history was "not the way to proceed". No expression of remorse could be found in his speech for the British abandonment of responsibility for underdevelopment in the West Indies. Neither was there an indication of concern for the plight of Windrush West Indian workers in Britain, who occupy the lowest socio-economic rung of the national ladder.

Cameron did, however, offer an aid package to the region – £300 million earmarked for infrastructural projects in nations that qualified. He ended his speech with the following declaration:

> Indeed, in recent years, some people here have asked whether Britain remains as committed and interested in this region as we once were. Well, today I want to answer that in the clearest terms possible. I hope this visit, and the concrete support I've announced, will ensure that no one should have reason to question the UK's commitment to the Caribbean future. My commitment to a full-on re-engagement here is absolute. And, ultimately, the reason for this is about so much more than trade and assistance. I passionately believe that the UK should remain the partner of choice for the Commonwealth Caribbean – now and in the future.[14]

Press reports highlighted the regional public response: "David Cameron rules out slavery reparations during Jamaica visit"; "David Cameron calls on Jamaica to 'move on' from painful legacy of slavery"; and "British prime minister David Cameron rules out slavery reparations in Jamaica", tells country "to get over it".[15]

The red media headlines reflected the continuing West Indian concern with the matter of financial compensation for native genocide, slavery, indenture-ship and colonization. Earlier that year, the Caribbean Community's newly constituted Reparations Commission had been active regionally and globally, laying the legal and political foundations for a formal approach to the British government. The Caribbean told Cameron there could be no new beginning without moral sincerity and integrity in dealing with the history of wealth extraction from the region and its creation of underdevelopment.[16]

---

14. Ibid.

15. Ibid.; Selena Hill, "British PM David Cameron Rules Out Slavery Reparations for Jamaica, Tells Country to Get Over It", *Latin Post*, 4 October 2015.

16. Beckles, "Open Letter".

The following year, 2016, the United Nations Development Programme published its report detailing the economic obstacles and social challenges facing the Caribbean. It showed with stark empirical data the limited extent to which the region has progressed on expected development fronts since the British government had rejected, over a period of sixty years, the claims of regional leaders for reparatory-development funding. There had been no significant movement in this regard between the Moyne Commission Report (1945) and the first phase of regional independence (1962–66).

The report begins with an assessment of regional economic vulnerabilities, the result of "growing multidimensional poverty". "Economic growth," it also states, "is insufficient on its own for lifting and keeping people out of poverty." Looking beyond the poverty indices, the research data show that the biggest challenges facing the region are the legacies of extractive colonialism – growing inequalities, gender discrimination and long-standing issues of racial exclusion.[17]

It noted:

> Poverty and unemployment rates, especially among youth, remain high . . . combined public social protection and health expenditures, which contribute to resilience and adaptive capacity, lag for all Caribbean countries as a proportion of GDP. . . . In this regard, the Caribbean faces a distinct challenge amongst developing countries since poverty as traditionally measured, and growing multidimensional poverty, which takes account of the near-poor and vulnerable, exist alongside persistent low growth.[18]

The report also shows that "most CARICOM countries have had a negative evolution in the Human Development Index ranking over the last five years". Youth exclusion and economic underperformance are particularly striking. Poverty, juvenile crime and unemployment are linked to poor achievement in secondary school, in itself a function of poverty. Youth unemployment ranges between 18 per cent and 47 per cent, except in Trinidad, where it is 10 per cent. The youth "comprise between 28% and 50% of all unemployed persons and females are more likely to be unemployed".[19]

Three years prior, regional academics gathered to celebrate the fortieth anniversary of the publication of George Beckford's classic text *Persistent Poverty:*

---

17. UNDP, *Multidimensional Progress*, 4.
18. Ibid., 3.
19. Ibid., 9.

Underdevelopment in Plantation Economies of the Third World. The book was published in 1972 by the University of the West Indies professor of economics and it has remained central to attempts at explaining the poor economic performance of the region.

Beckford argued that "persistent poverty" is rooted in the economic structures that were historically designed by the British as models for maximum wealth extraction. The resilience of the plantation mode of production, with minor modification, he added, when applied to newer, non-agricultural sectors, has served to assure the reproduction of poverty. Underdevelopment, he concluded, has been the inevitable result of colonial market relationships and entrepreneurial mentalities that have remained structurally unaltered.[20]

It is within this context that the revived reparatory justice movement has attached itself, once again, to regional economic underdevelopment discourses. Inasmuch, therefore, as Britain's extraction of wealth from the region was the most efficient of the European nations', it should not be considered phenomenal that the English-speaking subregion has the highest poverty in the newly independent Caribbean.

This book, then, addresses the economic impact of the British debt owed to the West Indies, and, critically, the efforts Britain has made since emancipation to keep capital away from the region. It focuses on financial strategies used to underfund development projects such as the 1958 federation and other major initiatives in the independence era. The politics of persistent poverty as an expression of economic underdevelopment is revisited and presented within the context of compelling new evidence about British imperial actions and intentions.

Slums of Empire

David Lloyd George, British prime minister from 1916 to 1922, entered the mainstream of Caribbean history for two significant reasons. First, as a British national hero of the First World War, he successfully demanded and extracted reparations for his country from defeated Germany. As a lead architect of the 1919 Treaty of Versailles, and then at the follow-up London Conference in 1921, he demanded from Germany a reparations payment of US$33 billion for

---

20. Beckford, *Persistent Poverty*, xxii–xxvii.

civilian damage. Second, in 1926, while reflecting on the causes of the rising anti-colonial movement in the West Indies, he described the region most graphically as the "slums of Empire".[21]

Britain's intention in extracting massive reparations from Germany was to slow and stultify its economic recovery and to promote its own competitive economic advantage. In the case of the West Indies, where three centuries of wealth extraction had served Britain well in respect of its industrial development, the former prime minister's intention was to draw attention to its economic decay and decline and its incapacity to further offer business benefits. In this ironic fashion, he presented the basis for a reparations response from the Caribbean to British economic exploitation.[22]

The "slums of Empire" were Britain's first primary site of large-scale wealth extraction. The inhabitants today are mostly the descendants of the chattel enslaved from Africa and the indentured servants from India who did not generally receive the terms and conditions agreed by their contracts. The wretched of these communities live in deep, persisting poverty and social despair. These West Indians are the casualties of Britain's spectacular economic development and imperial pride.

But in the West Indian slums, there is more political struggle for justice than economic increments. There is in the twenty-first century a historic hegemonic, persistent demand for reparations and equal economic opportunity. These expectations fill the political space with a sense of urgency about democracy and development. From these very slums came the first successful workers' revolution against the British Empire. Within less than a decade of Lloyd George's declaration, the struggle in the slums had confronted and laid bare the brutality of British colonialism. Taking to the streets from the fields, the workers struck a mortal blow to the imperial order.[23]

---

21. George Padmore, "England's West Indian Slums", *Crisis* 47, no. 10 (October 1940): 317. See also by Padmore, "Poverty, Disease Is Natives' Lot in West Indies", in J.R. Johnson's column, "The Negro Fight", in *Labour Action* 4, no. 10 (17 June 1940).

22. Under the terms of the London Accord that followed in 1921, Germany was asked to pay the sum of 132 billion gold marks, US$33 billion. Between 1919 and 1932, Germany paid US$21 billion. The reparations payment was cleared in 2010 with the final instalment of £60 million.

23. Richard Hart, *Labour Rebellions of the 1930s in the British Caribbean Region Colonies* (London: Caribbean Labour Solidarity and the Socialist History Society, 2002). See also O. Nigel Bolland, *On the March: Labour Rebellions in the British Caribbean, 1934–1939* (Kingston: Ian Randle, 1995).

The popular eruption of the 1930s advanced the move towards nationhood and political democracy. It culminated in an intensification of the demand for economic development and social equity. The "slums" sought to sever themselves from their imperial parent and declared their intention to be free. Leaders of the successful anti-colonial movement placed before the retreating empire the demand for reparations in the form of capital support for economic development as the cure for endemic impoverishment.

The effort to uproot this poverty has produced many critical questions and fewer acceptable answers. In every town in each territory, slums have remained a hallmark of identity. They represent a visual legacy of British wealth extraction that continues to pose an existential threat to sovereignty. They are the core of the colonial mess left behind by Britain.

Cleaning up this mess has been the primary work of three generations of nationalist leaders, for whom the task is considered a precondition for development. From the outset they conceptualized nation-building within this understanding. Their efforts have served to focus popular attention on the debt Britain owes to the region. Its payment continues to occupy a central place in political and academic thinking about social justice, racial pride and economic development.

From the 1920s to the 2020s, economic development thinking has reflected this paradigm. Urban and rural poverty is the top agenda item in strategic planning, and the region has globalized its call for development reparations. The postcolonial economy has remained poor, fragile, an embarrassment to market developmentalism. Despite decades of heroic efforts by state and civil society, the postcolonial headwind, originating principally from Britain's resistance, has thwarted the region's ability to bring about sustainable development.

The sum effect of unsuccessful efforts has remained poverty and underdevelopment. A 2018 economic survey of the region confirms what decades of academic study and political activism have proven: that the oppressive, anti-development institutional and ideological structures of British rule, in both sociocultural and economic aspects, remain deeply ingrained and are spectacularly resilient.[24]

The ecosystem of this heritage and its capacity to suppress and distort development policy have been extensively analysed. The regional economy has remained

---

24. UNDP, *Multidimensional Progress*, iv–v.

"low growth and high debt". It is deemed, as a postcolonial construct, to have underperformed, and its leaders, both entrepreneurial and political, are considered development failures. Unemployment rates in 2015 across the region average within the 21–26 percentile range, with the youth cohort stretching outward to the upper band.[25]

The consequence has been the consolidation of hardcore poverty. Social and economic indicators suggest dynamic underdevelopment with a negative future outlook. Basic prosperity has eluded generations of the post-plantation poor. Political leaders, until recently, have avoided demanding reparatory development from Britain and its partners in the multilateral system. As a result, they have been ushered down the dead-end track of crippling debt. The region today has one of the highest debt-to-gross-domestic-product ratios in the world, standing in excess of the 100 per cent threshold which nullifies the potential for growth. Its economic underdevelopment status is its primary feature.[26]

The call here is for a discursive return to the reparatory justice approach to economic development that provides an opportunity to transition from the aid-debt entrapment to an investment orientation. It insists, as did Arthur Lewis in 1938–39, that the debt that Britain and Western countries whose economies have their basis in slavery owe the West Indies – for three centuries of native genocide, black chattel enslavement, Indian indentured servitude, and the overall crimes of colonization – must be acknowledged, adjudicated and settled in a manner supportive of development.

The liability on Britain's side of the balance sheet must be converted into a performing asset on the West Indian side. This shift will enable the creation of a sustainable development framework. It will make possible relief from the monumental multilateral debt in the region. Critically, it will serve to refocus attention on the enormous growth potential that exists in the region.[27]

This requires an epistemic shift from the full-blown notion of West Indian development failure to a balanced and mediated explanation in which greater significance is given to making amends for the debilitating colonial inheritance. Such a discursive movement will promote a clearer understanding of the enormous economic potential of the region once placed in a competitive circum-

---

25. Ibid.
26. Ibid.
27. See Hilary McD. Beckles, *Britain's Black Debt: Reparations for Caribbean Slavery and Native Genocide* (Kingston: University of the West Indies Press, 2013).

stance. The reaffirmation of the conceptual integrity and academic soundness of earlier Caribbean research on postcolonialism and nation-building is the basis upon which the Western world should rise to an investment partnership with the region, as part of the growing global call for equity in the world economy.[28]

This book, then, seeks to recentre the history and heritage of the wealth-extraction model Britain used in the West Indies for three hundred years. It also exposes the strategies it used to exit its obligations to the region on the cheap by escaping responsibility for the mess it left behind. The evidence, both old and new, shows that beyond the issue of minimal social welfare, it was never Britain's intention to promote development in the West Indies.

In freeing themselves of colonialism, first with popular protest and then by constitutional negotiation, West Indians provided Britain with an opportunity to punish the region by way of diplomatic double standards. The evidence that shows the railroading of decades of reparations demands for development is to be found in the official records.[29]

Britain's persistent public denial of its Caribbean debt sits alongside its private admission of it. The doublespeak has been the standard strategy of avoidance. This much was demonstrated during the emancipation reform of the 1830s, the federation fiasco of the 1950s and the independence detachment of the 1960s. At each moment, West Indians were entrapped within this deceptive diplomacy. In every instance, they set sail on a journey to freedom and development on a turbulent ocean, in a rotting ship burdened by British debt.

Finally, this book calls for new rules. It looks to the future and calls to Western nations that grew fat on the crimes committed against humanity in the region to settle, in a global summit, the debt owed the Caribbean, to facilitate healing and the dignified induction of the region within the twenty-first-century global economic order.

---

28. See Beckford, *Persistent Poverty*; see also George Beckford, ed., *Caribbean Economy* (Kingston: Institute of Social and Economic Research, University of the West Indies, 1975); Girvan, *Foreign Capital*.

29. See Escobar, *Encountering Development*, 10–17.

CHAPTER 1

Roots of Poverty
Emancipation Business Model

So far as purely British interests are concerned, this might not greatly matter. We have no great commercial or defence interests in these islands any longer; and the ties that we have with them are largely cultural, moral and sentimental. Our principal ally, the United States, is, however, very sensitive about anything that happens in these territories and would not welcome a situation developing in which Britain withdrew and left seven potential little Haitis or Cubas on their door step.

—Sir H. Poynton to Sir P. Gore Booth [permanent undesecretary of state] 28 September 1965, FO 371/179142, no. 5

THE CUMULATIVE EFFORTS OF THREE HUNDRED years of British colonial trade policies constitute the principal causes of the West Indian economy entering the mid-twentieth century structurally underdeveloped and unprepared for the economic challenges associated with nationhood. The legal creation and commercial management of the slavery-based economies between the 1630s and 1830s, and a subsequent century of white-supremacy governance, assured the region's impoverishment and social degradation.[1]

Containing the nineteenth-century economic access, ownership and participation of the emancipated social majority, and later the indentured Asians, effectively ruled out the concept of a Caribbean, broad-based economy.

---

1. See Dispatch from Metcalfe to Russell, 30 March 1840, CO 137/248; Glenelg to Governors of West India Colonies, CO 318/141, Public Records Office (PRO), 2 April 1838. See also Thomas Holt, *The Problem of Freedom: Race, Labour and Politics in Jamaica and Britain, 1832–1938* (Kingston: Ian Randle, 1992); Hilary McD. Beckles, *Great House Rules: Landless Emancipation and Workers' Protest in Barbados, 1838–1938* (Kingston: Ian Randle, 2004).

Even when, in the 1950s, the resurrected concept was officially upheld by anti-colonial leaders, the imperial government received it with attitudes ranging from outrage to hostility.

The poverty of African and Asian communities was sustained as the colonial norm by Britain and considered necessary in order to assure white economic control. Rigidly embedded in the regulation of the post-slavery economy was the principle of white supremacy. It was for this reason, at the beginning of the twentieth century, that African and Asian majority communities were in consensus that only force of arms could uproot and replace this economic governance.[2]

Economic Extraction Model

The West Indies began their modern existence as a massive crime scene. The British state and its colonizing investors took the culture of commercial plunder and corresponding crimes against humanity to the highest global level. As the indigenous population collapsed from over three million to fewer than thirty thousand, British investors imported over three million enslaved Africans to replace them. In addition, investors enslaved millions of their offspring in the wealth extraction system. Profit-maximizing businesses were built around mining, farming and trading; all utilized the commodification of African labour. The principal form of investment in property was the enslaved African body.[3]

Britain was first among the European investors to legally codify the enslaved and enchained African as non-human. Over time, the legal designation gained commercial sophistication, and enslaved Africans were subject to all the characteristics of property.[4] They could be transferred by a bill of sale or oral agreement

2. O. Nigel Bolland, *The Politics of Labour in the British Caribbean* (Kingston: Ian Randle, 2001); Paul Rich, "Sydney Olivier, Jamaica and the Debate on British Colonial Policy in the West Indies", in *Labour in the Caribbean: From Emancipation to Independence*, ed. Malcolm Cross and Gad Heuman (London: Macmillan, 1988), 208–33.

3. Protest of Assembly of Jamaica, June 1838, Parliamentary Papers (PP) 1839, 35. See Michael Craton, *Testing the Chains: Resistance to Slavery in the British West Indies* (Ithaca: Cornell University Press, 1982); Hilary McD. Beckles, *The First Black Slave Society: Britain's "Barbarity Time" in Barbados, 1636–1876* (Kingston: University of the West Indies Press, 2016).

4. Beckles, *First Black Slave Society*.

and were generally accounted for as capital assets. In addition, they could be used as cash and presented as an instrument in a financial transaction.[5]

Profits from this economic system drove a factory-building frenzy in the rural and urban economy of Britain. The economics of slavery, furthermore, facilitated genocidal outcomes. No African population in a West Indian colony had as many members at the end of slavery in 1838 as it had imported from Africa.

Barbados, the economic model that produced massive financial success for investors, imported 600,000 Africans. In 1834, when emancipation legislation eventually recognized Africans as humans and ended the institution of slavery, there were 83,000. Jamaica imported some 1.5 million Africans and at emancipation contained just over 300,000. In general, no more than 20 per cent of imported Africans into a colony survived this holocaust.[6]

The West Indies, then, experienced at the hands of the British both an indigenous and an African genocide, a double crime against humanity that is yet to be officially acknowledged by Britain. The wealth extracted in the process generated British economic growth and institutional development. In this way, Britain was able to attain its national strategic goals. Investing elites thrived; the middle and working classes consumed more, better and cheaper food; and the nation's living standard had never been higher.

British political prestige was elevated in the exercise of the economic power that followed. This, along with profit and power, was the objective of the paradigm, which proved addictive to British national consciousness. The desire for sugar and other colonial products knew no limit. Wealth extraction was done effectively and with minimum injection of capital. The concept that best captures this method is "plunder". "Britishness" became synonymous with brutishness within the context of the extraction model.[7]

Slave owners responded to Adam Smith's magisterial academic work on the relationship between slavery and British economic growth. *The Wealth of Nations* was published in 1776 and it specified the positive and negative impact of the West Indian economy at the height of its wealth generation. Jamaica, the

---

5. Ibid.

6. See David Lambert, *White Creole Culture: Politics and Identity During the Age of Abolition* (Cambridge: Cambridge University Press, 2005); K.M. Butler, *The Economics of Emancipation: Jamaica and Barbados, 1823–1843* (Chapel Hill: University of North Carolina Press, 1995).

7. Lambert, *White Creole Culture*.

core of the eighteenth-century British colonial economy, was destroying and replacing enslaved Africans at a rate of nearly ten thousand per year.[8]

Smith questioned the financial efficiency of the mature slavery extraction model, its productivity and profitability, and the rationality of capital allocation. He presented an economic argument that situated the aging slave economy on the cost side of the national balance sheet. Wastage, he stated, was the hallmark of the century-old model; it could not be reformed, and should be abandoned. As a business enterprise, he concluded it was no longer adding value to the British economy, though it still enriched the diverse cohort of enslavers.[9]

Aid before Emancipation

Slave investors and managers responded to Smith's criticism with a comprehensive programme of labour-management reform. They considered themselves profit maximizers, market rationalists and efficiency optimizers. In the last quarter of the eighteenth century, they rolled out a policy of "better treatment" for their 600,000 enslaved workers to consolidate wealth extraction in the medium to long term. They called this first reform "the Amelioration".

The enslaved were stimulated by management policy to produce more in return for a package of benefits. They were offered better prenatal care for pregnant women and consistent access to improved nutrition. The "aid package" was in exchange for greater productivity and social stability. Critically, this was the first system of "aid" the British had offered to the oppressed poor in the West Indies.[10]

The audacity of the aid package was soon met with violent rejection by the enslaved. The period 1780 to 1820 was associated with an intensification of anti-slavery rebellion in the region, a crescendo of military opposition. In Jamaica, the Maroons went to war against the British for the final time, and in Barbados, after one hundred years with no organized violent rebellion, "General" Bussa, so named by his fellow rebels, led an island-wide anti-slavery war.

In St Vincent, Chatoyer led a coalition of enslaved Africans and indigenous

---

8. Adam Smith, *The Wealth of Nations* (1776; reprint, New York: Canna, 1937).
9. Ibid.
10. See Fitzherbert MSS, Turner Hall plantation account, Barbados, 1775–80, WI/17–18; for Antigua, see Tudway MSS, Box 15, Somerset Record Office DD/TD. See also J.R. Ward, *British West Indian Slavery: The Process of Amelioration, 1750–1834* (Oxford: Clarendon, 1988).

people against British enslavers and colonialists; and in Grenada, Fédon, a free multiracial man, pulled off, even if temporarily, a successful revolution against the British. These events signalled that aid for the enslaved had failed as a reform strategy.[11]

"Freedom", not "more food", was the message from the enslaved community. "Freedom first" was written in blood, rejecting compliance and capitulation. The economics behind the policy shift, that it had become "better to breed than to buy" the enslaved, required a sales pitch to the enslaved. The proposal of "aid instead of emancipation" was rolled out regionally. The enslaved looked to Haiti while imagining their options, and opted to idealize the lesson taught by Toussaint L'Ouverture: an uncompromising philosophy and praxis of freedom.[12]

The final step towards the 1833 Act of Emancipation also included a violent experience, in the massive 1831 Jamaica anti-slavery war. From then to the postcolonial period, the narrative speaks to the demand for freedom, development and reparatory justice. But simultaneously, the years between the 1830s and independence in the 1960s contained the evidence of British hostility to the aspirations of the West Indian people.[13] In these decades, the wealth extraction continued unchecked through the region, constituting today's detrimental legacy.[14]

---

11. Codrington account, 1784–90, MSS X/43–5, Plantation Accounts, Lambeth Palace Archive, London; Claude Levy, "Barbados: The Last Years of Slavery, 1823–1833", *Journal of Negro History* 44 (1959): 308–45.

12. Privy Council Report, PP 1789, 26 (646a), pt. III; Barbados no. 15 Senhouse MSS, Memoirs of Joseph Senhouse, vol. 2, fo. 287, August 1778; Monson MSS, Thistlewood Diaries, 9 August 1780; Hilary McD. Beckles, *Natural Rebels: A Social History of Enslaved Black Women in Barbados* (London: Zed Books, 1989); Hilary McD. Beckles, "Property Rights in Pleasure: The Marketing of Enslaved Women's Sexuality", in *West Indies Accounts: Essays on the History of the British Caribbean and the Atlantic Economy*, ed. Roderick McDonald (Kingston: University of the West Indies Press, 1996), 169–87; Hilary McD. Beckles, *Centering Women: Gender Discourses in Caribbean Slave Societies* (Kingston: Ian Randle, 1999)

13. Abolition of Slavery Act, 1833; PP 1833, 3–4, Will. IV, cap. 73. See Malcolm Cross and Gad Heuman, eds., *Labour in the Caribbean: From Emancipation to Independence* (London: Macmillan, 1988); Cary Fraser, *Ambivalent Anti-Colonialism: The United States and the Genesis of West Indian Independence, 1940–1964* (Westport, CT: Greenwood, 1994); William Green, *British Slave Emancipation: The Sugar Colonies and the Great Experiment, 1830– 1865* (Oxford: Clarendon, 1976); Howard Johnson, "The West Indies and the Conversion of the British Official Classes to the Development Idea", *Journal of Commonwealth and Comparative Politics* 15, no. 1 (1977): 55–83.

14. See Franklin Knight, *The Caribbean: The Genesis of a Fragmented Nationalism* (New York: Oxford University Press, 1978).

Reforming the Slavery Business Model

The search for greater profits from trading in enslaved people and sugar production drove enslavers and investors, and their parliamentary protectors, consistently to revise the terms and conditions of the economics of extraction. The final parliamentary debate of 1833 and the decision to terminate slavery constitute at best a significant reform of the colonial extraction model.[15]

The rebellions across the region showed the non-sustainability of slavery.[16] After 1838, the domestic supply of locally born black people was just enough to sustain commodity production. The sugar producers were discontented with the state of affairs and pushed the British government to open up the Asian labour market to their plantations.[17]

In capturing the majority vote, abolitionists bombarded public consciousness with the idea that the legal ending of slavery was one and the same thing as freedom for the black community. Reformers, however, for the most part, did not intend the legal end of slavery to translate into black freedom in real terms.[18]

In at least one aspect, the Abolition Act was the most deceptive and racist legislation passed by the British legislature in the nineteenth century. It was approved by Parliament on 28 August 1833. The title given to the law was "An Act for the Abolition of Slavery throughout the British colonies; for promoting the Industry of the manumitted Slaves, and for compensating the Persons hitherto

---

15. See Report of Special Magistrate Doughtry, 30 June 1835, PP 1835, 1; Hilary McD. Beckles, "The Wilberforce Song: How Enslaved Caribbean Blacks Heard British Abolitionists", in *The British Slave Trade: Abolition, Parliament and People,* ed. Stephen Farrell, Melanie Unwin and James Walvin, 113–26 (Edinburgh: Edinburgh University Press, 2007); Robin Blackburn, *The Overthrow of Colonial Slavery, 1776–1848* (London: Verso, 1999).

16. Dispatch from Smyth to Glenelg, 19 March 1836, PP 1836, 49; Hilary McD. Beckles, "The 200 Years War: Slave Resistance in the British West Indies: An Overview of the Historiography", *Jamaican Historical Review* 13 (1982): 1–10; Alex Tyrell, "A House Divided against Itself: The British Abolitionists Revisited", *Journal of Caribbean History* 22, nos. 1–2 (1988): 42–67; Eric Williams, "The British West Indian Slave Trade after its Abolition in 1807", *Journal of Negro History* 27, no. 2 (1942): 17–91.

17. See Beckles, *First Black Slave Society.*

18. See Dispatch from Barkly to Newcastle, 26 May 1854, CO 137/322; Dispatch from Sir Lionel Smith to Glenelg, 3 December 1838, PP 1839, 35; Eric Williams, *Capitalism and Slavery* (Chapel Hill: University of North Carolina Press, 1944), 154–78; Nicholas Draper, *The Price of Emancipation: Slave Ownership, Compensation and British Society at the End of Slavery* (Cambridge: Cambridge University Press, 2010); Christopher Brown, *Moral Capital: Foundations of British Abolitionism* (Chapel Hill: University of North Carolina Press, 2006).

entitled to the Services of such Slaves". It was the first time, after two hundred years of successfully dodging the issue, that Parliament had admitted that the legal identity of enslaved black people was that primarily of private property and not human.

The act provided that enslavers were the lawful property owners of their enslaved and were entitled by law to compensation, since the state intended to deny them the usage and enjoyment of their property rights. The Emancipation Act, then, effectively deemed enslaved people non-human. Parliament proceeded to compensate slave owners as a matter of property-rights reparations.[19]

The property status of blacks had been for centuries a stain on the social fabric. Emancipation was crafted and designed as a legal adjustment to the extraction model; the intention was to upgrade the system of labour exploitation. Long-term bondage was inscribed into the provisions of the law. Two hundred years of enslavement, the act implied, had not achieved their objective completely.[20]

Meanwhile, supporters of black freedom insisted that enslavement was best understood as the theft and plunder of the African's body, a personal resource. The plantation economy for blacks, therefore, was never legitimate; it was a system built upon stolen labour resources. Furthermore, they continued to conceptualize the British government, and their protected enslavers, as robbers, pirates and plunderers.

Thomas Clarkson had insisted in his public anti-slavery speeches that the British government was the primary criminal party in the illegal enterprise of African enslavement. It could not, therefore, be considered anything other than an enemy of the African people and the West Indies. This argument was also made by Augustus Beaumont in an 1826 literary contribution, in which he said that slavery was best described as the robbery of the Africans and that the crime of the British state was to declare it in the national interest.[21]

A letter published by the *Times* in 1824 made the same argument, though more forcefully, suggesting that "creating" and "upholding" slavery in the West Indies were "a national crime, and not the crime of the slaveholder alone". The entire nation, and its government, the author stated, participated in and benefited from the criminal conversion of African personhood into a commercial

---

19. See Resolution of Parish of Portland, Jamaica, 2 February 1839, PP 1839, 35; Dispatch from Metcalfe to Russell, 2 August 1841, CO 137/256; see also Beckles, *Britain's Black Debt*.
20. See Draper, *Price of Emancipation*, 100.
21. Ibid., 86–87.

unit of property, and framed the West Indies as host of the most exploited economy and society in the world under British power.[22]

Making the Enslaved Pay for Their Freedom

The Abolition of Slavery Act called for "compensating the person entitled to the services of such slaves". Emancipation, in theory, represented the transfer of the slave owner's alleged rights in the personhood of the enslaved back to the self of the enslaved. By the act, the state agreed to pay the replacement value of the enslaved to the enslaver and not to the enslaved. This meant the transfer of £47 million (the value of the enslaved West Indian community) to the slave investor class and British nation. It was a movement of £47 million from the West Indies to Britain. It was the largest financial extraction from the region: a skilful scheme by which the British state plundered the West Indies under the guise of humanitarianism.

This act enabled a massive injection of West Indian wealth into Britain's economy. After a decade of haggling over the size of the extraction and methods of transfer, slave investors eventually settled for the double gift – property rights in black bodies assured and cash pay-outs for the adjudicated replacement value of each body.

Beaumont eloquently responded that the so-called property right in blacks, to the extent that they existed, was the "born rights of the Negro – a right to his labour – to all he can acquire". Several significant people voiced the opinion that the enslaver had "no claim to a right of property in the body and soul of any human being whatsoever". The government, having defined the African as non-human, saw no need to answer the charge.[23]

It followed, then, that the British state did not intend to compensate or pay reparations to the enslaved. Clarkson argued that reparation for the crime of enslavement was due to Africa and the Africans in the West Indies because they were the victims of robbery and rape by the British. In any other part of the civilized world, he said, the enslaving criminals would "have been condemned to death".[24]

---

22. Ibid., 93.
23. Ibid., 81, 87–88.
24. Ibid., 86.

The British Parliament rejected the argument that the enslaved were entitled to any form of compensation and blocked all attempts to place reparatory resources in their hands. The policy of "no wealth for the West Indies" was an extension of the concept that the role of blacks in the colonies was to create and not to receive wealth.

Trickery in the Treasury

The sum agreed to compensate enslavers was £20 million. In the West Indies there were 664,970 enslaved people. The British government, after detailed actuarial studies, estimated that the market worth of enslaved people in the British colonies, Mauritius and the Cape of Good Hope was £45,281,738. The agreed reparations strategy was that enslavers would receive from the government £20 million in cash, and the enslaved would pay them the remainder in "free labour" for an additional six years after they were freed. The enslaved, then, gave more to their enslavers than the British government did.[25]

Generations of historians in the Caribbean and elsewhere fell for the deception associated with the British narrative of emancipation. The official fable suggests that the British government had designed the "apprenticeship" period to give the formerly enslaved "time" to become "industrious", and the enslaver the opportunity to become a responsible and fair wage-labour employer.

This deception found its way into the popular and academic literature. In fact, the principal purpose of the transition was to make the enslaved pay 50 per cent of the cost of their emancipation. It was a stealth strategy by the British government to extract maximum wealth from the enslaved population. Slave owners with £20 million in cash ran to the bank. The £25 million paid "in kind" by the enslaved added to the plunder. Nicholas Draper has shown that the £20 million represented 40 per cent of British national expenditure in 1834, which would equate to about £200 billion in 2010, given the relative size of the economy. In 2010, the value of £20 million in cash would be about £76 billion. He states, furthermore, in reference to the calculations of Paul Fogel and Stanley Engerman, that the "package of cash plus interest, plus the value of the six-year apprenticeship, totalled 96 per cent of the market value of the enslaved", and that the deal comprised "49 per cent cash and 47 per cent from the apprenticeship". He concluded that "despite the efforts of [Thomas]

---

25. Beckles, *Britain's Black Debt*, 150.

Buxton, the enslaved therefore paid between a fifth and one-half of the cost of freedom".[26]

Buxton and other prominent emancipation leaders tried and failed to prevent the financial extraction from the enslaved West Indians. They opposed the apprenticeship strategy and argued that the compensation paid to enslavers should be paid fully by the government, since the House of Commons majority was determined to "oppose the payment of a single farthing to the Negro". But after two hundred years of free labour from enslaved Africans, enslavers received an additional £47 million, a debt owed to the West Indies by the British government.[27]

The Emancipation Act was greeted by black West Indians with a sophisticated blend of revelry and resistance. The sugar plantation owners dug in and prepared for a militant counter-attack.[28] Across the region, governors called out the troops and militia to contain the rebellious.[29] The emancipated maintained their position: "No wages, no work." The death penalty was promoted and the result was an intensification of militancy in the colonies.[30]

West Indian freedom, then, began in 1838, in conflict over the conditions of emancipation. The black people demanded "full freedom" and "justice", which included access to economic and productive resources. The British government had an opposing view. It was that the manumitted community, as a rule, should have no independent access to productive resources, or high-level social status, and should not be allowed to be custodians of a viable Caribbean economy. They were to labour for prior "owners" in order to survive, and wages should be paid at subsistence levels, leaving no room for significant wealth accumulation.

Black workers were expected to fear freedom and not to consider it the basis of an indigenous nation. Manumission was given to the enslaved, noted a British official, but a free society "has not been formed".[31]

---

26. Draper, *Price of Emancipation*, 106. Thomas Buxton was an anti-slavery parliamentarian.

27. Ibid.

28. See Robert Shelton, "A Modified Crime: The Apprenticeship System in St Kitts", *Slavery and Abolition* 16, no. 3 (1995): 331–46; Minutes of Stephen, 15 September 1841, CO 137/256; Resolution of House of Commons Committee on the West India Colonies, PP 1842, 18.

29. Shelton, "Modified Crime", 332.

30. Ibid., 333.

31. Bonham C. Richardson, *Economy and Environment in the Caribbean: Barbados and the Windwards in the Late 1800s* (Kingston: University of the West Indies Press, 1997), xi. See also Dispatch from Elgin to Stanley, 5 August 1845, CO 137/284; Eighth Report of the House of Commons Committee on Sugar and Coffee Plantations, PP 1847–48, 18; Dispatch from Bartly to Newcastle, 26 May 1854, PP 1854, 43.

CHAPTER 2

"The Nigger Question"
Racial Terrorism

The real truth is, that of late years injustice has been done to the character of the negroes, in consequence of the disappointment resulting from the overestimate put forward on all sides of their advancement in civilisation at the epoch of emancipation; the advocates of that measure gladly suffering themselves to be deceived by mere external demonstration, whilst its opponent found their account in allowing it to be proved for them that slavery was not so brutalising and debasing in its effects as the antislavery party at other times somewhat inconsistently asserted.

—Dispatch from Henry Barkly to Newcastle, 26 May 1854, CO 137/322, PRO

GOVERNMENT-SPONSORED EMANCIPATION WAS FOLLOWED BY A century of ideological, cultural and military terrorism unleashed upon the black community. British intellectuals and academics who supported the white-supremacy perspective on black freedom elevated to an unprecedented level the literary and civil-society assault. The anti-black onslaught that followed endorsed the government policy that emancipation would not translate into liberation.

Meanwhile, economics, as a formal academic discipline, was taking its modern form after two developing methods of measuring the effectiveness of extraction practice. Political scientists and philosophers joined the economic debate about the role of free blacks in the future of West Indian colonization, and in so doing enhanced the popular perception of their disciplines. How to ensure that emancipation enhanced the economic benefit to Britain was the heart of national debate.[1]

---

1. See Mulgrave to Goderich, 2 March 1833: Ripon Papers, 1833–42, Add. MS, 40, 862–63; Mulgrave to Stanley, 14 March 1834, CO 137/192; Glenelg to Governors of the West Indian

The economics of emancipation also dominated parliamentary debates. The sustainability of the plantation system was the nation's top priority. The need to convert the labour of freed blacks into a continued bonanza for British investors required a comprehensive, compelling analysis. Pro-slavery intellectuals from the seventeenth century, such as the philosopher-enslaver John Locke, had condemned Africans in the West Indies to lifelong enslavement in their service of British economic advancement. Other philosophers, like David Hume, followed in the eighteenth century. In his 1753 essay "Of National Character", Hume formulated the concept of white supremacy as the inevitable West Indian governance model.[2] With legal emancipation in 1838, the region entered its freedom phase, and the focus of British public opinion-shapers turned aggressively to the issue of black cultural identity and its future.

The matter of the right of blacks to independent cultural and economic self-development outside white domination was the hot topic, not in the tropics, but in the political heartland throughout Great Britain. Philosophers, economists and sugar planters upgraded their political alliances and reignited the racial discourse that had been embedded in the debate over slavery and emancipation. Reasserting the argument that the Emancipation Act was a strategic error, the anti-black alliance sought to show that the emancipated were better off in a state of actual or near-enslavement and that the West Indian economy would decline and decay as a consequence of their liberty.[3]

The Emancipation Act itself laid down the foundations and set the parameters for the debate. The British Parliament had finally declared that blacks were not human. The act was a path through which blacks would shed their

---

Colonies, 16 November 1835, PP 1836, 166; Gordon K. Lewis, *Main Currents in Caribbean Thought: The Historical Evolution of Caribbean Society in Its Ideological Aspects, 1492–1900* (Kingston: Heinemann Caribbean, 1983), 94–120; Beckles, *Great House Rules*.

2. See Eric Williams, *British Historians and the West Indies* (Port of Spain: PNM Publishing, 1964), 5.

3. See Henry Barkly to the Duke of Newcastle, 14 January 1854, CO 137/322, no. 8. See also Gad Heuman, "'Is This What You Call Free?' Riots and Resistance in the Anglophone Caribbean", in *Contesting Freedom: Control and Resistance in the Post-Emancipation Caribbean*, ed. Gad Heuman and David Trotman (Oxford: Macmillan, 2005), 104–18; Brian Moore, *Race, Power and Social Segmentation in Colonial Society: Guyana After Slavery, 1838–1891* (New York: Gordon and Breach, 1987); Swithin Wilmot, "'Females of Abandoned Character'? Women and Protest in Jamaica, 1838–65", in *Engendering History: Caribbean Women in Historical Perspective*, ed. Verene Shepherd, Bridget Brereton and Barbara Bailey (Kingston: Ian Randle, 1995), 279–95.

property status. It also denied them compensation for their two hundred years of unpaid labour.

Thomas Carlyle: Campaign Leader of Black Haters

These conversations constituted a campaign led by Britain's leading public conservative intellectual, the controversial Scottish political philosopher Thomas Carlyle.[4] The Emancipation Act had outraged Carlyle. He considered the rhetoric of black freedom unrealistic and hypocritical. Maintaining that enslaved black people were correctly designated by the British state as property, he vilified the reasoning that led to their changed status. The noble enslavers, he said, were betrayed and should have been rewarded and further empowered by their government with an extension rather than an abolition of slavery. With the use of more military might to keep the blacks in chains, he suggested, the plantations could have been saved. As a popular opinion-shaper, he proceeded on the assumption that the right-thinking majority in society shared his views.[5]

In 1849, Carlyle assembled his opinions, well known for a decade, and published them in an anonymous essay entitled "Occasional Discourse on the Negro Question". It appeared in the influential conservative journal *Fraser's Magazine for Town and Country*. In 1853, the essay was revised and republished as the pamphlet *Occasional Discourse on the Nigger Question*.[6]

The publications ignited and sustained for the rest of the century the first British national debate on the subject of black West Indians in the emerging world economy. The public was provided with a forum in which to reflect on the condition of the West Indian economy. Progressive thinkers critiqued conservative, Establishment opinion, and confronted elements of the Carlylian campaign with a radical call for black liberation and reparatory justice.[7]

Carlyle's thesis was that enslavement had become an acceptable national

---

4. Thomas Carlyle, "Occasional Discourse on the Negro Question", *Fraser's Magazine for Town and Country* 40 (December 1849): 670–79.

5. Ibid. See also testimony of John Morris in "Report from the House of Assembly on the Injury Sustained during the Recent Rebellion", PP 1831–32, 56; PP 1831–32, 258.

6. Thomas Carlyle, *Occasional Discourse on the Nigger Question* (London: Thomas Bosworth, 1853). See Catherine Hall, *Civilizing Subjects: Metropole and Colony in the English Imagination, 1830–1867* (Chicago: University of Chicago Press, 2002).

7. See John Stuart Mill, "The Negro Question", *Fraser's Magazine for Town and Country* 41 (January 1850): 25–31.

institution in the best traditions of British labour culture. The idea of emancipation, he said, had therefore emerged from a pseudo-philanthropic campaign against national norms. The correct path, he opined, should have been the deeper induction of the enslaved into the mores of British civilization.

Such a strategy, Carlyle said, would have prepared blacks in the long term for an upgrade into the human family, with a corresponding social identity. Blacks, he insisted, simply had an inadequate quota of intelligence to live in the modern world as equals to whites, and would degrade themselves even further with the imagined freedom they received as a gift from politically weak, ultra-moralizing liberal parliamentarians.[8]

Emancipationists, Carlyle insisted, in winning support from some conservative politicians and liberals with a religious cause, had made a tragic error in judgement. The mistake, he said, had led to the political and economic weakening of Britain and the West, in relation to the rest of the world. Situating his racist discourse in notions of British nationalism, he successfully mobilized powerful elements of public opinion against the idea of a Caribbean economy based on black liberty.

So influential was Carlyle's campaign that he succeeded in facilitating colonial administrators in the West Indies in developing harsher and more repressive social and economic measures to subjugate the black community. He became the unofficial voice of successive British governments in respect of manumitted blacks. Official West Indian policies were based on Carlylian principles that intended the manumitted to be imprisoned on plantations as a socio-economic norm.

Blacks had been allowed, wrote Carlyle, to fall back into the African barbarism from which enslavement had partially rescued them. Everywhere in the West Indies, he suggested, they were to be seen lying around under mango trees with no interest in sustained labour, representing a description of hell in which the accumulation of white capital was threatened by black laziness. The West Indies, long a significant slave-based contributor to British economic growth and development, had become, with emancipation, a drain upon the nation, on account of the corrosive effect of blackness unchecked.[9]

---

8. Carlyle, *Occasional Discourse.*

9. Ibid. See also Charles Roundell, *England and Her Subject-Races, with Special Reference to Jamaica* (London: Macmillan, 1866).

Freedom for blacks in the West Indies, therefore, in Carlyle's thinking, was not only a force of subversion with respect to British economic development, but a blow to the advance of the white race that was destined to rule them in the West Indies. His assault on the black community was expressed in statements such as:

> "Sweet blighted lilies", as an American epitaph on the nigger child has it, "sweet blighted lilies, they are holding up their heads again". . . . How pleasant to have always this fact to fall back upon; our beautiful black darlings are at least happy; with little labour except to the teeth, which, surely, in those excellent horse-jaws of theirs, will not fail.[10]

> Black persons rendered extremely "free" indeed! Sitting yonder, with their beautiful muzzles up to their ears in pumpkins, imbibing sweet pulp and juices; the grinder and incisive teeth ready for every new work, and the pumpkins cheap as grass in those rich climates, while the sugar crops rot around them uncut, because labour cannot be hired, so cheap are the pumpkins.[11]

> In Demerara, as I read in the Blue Book last year, the cane-crop, far and wide, stands rotting; the fortunate black gentlemen, strong in their pumpkins, having all struck till the "demand" rise a little. Sweet, blighted lilies, now getting up their heads again![12]

> Do I, then, hate the negro? No, except when the soul is killed out of him. I decidedly like poor Quashee; and find him a pretty kind of man. With a pennyworth of oil, you can make a handsome glossy thing of Quashee; when the soul is not killed in him, a swift, supple fellow; a merry-hearted, grinning, dancing, singing, affectionate kind of creature, with a great deal of melody and amenability in his composition.[13]

> If Quashee will not honestly aid in bringing out those sugars, cinnamons and other nobler products of the West-Indian Islands . . . [he] will get himself made a slave again (which state will be a little less ugly than his present one), and with beneficent whip, since other methods avail not, will be compelled to work. Or alas, let him look across to Haiti, and trace a far sterner prophecy. Let him by his ugliness, idleness, rebellion, banish all white men from the West Indies, and make it all one Haiti.[14]

---

10. Carlyle, *Occasional Discourse*, 4.
11. Ibid., 5.
12. Ibid., 6.
13. Ibid., 14.
14. Ibid., 38.

The "Nigger Question" was demonstrably the demagogic manifesto of British government officials, with traction throughout the colonial governance system. Carlyle was hailed the ideological leader of imperialism, defending the nation against the weak emancipators of unproductive, subhuman black West Indians. Those who, on economic grounds, from Adam Smith in the 1770s to John Stuart Mill in the 1830s, suggested that slavery, in addition to being an immoral institution, had become an economic drain and cultural curse upon the nation, were condemned by Carlyle as subscribers to the "Dismal Science" – the emerging discipline of "Economics" – that celebrated Mammon above all else.[15]

Black freedom for Carlyle was a new West Indian fad, while slavery was a respected pillar of ancient Western civilization. The blacks, he implied, had placed the concept at the centre of a West Indian cosmology – they waged wars, actual and cultural, against their British masters. Their commitment to freedom, he noted, was demonstrated in their daily resisting work and discipline.

His attack on them included the use of the word "Quashee", a description that covered the social ascriptions he assigned to all blacks. He used it as a literary code to successfully focus British policy and public opinion on the idea that freedom was foreign to blacks, and that submissiveness to the British state should be their long-term lot.[16]

"Quashee" was the West Indian black who slept all day and partied all night, surrendering productivity to pleasure. Quashee rose from the ashes of slavery and became the carrier of an undeserving, regressive culture of liberty and equality. This was the condition British officials were programmed to despise and oppose with all their Carlylian might. Panic took hold in the corridors of the British Parliament. The Carlylians accused it of unleashing the unthinkable – an unemployed African.

The black male, furthermore, as Quashee, Carlyle sought to show, was no man, and should therefore be excluded from the conversation about the rights of man. It is the "might" of man, British men, white men, he said, which was threatened in the age of black emancipation. Quashee should be subordinated within white domestication, he insisted, and the British, by showing sustained strength and wisdom in the West Indies, would best promote the truth of the case – that "Might is Right in the long run". And critically, he concluded,

---

15. Ibid., 5.
16. Ibid.

"might" and "right" would be found to occupy the same discursive space in the fullness of time.[17]

The best-case post-slavery governance model for the West Indies, he insisted, called for ethnic ranking with the wisest (white men) in charge, then to the "next wisest, and so on till we reach the Demerara Niggers (from whom downward, through the horses, etc.)". This view, noted Williams, provided the context for the fascist colonial policy that led to the imperial impulse to massacre blacks in the West Indies. Carlylian colonial policy in the aftermath of emancipation targeted black West Indians in the morning, and later in the century, brown East Indians in the evening.[18]

Pushback from the few progressive opinion-shapers was significant but meek and mild. Their commitment to black liberty had been persistent and intellectually informed. But they lacked the passion necessary to back their principles. Wordsworth's petition, three decades earlier, for example, in support of Toussaint's Haitian Revolution, had won a few influential followers, but only John Stuart Mill, considered the mildest of men, was prepared to make a robust rebuttal to Carlyle. In 1850 he offered a significant literary response, also published in *Fraser's Magazine*.[19]

Mill was a supporter of the emancipation process and considered part of a wider radical mobilization that included equal rights for women, the right of workers to combine, and the independence of Haiti. His brush was broad, as was his contribution to progressive discourse without rancour. He suggested that emancipated blacks were a part of the rising progressive diversity of humanity and that the West Indies were set on the path to development.[20]

While Mill did not campaign for financial compensation for blacks, he defended them as men and women equal to all others. He suggested that classical Egyptian culture was, in large measure, an expression of black Africans, and therefore a part of the heritage of Africans in the West Indies. Hence he rejected the racist reasoning of Carlyle by illustrating its historical inaccuracy and intellectual weakness.[21]

Mill stood on the side of emancipation as a progression in West Indian development. He imagined the effects of black freedom leading to a democratizing

---

17. E. Williams, *British Historians*, 45.
18. Ibid., 51.
19. Ibid. See also Mill, "Negro Question".
20. Ibid.
21. Ibid.

economy. He challenged the backward fantasy embedded in Carlyle's call for further black entrapment. His public empathy for blacks, however, was less well known than Carlyle's antipathy.[22]

The British government revealed at each significant moment its attachment to Carlylian philosophy. Blacks were expected to fear the consequences of freedom, as robust pursuit of it would trigger oppressive responses. The British, then, had framed a minimalist emancipation model in the West Indies. This was expected to give them time to conceal the tracks of the crimes against humanity that slavery represented. Carlylian racism was used to legitimize the widespread incidence of murders and other atrocities committed against blacks by colonial administrators.

The ideological bombardment of blacks with Carlylian caricatures was a critical part of British official policy that rejected their claims for economic empowerment and political self-determination. The failure of abolitionists to protect the emancipated from this extended bondage was, in part, a consequence of their inadequate advocacy for black freedom, since, on this issue, the two sides of Parliament were in unity. Both were ultimately committed to a West Indian economy in which the reign of white supremacy was left intact.

Government commitment to the traditional plantation economy, structured on the principle of economic extraction, was intensified and governed by white supremacy. The reformed labour system called for a further period of profit extraction at the expense of the manumitted.

British government policy – to keep blacks in bondage and on the lands of former enslavers – led to a second wave of black freedom struggles. From Belize to Barbados, and Jamaica to Guyana, the West Indies in the second half of the nineteenth century erupted into a theatre of anti-colonial warfare. From William Gordon and Paul Bogle in Jamaica to General Green and Samuel Prescod in Barbados, generations of extraordinary black leaders with democratic principles were motivated to confront the deception the Emancipation Act represented and present an indigenous vision for a new economic order.[23]

---

22. Ibid.

23. Glenelg to Governors of West Indian Colonies, 6 November 1837, in "Papers in Explanation of the Measures Adopted for Giving Effect to the Act for the Abolition of Slavery", PP 1837–1838, 154; Sligo to Glenelg, 5 March 1836, "Papers Relating to the Abolition of Slavery", PP 1836, 166. See also Holt, *Problem of Freedom*; Andrew Lewis, "'An Incendiary Press': British West Indian Newspapers during the Struggle for Abolition", *Slavery and Abolition* 16, no. 3 (December 1995): 346–62.

CHAPTER 3

Black Bloodbaths

Dying for Democracy

The prosperity of the labouring classes, as well as all other classes depends in Jamaica, and in other countries, upon their working for Wages, not uncertainly or capriciously, but steadily and continuously, at the times when their labour is wanted, and for so long as it is wanted; and that if they would use their industry, and thereby render the Plantations productive, they would enable the Planter to pay them higher Wages . . . and they must be assured that it is from their own industry and prudence . . . and not from any such scheme as have been suggested to them, that they must look for an improvement in their condition.

—Cardwell to Eyre, 6 May 1865, CO 137/390, no. 128

IN 1868, HENRY BLEBY DESCRIBED BRITISH post-slavery rule in Jamaica as "the Reign of Terror". Carlylian racism held a stranglehold on British policy. The effects were obvious: increased police and military repression and psychological terrorism. The result was a century of bloodletting.

At no stage following emancipation did the British government agree with the leaders of the black community that the future of the region could be based on a model of black economic empowerment. There was a clear imperial perspective that the role of the black community was to provide labour, not entrepreneurship.[1]

---

1. Henry Bleby, *The Reign of Terror: A Narrative of Facts Concerning ex-Governor Eyre, George William Gordon, and the Jamaica Atrocities* (London: William Nichols, 1862); Trial of Samuel Sharpe, 19 April 1832, CO 137/185; PP 1831–1832, 561; McNeel to Smith, 23 July 1839, Evidence of Robert Murray, PP 1840, 212; Eyre to Cardwell, 20 October 1865, CO 137/393; Evidence of Captain Ross, 22 October 1865, CO 137/397. See Gad Heuman, *Between Black and White: Race, Politics, and the Free Coloureds in Jamaica, 1792–1865* (Oxford: Oxford University Press, 1981); Gad Heuman, *"The Killing Time": The Morant Bay Rebellion in*

While multiple efforts were made at the parliamentary level to expand constitutional democracy in Britain, the "Nigger Question" discourse was producing military-style fascism in the West Indies. This duality was central to the governance of the empire. When Justice Mansfield, for example, made his famous ruling in the Somerset case in 1772, in which he defined blacks as non-humans, the politics of his judgment was evident: that chattel slavery was a West Indian institution not compatible with British law and the ideals of its people, who had for centuries inhaled the fresh air of liberty.

The "foul" stench of enslavement, the judge said, should be far removed from the reach of the inhabitants of the nation.[2] However, he did admit, slavery as an institution was conceptualized, put into practice and managed from the metropolis for the benefit of Britain.

After black enslavement, the colonial agenda called for the mass importation of workers from India to constitute a revised labour regime that would help to sustain the plunder of the West Indies. Queen Victoria became extractor in chief of both the East Indies and the West Indies. Carlyle was as addicted to the "Coolie" conversation as he was to the discourse on the "Nigger Question" that linked West Indians and East Indians to the survival of the plantation project.[3]

Gladstone, Prime Minister and King Enslaver

When William Ewart Gladstone became prime minister of Britain in 1868, it was generally understood at home and abroad that he represented the political power of the West Indian slavocracy. Who better than a son of the sugar plantations to consolidate control over the West Indies and management of the emancipated? His journey to leadership was predictable and detrimental.

Gladstone was the fourth son of the enslaver and plantation owner John Gladstone, who had made his fortune in the slave-trading and sugar business in the islands, as well as Guiana. The Gladstone clan was part of the Liverpool

Jamaica (London: Macmillan, 1994).

2. See Debbie Lee, *British Slavery and African Exploration: The Written Legacy* (Philadelphia: University of Pennsylvania Press, 2002); James Walvin, *Black Ivory: Slavery in the British Empire* (Malden, MA: Blackwell, 2001).

3. Carlyle, *Occasional Discourse*; see also Eyre to Caldwell, private papers, 23 October 1865, PRO 30/48/42.

colonial trading culture and was linked to its Scottish homeland through the slave-trading financial houses of Glasgow.[4]

> William was born in 1809, two years after the ending of the British trade in enslaved Africans that had enriched his father en route to the status of slavery royalty in Guiana. He opposed black emancipation and eagerly supported the importation of indentured Indian workers to rebuild and renovate his plantations. By the time of his death in 1898, just three years ahead of his beloved queen, he had served as prime minister for four terms, lasting twelve years. He was also a manager of British imperial loot, serving on four occasions as chancellor of the exchequer.

John's West Indian fortune provided William with the most expensive English elite education – Eton College, Oxford University and, finally, Lincoln's Inn, which he entered in 1831 to train as a lawyer. As a student at Oxford, he denounced the liberalism that had empowered anti-slavery advocacy, reforming consciousness and emancipation legislation.

William declared himself a Conservative and an ardent supporter of slavery. He entered the House of Commons at twenty-two under the political tutelage of a well-known investor in enslaved labour, the Duke of Newcastle. His inaugural speech was in defence of his family's plantation business in Guiana, much to the satisfaction of his pro-slavery colleagues on both sides of the house.[5]

The "scion of one of the largest slave-holding families in the world", William fought ferociously to keep blacks in bondage, and the West Indies a sugar plantation paradise. With his legal training, he successfully extracted a massive fortune from the British government in compensation for his family's enslaved blacks. They owned 2,508 enslaved people on nine plantations in Guiana and the islands. They received compensation to the value of £106,769 from the state, the equivalent of nearly £100 million in today's average earnings.[6]

---

4. See S.G. Checkland, *The Gladstones: A Family Biography, 1764–1851* (Cambridge: Cambridge University Press, 1971). See also H.C.G. Matthew, "Gladstone, Sir John, 1764–1851", *Oxford Dictionary of National Biography*, https://doi.org/10.1093/ref:odnb/33417.

5. See Madhavi Kale, *Fragments of Empire: Capital, Slavery, and Indentured Labor Migration in the British Caribbean* (Philadelphia: University of Pennsylvania Press, 1998).

6. "Jamaica", Lewis Bowerbank, CO 38/48/44, PRO; David King, *A Sketch of the Late Mr G.W. Gordon, Jamaica* (London: Oliphant, 1866); Richard B. Sheridan, "The Condition of Slaves on the Sugar Plantations of Sir John Gladstone in the Colony of Demerara, 1812–1849", *New West Indian Guide* 76, nos. 3–4 (2002): 243–69; "John Gladstone: Profile and Legacies Summary", Legacies of British Slave-Ownership, Department of History,

When the Americans went to civil war in April 1861 over slavery at home, Gladstone defended Southern enslavers as he did his West Indian colleagues. On 7 October 1862, he called for British parliamentary support for the Southern Confederates who intended to sustain their own United States of America on the slavery system. He was also a dedicated admirer of slavery advocate and defender Jefferson Davis, whose slave-owning credentials he considered impeccable.

As a pro-slavery advocate, William became leader of the Liberal Party in 1867, linking his old conservatism to his new liberalism. The consequence was the effective unification in Parliament of the plantation cause. At his end, in 1898, he was defined by anti-slavery advocates as a British statesman and Liberal politician who represented during the sixty years of his parliamentary career the enslavement of blacks and deception of indentured Indians.

Slavery Still Desired

In 1869, two decades after emancipation, the Englishman the Reverend Greville John Chester visited Barbados on a tour of the plantation world. Slavery, Gladstone had stated seven years earlier, was as good an economic and social institute as any. Dining with the plantation elite at the governor's residence, Chester participated in many conversations on the "loss of slavery" and hope for its return.[7] Chester recorded:

> The fact is – though they are ashamed to avow it openly, – there still exists a strong feeling in favour of slavery amongst the planters, and especially amongst the planters' wives, and there is still a strong disposition to grudge the negroes their civil, educational, and religious privileges. This detestable feeling of exclusiveness, sad to say, is in some degree fostered by the clergy . . . who are the very humble servants of what they call the "respectable people".[8]

Furthermore, he suggested,

> One predominating characteristic of the white people is their abject fear of the negroes. Whether, on the principle that "conscience makes cowards of us all",

University College London, https://www.ucl.ac.uk/lbs/person/view/8961.

7. Rev. Greville John Chester, *Chester's Barbados: The Barbados Chapters* from *Transatlantic Sketches (1869)*, Barbadian Heritage Reprint Series (Bridgetown: National Cultural Foundation, 1990), 43; "A Narrative of the Arrest and Imprisonment of the Rev. E. Palmer", CO 137/409, no. 7.

8. Chester, *Chester's Barbados*, 40.

"this feeling be only the natural offspring of past tyranny and present scant or unwillingly rendered justice, or has any more solid foundation, I am unable to say". But exist it does. One is continually being told that if the English troops were to be withdrawn, the black West Indian regiments would immediately fraternize with the creole Negroes, and that a great massacre of whites would ensure.

The more likely outcome of these and such conversations, however, was the obverse – the bloody massacre of West Indian blacks. With Gladstone and his cohort in control of the British government, it seemed near certain that this would happen. And, indeed, it did occur, across the West Indies. Guiana, and then Jamaica, became the epicentres of mass killings.

At emancipation, Jamaica was home to some 311,070 enslaved people. Barbados trailed second with 83,150. Jamaican enslavers valued their human property at £13,951,139, the largest sum in the West Indies. Barbados was third with £3,897,276. Jamaican enslavers received £6,161,927 in reparations from the British government, while the Barbadians received £1,721,345; Gladstone's Guiana, whose 64,185 enslaved were valued at £9,729,047, received £4,330,665.[9]

It was Jamaica, as a result, that occupied the financial centre of British concern about the future of the West Indies as a sustainable plantation economy. It was also Jamaica that had the largest community of blacks willing to wage war in all forms in pursuit of economic empowerment and political liberty.

Uppermost in their mind was the acquisition of land. But imperial policy was clear: no freehold land for blacks and therefore, no land reform to facilitate political and economic enfranchisement. But they were not deterred. The number of freehold units they owned of ten acres and less increased from 883 in 1840 to 20,724 in 1845, and those between 10 and 19 acres increased from 938 to 2,112 in the same period. This ownership came with a price tag – written in their blood.[10]

The significant acquisition of small farms and subsistence peasant allotment inflamed the racism of local whites and the British government. The result was increased racial conflict in the colony. The relationship between black economic empowerment and white economic superiority, considered contradictory in Gladstone's Britain, was the inevitable flashpoint in the framing of post-slavery economics. Whites feared that blacks were targeting land ownership not only

9. Beckles, *Britain's Black Debt*, 149, 151.
10. E. Williams, *British Historians*, 62.

for enhanced food supplies but to meet eligibility for the political franchise. Farms and franchise constituted freedom, but standing in defiance of this development were garrisons and domestic militias.

Workers withdrew interest in accommodating former enslavers with the supply of adequate and reliable labour. They offered some work; however, at levels of remuneration the planters considered unreasonable and unaffordable. The economics of the labour market favoured the self-empowerment agenda of labourers, especially those in possession of land. They were keenly aware of the hostility embedded in imperial policy, but moved nonetheless with alacrity to acquire larger tracts of land.

Carlyle's recommendation was to facilitate Conservative policymakers in devaluing the legal advantage of black labourers and to impose market restrictions on land availability. The keenness of the plantation interest to abandon laissez-faire economics revealed his desire to change the labour market rules of supply and demand. As sugar production in Jamaica fell from 68,198 tons in 1828 to 29,624 tons in 1850, and its share of world production fell from 15 per cent to 2.5 per cent in that period, the economic opportunity for blacks to establish the basis of an indigenous economy became the central political concern of the British government and its colonial governors.[11]

Evidence of black entrepreneurial agility stood in stark contrast to the island-wide abandonment of white-owned farms. The decline of these enterprises was discussed in the British Parliament and was attributed by Conservatives to the imperfection of emancipation legislation. The largest plantation colony, Jamaica, was described as creeping inexorably into the clutches of grasping manumitted blacks.

The increasing production and export of non-sugar agricultural commodities were likewise attributed largely to the success of black farmers. It was noted that "exports of ginger increased from 382,326 pounds in 1841 to 613,479 in 1846; exports of coconuts from 103,452 to 245,450". On the other hand, it was recorded that "imports of soap rose from 18,866 cwt in 1834 to 46,308 in 1851; and of flour from 53,998 barrels to 66,106".[12]

Black economic creativity and consumer participation presented an image of industry and energy contributing to the island's economy. As the evidence

---

11. Ibid.
12. Ibid., 63.

of market engagement and community development became more substantial, political and military preparations for the pushback were put in place.

The idea of flooding the West Indian labour market with deceived and oppressed Indian indentured workers, with other workers coming from China, was rolled out in London by the Gladstone group, and ably supported by political officials. Wage suppression and reduced land availability were considered the primary imperial response to subvert black achievement and restore the destitution that had been the dominant feature of slavery.

Williams argued that the Jamaican elite and their imperial supporters looked around the free and colonized world for cheaper labour, and had considerable success in short time: "Between 1834 and 1842, no fewer than 4,496 workers were introduced from Britain, Germany, Bahamas, Canada, and the USA, while 1,270 came from Africa. Between 1850 and 1858, a total of 4,551 contract workers were brought in from India, of whom 1,726 were repatriated; between 1860 and 1863, a further 6,482 immigrants were introduced."[13] Crushing Quashee, the policy objective of the Carlyle cohort and the Gladstone parliamentary group, was fully activated and deployed.

The Guiana Massacre

The foundations for Britain's first post-emancipation black bloodbath in the West Indies were laid systematically, one policy after another. Each was designed to ensure that neither plural democracy nor black economic enfranchisement would characterize the new era. Such policies to thwart black success in land and labour markets were vigorously deployed. Jamaica and Guiana governors, more so than others in the West Indies, placed their militias and garrisons on high alert. These colonies were the largest battleground, home to the grand standoff between the concepts and concrete realities of the "Rights of Man" and the "Might of Empire".

In Gladstone's Guiana, the new frontier of the old sugar plantation system, freed blacks and indentured Indians stood their ground and prepared for the violent onslaught. There was a high level of island-to-mainland migration as the manumitted sought out land to create free villages, the basis of their incipient self-determination movement.

---

13. Ibid.

Innovative and entrepreneurial, as were their counterparts in Jamaica, Guianese workers formed cooperatives to buy expensive arable land on which to grow crops for the local and export markets. As in Jamaica, they confronted official efforts designed to force them back to the plantation as labourers. The importation of thousands of indentured workers by plantation owners from India, Madeira, Portugal and China to break blacks' self-empowerment resolve met with minimum success.[14]

As political tensions mounted, blacks and Indians pressed their claim for just wages, fair food prices and access to land. At the same time, whites urged the governor to place the military options on the agenda. Governor Wodehouse defined black workers as living in a state of defiance, in a "life little less savage than that of beasts of the fields". His provocation of workers, blacks especially, reflected British policy. The response was rebellion. The Angel Gabriel, the name given to John Sayers Orr, leader of black workers, called for anti-colonial confrontation in 1856.[15]

Warfare broke out on 16 February, following the governor's summoning of Orr. He was formally accused of convening an illegal gathering of workers at which he recommended civil disobedience. He was also accused of targeting the Portuguese ethnic minority who commercially supported the British Empire. It was reported that in the rebellion, only Portuguese shops were looted, and their owners abused and beaten throughout Demerara, Essequibo and Berbice.[16]

The rebellion brought the colony to a standstill. The governor called out the troops in order to crush the rebels. He stated that the uprising demonstrated "beyond the possibility of doubt that the masses of the population are in no degree able to govern themselves". Furthermore, in this regard, he said, they have degenerated below where they were "at the time of Emancipation". One hundred captives were tried for rebellion; reports referred to prisons overflowing with black malcontents. The majority were sentenced to imprisonment with hard labour; terms ranged from one to three years.[17]

During the trials, Orr was treated with greater flexibility than his followers.

---

14. Kale, *Fragments of Empire.*

15. See Michael Craton, "Continuity not Change: The Incidence of Unrest among Ex-Slaves in the British West Indies, 1838–1876", *Slavery and Abolition* 9, no. 2 (1988): 144–71.

16. Ibid., 146–147. See also V.O. Chan, "The Riots of 1856 in British Guiana", *Caribbean Quarterly* 16, no. 1 (1970): 39–50.

17. Craton, "Continuity", 149; Eyre to Caldwell, 20 November 1865, no. 291, CO 137/395.

He was sentenced to three years' imprisonment. The governor reported that "the people of England are no longer under the delusion that these people can be controlled by precisely the same forms of laws as prove sufficient in highly civilized communities". Furthermore, he said, "they no longer wish freedom from slavery to mean anything less than freedom from all legal control".[18]

The following year, Wodehouse departed the colony on vacation. The black community took the opportunity of sending him off at the docks with a salute of pelted stones. On his retirement from the governorship in May 1861, he thought it best to sneak away from the dock in a steamer in the "dead of night" to "avoid a salute of dead cats and dogs".[19]

"Vox Populi"

On the heels of Orr's rebellion in Guiana came the workers' uprising in St Vincent in 1862. The Vincentians considered themselves at the centre of British policy that specified how emancipated blacks were to be kept as close as possible to the norms of slavery. Planters deemed it possible to remove social incentives and material benefits that were implemented during the last decade of slavery. The governor of the island encouraged them, if they saw fit, to abandon the prior industrial relations culture. The response of workers was the mass declaration of freedom of expression against the British government, the colonial administration and sugar planters.

Confrontation with blacks began on Mount Bentinck sugar estate, where the manager unilaterally threw out the labour agreement that gave workers access to small plots of land and other benefits, such as health care and cash wages for extra or overtime work. The cumulative effect of these reductions was to undermine living standards and restore slavery-like conditions.

From Mount Bentinck, workers' protests spread across the island, with intense concentration in Charlotte and St George, where Portuguese dry-goods retailers had settled in large numbers. As in Guiana, the rebellion that targeted sugar planters as the primary enemy of the people did not spare their allies.[20]

---

18. Eyre to Caldwell, 20 November 1865, no. 291, CO 137/39.

19. Craton, "Continuity", 150. See also James Rose, *The Strike of 1848* (Georgetown: History Society, University of Guyana, 1989).

20. Woodville Marshall, "'Vox Populi': The St Vincent Riots and Disturbances of 1862",

From Thomas Carlyle to Anthony Trollope

In 1859, between the commencement of workers' rebellions in Guiana and St Vincent, the well-known British novelist Anthony Trollope arrived in Jamaica. In the same year, his considerable literary skills were celebrated with the publication of his book *The West Indies and the Spanish Main*. The title suggested that it was just another travelogue by a curious, critical observer of the emancipation process. But his core concern was the popular black discontent evident throughout the region.[21]

Trollope's West Indian commentary had been widely publicized. The British political community was eagerly awaiting his publication, promoted by his publicist as a tell-all account. Jamaica was already branded a powder keg in light of the Sam Sharpe war against slavery in 1831, the persistence of sporadic protest, the widespread appropriation of idle land by the manumitted, and the general unwillingness of blacks to accept the terms and conditions of work offered by employers. Trollope sought to inform the British audience about such activities that ostensibly constituted the true state of affairs on the island.

Williams described Trollope's account as "an expurgated version" of Carlyle's *Occasional Discourse on the Nigger Question*. But there was greater bitterness than in Carlyle's caricatures. Trollope also had more impact on the liberal elements of civil society that had been partly alienated by Carlyle's cursing blacks. Such groups wanted more objectivity from the novelist, yet they desired the acerbic commentary.

The reach of Trollope's writing, therefore, went beyond the conservative classes and permeated those sectors of society keen to know more about the West Indian economy and the mentality of the manumitted. He was aware of the greater influence his work would exert, and like an ambitious travel journalist, he was keen to make a lasting impression, but had no empathy for the feelings of blacks.[22]

Trollope's travel was intended to pave the way for what he had long wished, a career in politics in either the Liberal or Tory party. Little did the public know that his tour of Jamaica was part of a dress rehearsal for his bid to enter

---

in *Trade, Government, and Society in Caribbean History*, ed. B.W. Higman (Kingston: Heinemann Caribbean, 1983), 85–115.

21. Anthony Trollope, *The West Indies and the Spanish Main* (London: Good Press, 1859).

22. See E. Williams, *British Historians*, 64–65.

Parliament. His immediate plunge into Carlylian pro-slavery rhetoric represented the powerful prose-fiction extremism the Tory elite especially wanted to hear, and the squeamish liberals initially feared.

The "sugar estates in Jamaica", he said, and "more than half of the coffee plantations have gone back into a state of bush" and the colony, "rich with the richest produce only thirty years ago . . . has now fallen back into wilderness".[23] Allied to this were his lament of black freedom, his idealization of slavery and the chastisement of the British state for the undoing of the enslavers' paradise:

> Jamaica was a land of wealth, rivalling the East in its means of riches, nay, excelling it as a market for capital, a place in which money might be turned; and that it now is a spot on the earth almost more poverty-stricken than any other – so much is known almost to all men. That this change was brought about by the manumission of the slaves, which was completed in 1838, of that also the English world is generally aware.[24]

Following this description of declared grief for the loss of slavery, Trollope tells the tale of the specific losses to the world and England:

> The (British) families who are connected with Jamaica by ties of interest are becoming fewer and fewer. Property has been abandoned as good for nothing, and nearly forgotten; or has been sold for what wretched trifle it could fetch; or left to an overseer, who is hardly expected to send home proceeds . . . fathers no longer send their younger sons to make their fortunes there. Young English girls no longer come out as brides. Dukes and earls do not now govern the rich gem of the west, spending their tens of thousands in royal magnificence. . . . In lieu of this, some governor by profession, unfortunate for the moment, takes Jamaica with a groan.[25]

His entire literary project was a lamentation for those who still wished to return to slavery, and to soothe their sorrow:

> You cannot abolish slavery to the infinite good of your souls, your minds, and intellect, and yet retain it for the good of your pocket. Seeing that these men are free, it is worse than useless to begrudge them the use of their freedom. If I

23. Trollope quoted ibid., 65. See Grant to Duke of Buckingham, 9 October 1867, no. 200, CO 137/427.

24. E. Williams, *British Historians*, 65.

25. Ibid.

have means to lie in the sun and meditate idle, why, O my worthy taskmaster! should you expect me to pull out at thy behest long reels of cotton, long reels of law jargon, long reels of official verbosity, long reels of gossamer literature – why indeed? . . . [The] oil-fat negro, is a richer man than I. He lies under his mango-tree, and eats the luscious fruit in the sun, he sends his black urchin up for a breadfruit, and behold the family table is spread. . . . Yes, Sambo has learned to have his own way.[26]

Carlyle's "Quashee", then, morphed into Trollope's "Sambo", and with these imperial icons, the British cultural condemnation of the black West Indian was complete. Sambo was considered lazier than Quashee, and was not willing to work for former enslavers, now enriched with £20 million of reparation cash.

Sambo was Trollope's trope and the key to understanding British racial rage driven by the fear of a black takeover in Jamaica. No mention was made of the regional economic crisis being in great part a result of the Sugar Duties Act of 1846, which made West Indian sugar less competitive on the British market. It was Sambo's ascendency to a free life that threatened the white supremacy represented by the plantations.

While Trollope was keenly promoting racist stereotypes about the emancipated in the region, black Jamaicans were busy, under his nose, accumulating land to qualify for the electoral franchise. The right to vote was property-qualified, and the strategy of electing their own to parochial positions and to the House of Assembly was as shrewd a political move as could be contemplated. This, too, outraged the parliamentary supporters of Jamaican enslavers. Trollope noted:

At present, when the old planter sits on the magisterial bench, a coloured man sits beside him; one probably on each side of him. At road sessions he cannot carry out his little project because the coloured men out-vote him. There is a vacancy for his parish in the House of Assembly. . . . A coloured man is therefore chosen, and votes away the white man's taxes; and then things worse and worse arise. Not only coloured men get into office, but black men also. . . . "Fancy what our state is," a young Planter said to me; "I dare not die, for fear I should be sat upon by a black man!"[27]

26. Ibid., 66. See also Baptist Noel, *The Case of G.W. Gordon, Esq., of Jamaica* (London: Nisbet, 1866).

27. Trollope quoted in E. Williams, *British Historians*, 67. See also Swithin Wilmot, "From

Jamaica, both Carlyle and Trollope wrote, was the place in the West Indies where the British Parliament, with its emancipation proclamation, had unleashed the hydras of destruction.

Hate of Haiti: British Massacre at Morant Bay

"Haitianization" became the metaphor for the hell imagined to lie within British emancipation policy. The fear of black political and economic enfranchisement in Jamaica was simply too much for Mother Britain to bear. Haiti, therefore, independent since 1804, was the hated place. The book that sought to batter Haiti's blacks was titled *Where Black Rules White: A Journey Across and About Haiti*. It was written by the Englishman Hesketh Prichard, and was not yet published. That was to be 1909. But in 1859, forty years earlier, when Trollope traversed Jamaica, the general thesis proposed by both authors was already popular in Britain.

Haiti was the Caribbean society where blacks took everything held precious from the whites – the French and other Europeans.[28] France considered St Domingue, the name it ascribed to the colony, its most prosperous possession. With nearly 500,000 enslaved Africans before the black revolution, it overshadowed Jamaica, which came second in the numbers race with 300,000 enslaved. The British, and all of western Europe, craved the recapture of this enormous pool of human capital and longed for a future in which the blacks could be reenslaved.

France's failed attempt to reestablish possession of Haiti at the end of the 1790s led to its decision to cede ownership of the colony and its hitherto enslaved people to Britain. With little division, the British Parliament voted to invade and reestablish slavery. Thousands of British soldiers followed their French counterparts to bloody graves as the revolutionary army of Toussaint L'Ouverture swept Europe's military might before it. Crushed and humiliated, the British military high command licked its wounds while the state and elements of civil society nurtured hatred for the country that emerged in 1804, black, free and independent – Haiti.[29]

Falmouth to Morant Bay: Religion and Politics in Jamaica, 1838–1865" (paper presented at the Association of Caribbean Historians conference, Havana, Cuba, April 1985).

28. H. Hesketh Prichard, *Where Black Rules White: As Reported by the First White Man to Traverse Haiti in Nearly 100 Years* (New York: Scribner's, 1900).

29. See Hubert Cole, *Christophe, King of Haiti* (New York: Viking, 1967); David Geggus,

It was the only country in the hemisphere where "blacks ruled whites"; a place despised and feared by the British. Jamaica, Britain's prized property in the West Indies, was Haiti's neighbour, a simple voyage across a narrow strait known well by blacks on both sides. The mosquito easily managed this passage, it was said, and the British dreaded violent black revolution blowing from the east.

With Carlyle at the centre of British policy, and Haiti as the symbol of anti-black racism, the stage was set for the trigger-happy British government. Angered by two decades of failure to keep blacks in slave-like bondage, the colonial government was keen to implement imperial policy. Britain had recently sent out a new governor, Edward John Eyre, described by Williams as "one of the worst cases of gubernatorial rubbish ever exported to the West Indies". Eyre embodied the ire of the British, who could hardly contain their anxiety in the face of black empowerment in Jamaica against the background of Haitian nation-building.[30]

Some 550 enslaved blacks had lost their lives to white violent repression in the 1831 Jamaican anti-slavery revolution. Thirty-four years later, another 450 lives were to be sacrificed in the revolution's second phase. Since the publication of Trollope's treatise in 1859, there had been evidence of mounting black protest sweeping across the island – erupting in coordinated military action in the parish of St Thomas-in-the-East.[31]

It was October 1865, and anti-slavery revolution was also spreading across

Slavery, War and Revolution: The British Occupation of Saint-Domingue 1793–1798 (London: Oxford University Press, 1982); C.L.R. James, *The Black Jacobins: Toussaint L'Ouverture and the San Domingo Revolution* (New York: Random House, 1963); David Nicholls, *From Dessalines to Duvalier: Race, Colour and National Independence in Haiti* (New York: Cambridge University Press, 1979).

30. E. Williams, *British Historians*, 78; Henry Mais, Evidence, 12 October 1865, CO 137/400, Jamaican Royal Commission (JRC); Ashwood to Eyre, 6 January 1866, no. 1, JRC; Eyre to Caldwell, 7 November 1865, CO 137/394, no. 271; Storke to Caldwell, 19 February 1866, CO 137/499, no. 28.

31. See Heuman, "The Killing Time"; Special Commission, 6 March 1866, the Queen v. Bogle, for Felonous Riot, Papers; Evidence of Brookes Cooke, Arthur Warrington, JRC; Evidence of Edward Eyre, Custos of St Thomas-in-the-East, 10 October 1865; Description of the Disturbance, 30/48/44, Cardwell Papers; W.F. Finlason, *The History of the Jamaica Case* (London, 1869); H. Hume, *The Life of Edward John Eyre* (London, 1867); Douglas Hall, *Free Jamaica: 1838–1865: An Economic History* (New Haven, CT: Yale University Press, 1959); B. Semmel, *Jamaican Blood and Victorian Conscience* (Cambridge: Cambridge University Press, 1963).

the United States. There was drought in Jamaica, destroying families among the poor, who appealed to colonial authorities for relief, but to no avail. The northern community of St Ann petitioned Queen Victoria requesting food. The message embedded in the royal response was predictable. It was based on the language of the Emancipation Act: more "industry" was recommended as the cure for poverty and famine.[32]

Increased repression by Jamaican officials was the predictable outcome. This is what the British government had mandated. Large numbers of blacks were arrested, charged and imprisoned for illegal occupation of crown lands, inability to pay rent and causing disturbances of the public peace. Paul Bogle, a Baptist deacon in the ministry led by George William Gordon, the coloured, charismatic civil rights advocate, had created a black coalition of self-defence organizations described by Governor Eyre as seditious.[33]

Sporadic actions, such as liberating innocent people from police cells, provided opportunities for Bogle to address large gatherings. When his brigade descended on the compound of the Morant Bay Courthouse, the militia fired bullets into their ranks, killing seven people and wounding dozens. In response, the brigade stormed the courthouse and released fifty captives, while others seized food supplies from plantation stores in the vicinity. In these events, twenty white people were reported killed. The custos of Morant Bay was put to death while sending a message to Eyre. The rebellion did not contain itself to Morant Bay, but spread across the north and west of the island.[34]

Eyre was known as a colonial administrator experienced in putting down native rebellions. He had done so during stints of service in Australia and New Zealand, where the indigenous people were demanding freedom and self-determination. In addition, his racist attitudes in dealing with Africans and Indian indentured servants in Trinidad and St Vincent were a part of the West Indian memory. In the corridors of the British government, however, he was respected as an effective political leader.

---

32. Craton, "Continuity not Change", 152.

33. Ibid., 152–55; Storks to Cardwell, 19 February1866, Enclosure 28; Evidence of William Fuller, 5 January 1866, CO 137/40; Bleby, *Reign of Terror*; Report of Captain de Horsey, 22 October 1865, CO 137/397; Thomas Harvey and William Brewin, *Jamaica in 1866* (London: A.W. Bennett, 1867); Oxley to de Horsey, 21 October 1865, CO 137/397; Evidence of Henry Ford, 25 October 1865, CO 137/397.

34. Craton, "Continuity not Change", 152.

Before arriving in Jamaica, Eyre was radicalized in his disgust for "Sambo and Quasheba". He set about applying British policy. At Morant Bay, he gave the order to fire on the blacks. He also directed the setting up of the gallows. "It was necessary," he said, "to make an example which, by striking terror, might deter other districts from following the horrible example of St Thomas-in-the–East." Furthermore, he said, "the administration of summary justice became a necessity, and any hesitation would have been fatal to the success of the military operation".[35]

The order to massacre the blacks across the island created a bloodbath in which peasants with pitchforks seeking food were sacrificed. His contempt for black life was fully displayed. Eyre's biographer sets out his views in this way: "emancipation has only made (the Negro) more lazy, more cunning, more sensual, more profligate, more prone to mischief, and more dangerous".[36]

Fear and hatred of blacks drove Eyre to vengeance, and the viciousness of his vision turned Jamaica into a British killing field. Summarizing the killings, Michael Craton concludes: "More than 430 men and women were shot down or put to death after trial – with 600 publicly flogged and more than 1,000 houses burnt. Paul Bogle, caught by the Maroons in a cane piece, was hanged from the burnt-out Courthouse. George William Gordon, carried by ship to Kingston to Morant Bay so that he could be tried by court martial, was hanged within three days, on 23 October."[37] Eyre's ruthless abuse of power achieved its desired effect. Blacks across the West Indies heard of him: the governor as butcher. Bogle's name was also canonized in the community as news of the rebellion and his execution spread.

In the face of the demand for democracy, planter politicians, in association with the governor and the British Parliament, opted to abandon parliamentary representation and voted for direct rule from London. The legislature that comprised an elected House of Assembly, the seed of the future democratic order, was abandoned. The principle of political representation was set aside to secure imperial authority.

Rebellion, Bogle style, spread across the eastern Caribbean. In Barbados, the emancipated blacks rallied behind their leader "General" Green in 1876, and in Tobago, the Belmanna Rebellion took place in the same year. Vox populi

---

35. E. Williams, *British Historians*, 93.
36. Ibid., 96.
37. Craton, "Continuity not Change", 154.

was everywhere declared in the West Indies by the black community. British repression intensified as workers expanded their political and economic actions to bring an end to imperial brutality.[38]

These actions to subvert the quest for freedom were everywhere resisted. William G. Sewell, like Trollope, visited the West Indies in 1859, but no Carlylian was he. His writings from the region captured the emerging Caribbean political thinking. The British government defended and celebrated Eyre, while the progressive intellectual community, led again by the irrepressible John Stuart Mill, called for his conviction for mass murder.[39] He escaped criminal conviction, but he was convicted by Caribbean history.

Sewell's account, on the other hand, of West Indian demands for justice, in the context of British terrorism, illuminated and shaped blacks' demand for development. He wrote:

> The plantocracy of Jamaica is a thing of the past, and in its stead democracy is lifting its head. I am not so enthusiastic a democrat as to believe that the principles of our political faith, much less its practice, will flourish in any soil or in any climate. . . . Their power no longer predominates. They command no credit and no self-respect, and they obtain but little sympathy in their misfortune. Even from domestic legislation, they have sullenly retired, and their places are being fast filled by the people whom they have so long and so vainly tried to keep down.[40]

He noted, furthermore, how black blood was spilled in large quantities in the West Indies by British armed forces as manumitted communities sought to actualize the emancipation they imagined.

The policy of the British government of reforming slavery while keeping intact its structures and relationship was rejected by West Indians as rooted in racist thinking and policies. The lobbies that continued to defend slavery as a modern model for the West Indies persisted in the use of military power to crush the emancipated. British parliamentary governance forced blacks to pay the dearest imaginable price. But they emerged with resilience and fortitude as the nineteenth-century carriers of the modern dispensation called democracy.

---

38. Bridget Brereton, "Post-Emancipation Protest in the Caribbean: The 'Belmanna Riots' in Tobago, 1876", *Caribbean Quarterly* 30, nos. 3–4 (1984): 110–23; Marshall, "Vox Populi", 85–115.

39. William G. Sewell, *The Ordeal of Free Labor in the British West Indies* (New York: Harper and Brothers, 1861).

40. E. Williams, *British Historians*, 74.

Paul Bogle, leader of the 1865 freedom
struggle in Jamaica

Queen Victoria, who reigned in
the post-emancipation period and
consolidated white-supremacy racism
within imperial expansion

James Anthony Froude, British
historian and white-supremacy
advocate

Thomas Carlyle, British white-
supremacy philosopher and activist

PART 2

British Fascism against Caribbean Freedom

CHAPTER 4

Freezing Freedom
Blocking Black Progress

The black man in the islands does not enjoy the political liberty, that his white brother enjoys in the Mother Country; in this island [St Lucia] with a population of 40,000 inhabitants, not seven hundred are white; still they make laws to which we the 39,000 submit, they levy taxes, that we the 39,000 must pay, and . . . we have submitted patiently to this political slavery.

—"Memorial of J.E. Quinlan and Two Others", 22 July 1887, CO 321/101, no. 68

I have not yet been able to ascertain that any member of the Negro race in this colony [St Vincent] has attained such a character and position as would render it expedient to place him in a small council of nominated members. In an enlarged council having an elective element, room might be found for one or two of this class.

—Governor of the Windward Islands Walter Sendall, Minutes of the Legislative Council, 9 September 1886, CO 321/97

THE BRITISH GOVERNMENT DEALT A DOUBLE blow to the emancipated. It moved swiftly to consolidate white-supremacy governance on the foundation of the declining plantation system. It blocked and derailed the economic empowerment efforts of the majority of black and Indian communities. Every effort was made to inhibit the expansion and advance of the basic social freedom available to the black and brown populations. It fossilized the racialized economic and social structure in tandem with a repressive political framework intended to maintain the economic dependency of the region.[1]

---

1. Papers in Explanation of Measures Adopted for Giving Effect to the Abolition of Slavery Act, PP 1835, 177; Marquis of Sligo to Lord Glenelg, 9 July 1836, PP 1837, 521;

While the application in Britain of economic development theory informed the government's intention to improve living conditions for workers within the urban-industrial complex, white domination in the West Indies was intended to consolidate black poverty and political exclusion. There was nothing surprising about this. Prime Minister William Gladstone could not imagine a West Indian economy without sugar planters at the centre, and a society without military power in the hands of governors.[2]

The British government could see no other alternative. Royalty, aristocracy and government were aligned in the strategy. While the West Indies declined in economic value and financial importance, they remained nonetheless high-ranked in the political prestige of Empire. The plantation system was more than an economic institution. It was also a social culture with a distinct race-based ideology that gave white colonial elites power over all others, with no accountability.[3]

Colonialists were omnipotent on their plantations, with the right to take black life without penalty by illustrating that blacks were practising resistance of any kind. They had built their domestic sexual socialization on the right to

Charles Metcalfe to Lord Russell, 9 June 1840, CO 137/249, no. 84; Memorandum on the Progress of the Free System in the West India Colonies, 1840, CO 884/1, no. 6; S. Wilmot, "Emancipation in Action: Workers and Wage Conflicts in Jamaica, 1838–1848" (paper presented at the Sixteenth Annual Conference of Caribbean Historians, Barbados, 1984); Mary Turner, "Chattel Slaves into Wage Slaves: A Jamaican Case Study", in *Labour in the Caribbean: From Emancipation to Independence*, ed. Malcolm Cross and Gad Heuman (London: Macmillan, 1988), 14–32; Douglas Hall, *Five of the Leewards, 1834–1870: The Major Problems of the Post-Emancipation Period in Antigua, Barbuda, Montserrat, Nevis and St Kitts* (Aylesbury, UK: Caribbean University Press, 1971); Woodville Marshall, ed., *The Colthurst Journal: Journal of a Special Magistrate in the Islands of Barbados and St. Vincent, July 1835–September 1838* (Millwood, NY: KTO Press).

2. See "Third Report from the Select Committee on Sugar and Coffee Planting", PP 1847–48, 167; Checkland, *Gladstones*; S.G. Checkland "John Gladstone as Trader and Planter", *Economic History Review*, n.s., 7, no. 2 (1954): 216–29.

3. See Testimony of A.E. Bateman in West India Royal Commission (WIRC), *Report of the West India Royal Commission* (London: HMSO, 1897), 140–50; Annual Report for St Vincent, PP 1888, 73; "Depressed Condition of the Sugar Industry", 26 July 1884, CO 321/74; "Vaccination, Contagious Diseases, and the Registration of Deaths", 1 August 1891, CO 28/229, no. 142; "Central Sugar Factory", 12 July 1895, CO 321/160, no. 84; also 11 January 1895, CO 321/159, CO 884/7, no. 116; Report from the Select Committee on the Extinction of Slavery throughout the British Dominions, PP 1831–32, 20; David Lambert, "The 'Glasgow King of Billingsgate': James MacQueen and an Atlantic Proslavery Network", *Slavery and Abolition* 29, no. 3 (June 2008): 389–413; B.W. Higman, "The West Indian Interest in Parliament, 1807–33", *Historical Studies* 13, no. 49 (October 1967): 1–19.

exploit the enslaved. White sexual freedom and racial supremacy meant more to them than a marginal decline in profits. Sacrificing some income while maintaining full social authority seemed rational.

Sugar planters could survive on credit lines and suffer the shame of living on a bankrupt plantation. But maintaining social domination and political power was top priority in their existential reasoning.[4] Economic development of the colony as a whole was the lowest rung of the colonial priority ladder. Keeping blacks poor was a policy rooted in three centuries of economic extraction. Critically, it was linked directly to the broader imperial programme known as the "Scramble for Africa" and the "invasion of India".[5]

The West Indian economy, then, was marginalized for multiple market reasons, though it remained central to imperial interests. Economic extraction was again modified to promote British power and prestige on the global stage. Money was never exclusively the beginning and end of imperial thinking. As a consequence, everywhere in the West Indies, after the Morant Bay massacre of the Jamaican poor, British governments militarized politics. While destitution escalated to famine levels in Barbados and the eastern Caribbean, the sugar planters, in full military control of the production system and the political process, complained nonetheless about black rebelliousness.[6]

Critical-minded commentators, local and imperial, were in agreement that the solution to the regional food crisis resided in the creation of a productive black peasantry. Yet the British government could not imagine letting some measure of economic control pass to blacks from white colonial elites. Backed

---

4. See S.G. Checkland, "Finance for the West Indies, 1780–1815", *Economic History Review*, n.s., 10, no. 3 (1958): 461–69; Mary Butler, "'Fair and Equitable Consideration': The Distribution of Slave Compensation in Jamaica and Barbados", *Journal of Caribbean History* 22, nos: 1–2 (1988): 138–52.

5. See K.O. Lawrence, *Immigration into the West Indies in the 19th Century* (Bridgetown: Caribbean University Press, 1971); K.O. Lawrence, "The Evolution of Long-Term Labour Contracts in British Guiana and Trinidad, 1834–1863", *Jamaica Historical Review* 5, no. 1 (1965): 9–27; L.S.S. O'Malley, ed., *Modern India and the West* (London, Oxford University Press, 1941).

6. Richardson, *Economy and Environment*, xiii; Further Correspondence Relating to the Volcanic Eruption in St Vincent in 1902 and 1903, May 1903, CO 884/8, no. 26; Administrator to Governor, 7 June 1897, CO 321/173, no. 32; Grenada Government Gazette for 1895, CO 105/10; "Flogging for Praedial Larceny", 21 October 1900, CO 321/196, no. 229; "Federation of the Windwards", 2 December 1891, CO 321/129; "Disturbance between Soldiers and Police", 20 August 1891, CO 321/130, no. 136; "Report on the West Indian Incumbered Estates Court", PP 1884, 1.

by Carlylian pseudo-scientific pedagogy, colonial officials "held blacks incapable of managing tropical milieux". The colonies were "adjudged inaccessible, unviable, dangerously overexploited, and yet somehow also so fruitful as to encourage reversion to slothful savagery".[7]

By 1888, after fifty years of black emancipation, white elites still held full control of economic resources, in the face of widespread famine and destitution among the second and third generations of the manumitted. Rising black mortality coexisted with hegemonic retention of white wealth. Such extreme conditions constituted the ideal colonial order the British government envisioned. Black revolution simmered beneath, while above, white-supremacy systems prepared to see off the century.[8]

Progressive thinking in the West Indies and Britain, however, championed the cause of black peasant proprietorship as the sustainable solution to food security and social stability. In England, John Stuart Mill, commenting on the case for black entrepreneurship, called for a revised colonial policy that centred the economic enfranchisement of Africans and Asians. He argued that a small-farming culture could save the West Indies from the further spread of famine. As expected, he was condemned for his "communistic" concept, especially in Downing Street, where the plantations' champion, Gladstone, was prime minister.

The worsening of economic depression in Europe commenced in 1884, sending the black and Indian working class deeper into despair. In Barbados, St Vincent and Antigua especially, limited poor-relief systems crumbled under the weight of poverty. Whites were not prepared, even in the face of increasing mortality caused by famine, to release land for black and Indian self-reliance and survival.[9] Workers received no mitigating financial support from the British government. They were abandoned to perish by the sugar producers and other large landholders. The majority of communities understood that they were on their own, as it had always been.[10]

---

7. Richardson, *Economy and Environment*, xiii

8. Ibid., 4.

9. See C. Shepherd, "Peasant Agriculture in the Leeward and Windward Islands", *Tropical Agriculture* 24 (1947): 61–71; H.A. Will, *Constitutional Change in the British West Indies, 1880–1903* (Oxford: Clarendon, 1970); Michel-Rolph Trouillot, "Discourses of Rule and the Acknowledgment of the Peasantry in Dominica, 1838–1928", *American Ethnologist* 16, no. 4 (1989): 704–18.

10. Sydney Olivier, *White Capital and Coloured Labour* (1906; reprint, New York: Russell

Promoting Caribbean Development: Royal Commission, 1897

Famine and rising mortality at the end of the nineteenth century provoked condemnation globally, with strong expressions of concern in the United States. Cuba and Puerto Rico were experiencing a new era of capital investment in agriculture, linked largely to growing US business interest in the wider Caribbean. Political pressure from the north led to a British parliamentary decision to establish a Royal Commission of Inquiry in 1897.[11]

When the commission arrived at St Vincent in February 1897, a group of twenty-one workers had already prepared a document setting out the plight of the poor. In it, they likened the arrival of the commission to the coming of "Moses of yore into Egypt, delivering Israel from Pharaoh's bondage". The document, from the Barrouallie community, on the leeward side of the island, flattered the commissioners. They were subsequently shamed in oral sessions by workers lamenting the cruelty of British policy and the meanness of the colonial white elite.[12]

Everywhere the commission travelled in the West Indies and reviewed the records of poverty, death and the social indifference of elites, it grew in support for the peasant-proprietor solution. Daniel Morris, for example, agricultural consultant to the commission, commented on the core reason for the famine. He noted that 50 per cent of the land in the West Indies "is suitable for other cultivations than sugar-cane", and could therefore be mobilized by black proprietors to resolve the shortage of food.

This position found favour with other commissioners and was consistent with progressive advocacy in Britain. To solve the famine crisis, the report states, it would be necessary for the British government to promote a new policy calling with immediate effect for "the settlement of the labouring population on small plots of land as peasant proprietors".[13]

---

and Russell, 1971); George Carrington, *Our West Indian Colonies* (London: Anti-Bounty League, 1898), 20–30; James Stark, *History and Guide to Barbados and the Caribbee Islands* (Boston: Photo-Electrotype, 1893); Report: London Trades' Council, *Conference of Delegates from the Organised Trades of the United Kingdom in Favour of Free Trade and Condemnatory of Foreign State Bounties* (London: Co-operative Printing Society, 1888); Trouillot, "Discourses of Rule", 708–10.

11. Bonham C. Richardson, "Depression Riots and the Calling of the 1897 West India Royal Commission", *New West Indian Guide* 66, nos. 3–4 (1992): 169–91.

12. Richardson, *Economy and Environment*, 7.

13. Ibid.

Resistance in British politics to this democratic strategy was immediate. Fear of turning the West Indian social order on its head drove this opposition. The Colonial Office, led by Secretary Joseph Chamberlain, spoke out against the commission's recommendation. The labourers must be fed, he admitted, and some land should be allocated for their subsistence, but the threat of black idleness and refusal to work on the plantations which would follow were matters of great importance to Britain. The West Indies, he concluded, should maintain the paramountcy of the sugar plantation and the unflinching support of the white farming community. This must be the top priority, he said, while giving marginal room for responsible blacks to help themselves.[14]

Before it travelled to the West Indies, Chamberlain instructed the commission to familiarize itself with colonial perspectives by meeting with people of influence and interest in the colonies. Town-hall-style sessions were convened in London in early January. Chairman Henry Norman had been a governor in Jamaica, with experience in India and Australia. He was a soldier who supported colonial control by the suppression of natives. Sydney Olivier, the well-known Fabian socialist, was appointed secretary.[15]

In the West Indies, the commission collected a significant body of information. Public attention was focused on social conflict and the region's deep economic divide. Conversations revolved around whether there should be a retreat from the plantation system, or the black farmer should be the centre of a new development paradigm.

The region had reached a crossroads. Widespread famine constituted the evidentiary basis of the failed plantation system. However, with the exception of Olivier, the membership found it difficult to imagine the region without the economic dominance of sugar planters and their full control of political assemblies.[16]

---

14. Ibid., 7–8.

15. Ibid., 8–9; Michael Louis, "An Equal Right to the Soil: The Rise of a Peasantry in St Lucia (PhD diss., Johns Hopkins University, 1982); Bonham C. Richardson, "A 'Respectable Riot': Guy Fawkes Night in St George's, Grenada, 1885", *Journal of Caribbean History* 27, no. 1 (1993): 21–35; CO 321/133, no. 87; Glen Richards, "Collective Violence in Plantation Societies: The Case of the St Kitts Labour Protests of 1896 and 1935" (unpublished paper, Institute of Commonwealth Studies, University of London, October 1987).

16. WIRC, *Report*, see appendix C, part 3, Barbados; part 8, St Vincent; part 7, St Lucia; for riots in St Vincent, see CO 321/133, no. 87; for riots in Grenada and other colonies, see CO 884/9, no. 147; "To Enable Sugar Plantations to Be Cultivated and Managed for a Limited

The Froude Factor: British Fascism versus West Indian Democracy

The darkness that clouded British policy in the West Indies at the end of the nineteenth century, while famine ravaged the poor, suppressed the development of a Caribbean economy. Death from starvation increased in Barbados, parts of eastern Jamaica and most of the eastern Caribbean. These were a mix of old and new British colonies, but each was built upon the sugar-and-slavery plantation model. There was no effort to mobilize food supplies in Britain or reform land holdings in the islands to promote food security. British unresponsiveness until 1897 was the logical outcome of the emancipation edict that black political or economic empowerment should be officially discouraged and resisted.[17]

There was undoubtedly a significant Carlylian fanaticism that targeted the black community. It was associated with Anthony Froude, who had taken time off from his transimperial globe-trotting, promoting the alleged benefits of British colonialism, to focus specifically on the West Indies. He sought to rebuild his diminished academic reputation by elucidating the importance of the West Indies to British identity as an imperial nation. His writings recentred the issue that had been simmering since Governor Eyre was tried and freed for the mass murder of numbers of the Jamaican poor. He jumped into the fray, and with the support of soon-to-be prime minister William Gladstone, he unleashed his rage upon the blacks. British imperialism, now targeting Africans all over the continent, and Asians, revealed its darkest intention in the context of the West Indies.[18]

Froude's political reputation was public knowledge, as was his identity as Carlyle's professional colleague and ideological collaborator. In 1888, following

Period", 9 August 1886, CO 28/220, Act 20 of 1886–87; "Negro Rising", 10 July 1896, CO 28/241; C.S. Salmon, *Depression in the West Indies: Free Trade the Only Remedy* (London: Cassell, 1884); L. Westenra Sambon, "Acclimatization of Europeans in Tropical Lands", *Geographical Journal* 12, no. 6 (December 1898): 594.

17. Michael Craton, "The Transition from Slavery to Free Wage Labour in the Caribbean, 1780–1890: A Survey with Particular Reference to Recent Scholarship", *Slavery and Abolition* 13, no. 2 (1992): 37–67; Michael Craton, "Reshuffling the Pack: The Transition from Slavery to other Forms of Labor in the British Caribbean, ca. 1790–1890", *New West Indian Guide* 68, nos. 1–2 (1994): 23–75.

18. PP 1866–3682, 30; Official Papers Submitted to the Royal Commission of Inquiry by Governor Eyre; Report of the Jamaica Royal Commission, Evidence Reflected in the Minutes, part 2, 1866, part 3683, section 31.

his visit to the West Indies, he published his tour book *The English in the West Indies: or, the Bow of Ulysses*. He gave a warm endorsement to Carlyle's *Occasional Discourse*. Indeed, when Carlyle's pamphlet was republished, Froude had become its editor. As an Oxford history professor, he committed himself to validating the academic integrity of the text.[19]

The English in the West Indies became a popular book for officials with responsibility for shaping, guiding and defending British colonial policy. In some quarters, it was more influential than Carlyle's "Nigger Question", or Trollope's *The West Indies and the Spanish Main*. More readers looked to Froude for insights in the aftermath of Eyre's non-indictment by English grand juries.[20]

Froude's project in the West Indies was intended to shore up the foundation of Carlyle's ideological work. The targets were familiar: Carlyle's mythical Quashee and Trollope's imagined Sambo. Invented as tools to tell the tale of blacks' undeserved manumission, and therefore the policy error of emancipation, this literary construct was intended to make the case that the white race in the West Indies was weakening in resolve. Froude claimed to see "Sambos" everywhere he went in the West Indies. He presented a narrative of decline and decay that represented Britain's betrayal of its oldest global partner, the West Indian slave owner.

Froude celebrated the resilience of the Barbados enslavers, who fought to retain slavery to the bitter end. Despite emancipation, he boasted:

> Labour at any rate is abundant and cheap. In Barbadoes the negro is willing enough to work, for he has no other means of living. Little land is here allowed him to grow his yams upon. Almost the whole of it is still held by the whites in estates, cultivated by labourers on the old system, and it is to be admitted, cultivated most admirably. If the West Indies are going to ruin, Barbadoes, at any rate, is being ruined with a smiling face.[21]

---

19. Carlyle, *Occasional Discourse*; James Anthony Froude, *The English in the West Indies: or, The Bow of Ulysses* (1888; reprint, New York: Scribner's, 1897); John Clubbe, ed., *Froude's Life of Carlyle*, abridged ed. (Columbus: Ohio State University Press, 1979).

20. See James Anthony Froude, "England and Her Colonies", *Fraser's Magazine for Town and Country*, n.s., 1, no. 1 (January 1870): 1–16; James Anthony Froude, *Two Lectures on South Africa* (London: Longmans, 1880).

21. Froude, *English*, 33; Eugene August, ed., *The Nigger Question: The Negro Question* (New York: Crofts Classics, 1971); Carlyle, *Occasional Discourse*; W.H. Dunn, *James Anthony Froude*, vol. 2 (Oxford: Clarendon, 1963).

Other parts of the West Indies he adjudged to be heading over the cliff into "Haitianization".

Black rule, Froude said, was pretty much inevitable, given the weak emancipation posture adopted by Britain. The restoration of the elected House of Representatives in Jamaica in 1884, following its suspension after the Morant Bay massacre, he argued, was an example of liberal ideas running ahead of racial reality. Full military rule, no to the black franchise, no sharing of parliamentary power with coloureds, and no access to land by blacks were his policy prescription. Barbados, he intimated, came closest to this reality, and Jamaica was furthest.

Froude's call for military confrontation was advocated and promoted as the best path for the West Indies. There was widespread official support for this approach to colonial governance. West Indian resistance meant that further black bloodbaths were inevitable. By 1890, when his popularity soared with the sale of his books, worker resistance was intensifying, not only at the peasant base of West Indian society but in the emerging black professional community. His views held centre stage in British conservative public opinion, overshadowing the progressive movement that defied him and sought to expose the hate embodied by his imperial crusade.[22]

Mill's narratives minced to pieces Froude's racism by exposing his irritation with the evidence of black self-improvement. Froude fumed at Gladstone's concession to the coloureds in Jamaica with the restoration of the limited property-qualified franchise, and granting blacks access to political office. He might not have been aware that Gladstone's slave-owning dynasty in Guiana had spawned a coloured clan that had done well financially by serving as a support core in commerce. Gladstone was a student of mathematics and law at Oxford, and at an early age, understood that business numbers were critical in keeping subordinate social groups legally submerged.

Froudacity: The Blacks Write Back

The West Indian revolt against Froude came from his "Sambo" yard, in the form of the black writer John Jacob Thomas of Trinidad. Thomas was a champion

---

22. Froude, *English*; August, *Nigger Question*; Carlyle, *Occasional Discourse*; Dunn, *James Anthony Froude*.

of the emerging West Indian literary and intellectual scene. He was born in 1841, three years after the final legal collapse of the slavery system. He pursued the teaching profession to satisfy his considerable intellect.[23]

From teaching, Thomas transferred to the civil service. In 1869, at twenty-eight, he published a seminal book on West Indian language and linguistics, *The Theory and Practice of Creole Grammar*. He then launched a countercultural critique of Froude in the form of a brilliant, discursive book, published in 1889, *Froudacity: West Indian Fables Explained*.[24]

There could have been no more suitable writer to confront the mythologies emanating from the mentality represented by the Carlyle-Trollope-Froude triumvirate. The alliance of sugar planters, politicians and writers was no match for the erudite mind that represented the vision of the manumitted. Earlier revolutionary leaders such as Bussa, Sam Sharpe and Paul Bogle expressed the West Indian rejection of imperial injustice and offered liberty. Thomas seized the moment with his "up from slavery" narrative.[25]

There are those, Thomas wrote, who seek "to thwart political aspiration in the Antilles". The argument of such people, he noted, "is confidently relied upon to confirm the inexorable mood of Downing Street". The core of their contemptible argument, he identified, was that "the African element in the population of the West Indies is, from its past history and its actual tendencies, a standing menace to the continuance of civilization and religion". *The Bow of Ulysses*, he said, came into his hands in April 1888. He said, "It seemed to me, on reading that book and deducing therefrom the foregoing essential summary, that a critic would have little more to do, in order to effectually exorcise this negrophobic political hobgoblin, than to appeal to impartial history, as well as common sense, in its application of human nature in general, and to the actual facts of West Indian life in particular."[26]

Thomas proceeded to dismantle Froude's fetish with the intellect of black

---

23. J.J. Thomas, *Froudacity: West Indian Fables Explained* (London: T. Fisher Unwin, 1889).

24. Ibid.; See Edward Bean Underhill, *The Tragedy of Morant Bay: A Narrative of the Disturbances in the Island of Jamaica in 1865* (London: Alexander and Shepherd, 1895); J.J. Thomas, *The Theory and Practice of Creole Grammar* (Port of Spain: Chronicle Publishing Office, 1869).

25. See introduction to the 1969 reprint of Thomas, *Froudacity*, by C.L.R. James, and biographical note by Donald Wood (London: New Beacon Books, 1969); Trollope, *West Indies*.

26. Thomas, *Froudacity*, 51–52, 54–55.

people, his fairy-tale narrative on the "noble Haitian" effort to "realize the dreams of Toussaint", his dishonesty in respect of the benefits of black political participation in West Indian parliaments, and his lack of scientific inquiry in regard to the tremendous strides blacks had made to bring about a superior form of democratic governance. He wrote of the "glorious freedom" blacks had defended with their lives, and the power of their commitment to modern principles that are the basis of any progressive formal politics.[27]

In singling out the fanaticism of Froude and dismissing his claim to historical truth, Thomas wrote about the audacity of Froude, which reflected the theme of his book:

> Now, as to "the whites whom we planted as our representatives", and who, Mr Froude avers, are drifting into ruin, we confess to a total ignorance of their whereabouts in these islands in this jubilee year of Negro Emancipation . . . What are we Negroes of the present day to be grateful for to the US, personified by Mr Froude and the Colonial Office exportations? . . . Obliged to "us" indeed! . . . Really, are we to be grateful that the colour difference should be made the basis and justification of the dastardly denials of justice, social, intellectual, and moral, which have characterized the regime of those who Mr Froude boasts were left to be the representatives of British morality and fair play?[28]

Dismissing Froude, and his "fellow-apologists for slavery" and the gloss which they "endeavoured . . . to put on it", Thomas ended his book with the following statement:

> Finally, it must be borne in mind that the abolition of physical bondage did not by any means secure all the requisite conditions of "a fair field and no favour" for the future career of the freed men. . . . Even so have the conditions, figuratively, presented themselves under which the Blacks have been obliged to rear the fabric of self-elevation since 1838, while combating ceaselessly the obstacles opposed to the realizing of their legitimate aspirations. Mental and, in many cases, material success has been gained, but the machinery for accumulating and applying the means required for comprehensive racial enterprise is waiting on Providence, time, and circumstances for its establishment and successful working.[29]

---

27. Ibid.
28. Ibid., 114–15.
29. Ibid., 143, 193–94.

Racialized colonialism, then, was comprehensively rejected by a black West Indian intellectual who set aside the imperial intentions of Britain.

Thomas emerges as the first literary spokesman for the West Indian development agenda. He championed, for men and women of his post-slavery cohort, the project of replacing colonialism with a democratizing ethos.

In addition to Thomas's work, the 1888 publication of C.S. Salmon's *The Caribbean Confederation* offered another route to West Indian development. While Thomas wrote to defend the manumitted from British colonialism, Salmon broadcast a wider political message about the West Indies. First, he dismissed the fiction of Froude and his race-based recommendation. Then he offered a macroeconomic vision for regional economic development. The subtitle of his book reveals its thesis: *A Plan for the Union of the Fifteen British West Indian Islands.*[30]

Salmon built upon the foundations laid by Thomas and presented the case that the enterprising black and Indian communities of the West Indies were well on their way to end the plunder of the region by the plantation enterprise. He imagined it federated and liberated within a new ecosystem. The publication of his book in the jubilee year of emancipation enhanced the political importance of its message – that the black and Indian communities had the potential to make a transformative contribution to the region and the world. It was a message of hope and achievement. He opposed all that Froude stood for and sought to change the conversation from racial rhetoric to macroeconomic development and social change.

The effect of Salmon's book was to influence the thinking of the Royal Commission, which was bombarded with anti-black testimonies. Standing in direct contrast, and pivoting on Salmon's recommendation, the commission's report was futuristic, though not eminently feasible. Salmon was a colonial official with considerable practical experience, having served in the Seychelles and, critically, on the Gold Coast in West Africa. He was a keen supporter of political integration in West Africa and in the West Indies, believing it the basis of a non-racial West Indian economic order.

When Colonial Secretary Chamberlain received the commissioners' report, the two contending forces pulling apart the fabric of West Indian life were in

---

30. C.S. Salmon, *The Caribbean Confederation: A Plan for the Union of the Fifteen British West Indian Colonies* (London: Cassell, 1888).

Table 4.1. Percentage Sugar Products in Total Exports, 1897

Country	Per cent
Jamaica	18.0
British Guiana	70.5
Trinidad	57.0
Tobago	35.0
Barbados	97.0
Grenada	–
St Lucia	74.0
St Vincent	42.0
Antigua	94.5
St Kitts and Nevis	96.5
Dominica	15.0
Montserrat	62.0

Source: Report of the 1897 Royal Commission, 3; Richardson, *Economy and Environment*, 35.

full combat. The Carlyle-Trollope-Froude alliance, holding majority influence with the imperial government, was up against radical West Indian intellectuals such as J.J. Thomas and Samuel Jackman Prescod of Barbados. Gladstone had ceased to be prime minister in 1894, but in 1897, when the commission was established, Queen Victoria celebrated her jubilee and had declared herself "Empress of India". He wished for no progressive change in the West Indies. Queen, former prime minister and secretary of state were in alignment against black and Indian empowerment.

The report was released at the end of 1897. The commission had been established in December the prior year and arrived in the West Indies, at Georgetown, Guiana, on 27 January 1897. It held forty-five official sessions across the West Indies and collected data relevant to the past and present of the sugar plantations (table 4.1). Commissioners came down on the side of black peasant and smallholder entrepreneurship and proposed a revised model of West Indian development based on an economic strategy that balanced the white-owned plantation sector with the emerging black and Indian commercial smallholding and subsistence peasant sectors.[31]

---

31. See Richardson, *Economy and Environment*, 28–29.

There was no surprise, then, when the report was not well received by Secretary Chamberlain, whose respect for the old plantation system was well known. Three years earlier, he described the blacks in Jamaica as a backward and politically primitive lot not capable of participation, least of all managing a "liberal constitution". He added that such a system of governance, as developed by English colonists, was "not really suited to a black population".[32]

The report, then, fell upon the desk of a hardcore Conservative secretary for the colonies and died there. Colonies were given a free hand to assess and respond to its recommendations. In the Windward Islands, where the sugar culture was in its infancy, with labour shortages limiting their capacity for development, the white elite embraced some aspects of land distribution to facilitate peasant growth. In Barbados, Jamaica and St Kitts, where the sugar culture was deeply rooted, the report was set aside and largely ignored.

It was another moment in which the West Indies were placed at a political crossroads. The imperial interest ignored the time and offered no commitment to structural change; the Caribbean majority's views were rejected, with only small pockets of peasants benefiting. The drought that brought famine and deeper poverty to the villages of the poor proved insufficient motive to promote reform.

Fifty years later, an academic, reflecting on the continuous economic decline of the region, described the report as the "Magna Carta of the West Indian peasant". How wrong he was in that regard. It should best be described as a welcome West Indian economic development document that was ignored by the British. It was rejected by the imperial centre because it did not give full support to an economically and socially backward white-supremacy system in the West Indies.[33]

Between 1900 and 1930, the West Indian economic and political development project was rolled back on account of the imperial rejection of all forms of meaningful change. The opportunity embedded in the 1897 report receded into the inventory of ignored documents. Workers were rejected as strategic economic partners in West Indian progress. They moved on to address the importance of confronting and overthrowing colonialism. The land acquisition strategy was replaced by the aim of defeating the system of white supremacy by any means possible. Anti-colonialism became the focus of a new mass movement.

---

32. Ibid.
33. Ibid., 8.

CHAPTER 5

Plantations Are Forever

During the last few years . . . since the decline of the sugar cultivation . . . the labourer, naturally indolent, has become absolutely lazy and indifferent; he is half starved, half clothed, and sits all day on his plot of land indifferent to surrounding circumstances; his health and his character are rapidly deteriorating from sloth and starvation; he refuses to work for the small wages offered him (15 to 16 cents a day) for what he complains is very hard labour, and declares that he would rather starve than work for that wage.

—Testimony of Dr W. Bruce-Austin before the 1897 Royal Commission, St Vincent

BY 1930, THE BRITISH COLONIAL MACHINERY was triumphant in its repression of the black and Indian communities. The resistance of the masses that defined anti-colonialism for most of the nineteenth century was pushed back and considered defeated by the imperial government. The radical democracy movement in rural communities, which sought to pry land from the imperial fist, was instead losing ground to the urban franchise-rights rioters, who seemed a little more organized.[1]

Black bloodbaths across the region were largely rural experiences. Meaningful economic empowerment to assist starving urban workers and landless peasantry was effectively suppressed. The inclusive development model

---

1. Peter Fraser, "The Fictive Peasantry: Caribbean Rural Groups in the 19th Century", in *Contemporary Caribbean*, vol. 1, ed. Susan Craig (Port of Spain: Susan Craig, 1981), 319–47; Correspondence Respecting Measures for the Increase of Peasant Proprietary, March 1900, CO 884/5, no. 86; "Public Lands Acquisitions", 1900, CO 321/196, no. 218; "Land for Peasant Proprietary", CO 321/186; "Regulations under Land Settlement Ordinance", CO 321/212, no. 5; "Agricultural Development in the West Indies", 1899, CO 884/5, no. 88; Stanley Engerman, "Economic Change and Contract Labour in the British Caribbean: The End of Slavery and the Adjustment to Emancipation", *Explorations in Economic History* 21 (1984): 133–50; W.K. Marshall, "Notes on Peasant Development in the West Indies since 1938", *Social and Economic Studies* 17, no. 3 (1968): 252–63.

recommended by the Royal Commission Report of 1897 was predictably ignored. The government's willingness to carry unreformed colonialism long into the twentieth century was secure. This was the triumph of the racist, anti-democratic recommendations of those inspired by the Carlyle-Trollope-Froude faction.[2]

The readiness of Europe to engulf the world in its war to colonize Africa and Asia was predicated on the assumption that the West Indies was crushed, and the First World War between 1914 and 1918 projected global economic recession into the 1920s. The British government in 1930 was complacent in its suppression of the West Indians.

The economic and social data for the period describe the assured hegemony of Britishness in both private markets and parliaments. Colonial governors reported on the solidity of their power and presided with confidence over social and business functions at their residential palaces, each called "Government House".[3]

The sustainability of British power, however, was contingent on the effectiveness of the military suppression of working-class communities. Blacks were made to believe that their lives did not matter outside their capacity to labour in the service of estate owners. In Barbados, for example, a report from Acting Governor Broome settled any doubt there might have been in respect to this assertion: "If a sugarcane is stolen, or if a thief puts his hand through a window at night and robs an old woman of a saucepan, I receive an elaborate report on the matter from the police." If, however, he added, "one or two cases of undoubted yellow fever occur and end fatally, I hear nothing about it".[4]

---

2. "Agricultural Developments in the West Indies", 1899, CO 884/5, no.88; "The West Indies and Imperial Aid", 1905, CO 321/196, no. 92; "Peasant Proprietary: Confidential", CO 321/179; Grenada Blue Book, 1900, CO 106/94, 20–23; Memorandum Respecting the Saint Lucia Central Sugar Factory, 1902, CO 884/7, no. 116; Correspondence Relating to the Garrisons in the West Indies, London, 1906, CO 884/86; see Ronald Hyman, "The Colonial Office Mind, 1900–1914", *Journal of Imperial and Commonwealth History* 8, no. 1 (1979): 30–55. Johnson, "West Indies", 55–83; Margaret Olivier, ed., *Sydney Olivier: Letters and Selected Writings* (London: Allen and Unwin, 1948).

3. Rich, "Sydney Olivier", 208–33; Philip Curtin, "Scientific Racism and British Theory of Empire", *Journal of the Historical Society of Nigeria* 2, no. 1 (1969): 40–51; J.H. Davidson, "Anthony Trollope and The Colonies", *Victorian Studies* 12 (1968–69): 305–30.

4. R.W. Beachey, *The British West Indies Sugar Industry in the Late 19th Century* (1957; reprint, Westport, CT: Greenwood, 1978), 160–88; H.A, Will, "Colonial Policy and Economic Development in the West Indies, 1895–1903", *Economic History Review* 23 (1970): 138–39; J.W. Root, *The British West Indies and the Sugar Industry* (Liverpool: J.W. Root, 1899); Ralph Williams, *How I Became A Governor* (London: John Murray, 1913); G. Wright,

The mastery of colonial divide-and-rule tactics by imperial administrations was celebrated in this period of triumphalism. Desperation caused by widespread hunger and malnutrition presented the landless poor with two possible choices: they could emigrate to a neighbouring colony where survival opportunities seemed better, or serve where they were and pray for deliverance.

At the beginning of the twentieth century, over five thousand Barbadian workers had fanned out across the subregion; some twenty-six hundred of them were in St Lucia and a thousand in St Vincent. The sugar planters in St Lucia much preferred the Barbadians over domestic workers, who spoke French creole, which they hardly understood. St Vincent proved a more challenging island than St Lucia for emigrants, overburdened as it was with a relatively larger number of unemployed workers.[5]

The use of harsh fiscal measures to squeeze revenues from the working class was consistent with the long history of economic extraction associated with imperialism, and was perfected by the colonial government.[6] In this regard, three important early twentieth-century texts capture precisely the confidence of the British colonizers and the success of efforts to crush the democratic spirit of community resistance. Written in the period of widespread famine, these accounts detailed British brutality to workers and focused on their servitude. Blanshard's *Democracy and Empire in the Caribbean*, Thompson's *Black Caribbean*, and Macmillan's *Warning from the West Indies* capture with precision the legacy of slavery as it stretched into the fourth decade of the twentieth century.[7]

Blanshard's book depicts the white perception of black West Indians as they prepared to begin a major radical attempt to defeat British colonialism, which was digging in for the long century ahead. A new wave of rebellion on the horizon, however, was becoming clearer to the white elites. In addition,

---

"Economic Conditions in St Vincent, BWI", *Economic Geography* 5, no. 3 (1929): 236–59; see Richardson, *Economy and Environment*, 37.

5. Richardson, *Economy and Environment*, 41; see Benjamin Kidd, *The Control of the Tropics* (London: Macmillan, 1898), 2–10; W.P. Livingstone, *Black Jamaica: A Study in Evolution* (London, 1899); Memorial of the African Association on the Distress in the West Indies, CO 318/293.

6. Richardson, *Economy and Environment*, 51, 54.

7. Paul Blanshard, *Democracy and Empire in the Caribbean* (New York: Macmillan, 1947); W.M. Macmillan, *Warning from the West Indies* (Harmondsworth, UK: Penguin, 1936); Mona Macmillan, "The Making of Warning from the West Indies', *Journal of Commonwealth and Comparative Politics* 18, no. 2 (1980): 207–19; Sydney Olivier, "The Scandal of West Indian Labour Conditions", *Contemporary Review* 43 (March 1938): 282–89.

as the American "big daddy" identity in the region took shape with military invasions and occupations, particularly in Haiti, the willingness of workers to assert their right to freedom intensified.[8]

With these new developments, British governance revealed more of its fascist nature. The colonial facade of the region burst open and exposed inherently contradictory forces: the commitment to the sustainability of Empire, and the popular determination to destroy it.

The latter represented the growing West Indian sense of democracy and nationhood, standing in opposition to British control as a problem to be resolved. Incipient nationalism, building on the legacy of J.J. Thomas, and linking to a growing global socialist movement, was more determined than ever to subvert colonialism by any means possible and offer instead a Caribbean development paradigm. Meanwhile, British racism and its daily manifestation in anti-worker positions increasingly became an embarrassment to humanist decency in a rapidly decolonizing world.[9]

Keeping West Indian workers in bondage remained British policy, however, long after the death of Queen Victoria in 1901. West Indians had no reason to mourn her passing, especially as imperial officials saw to it that a new wave of white supremacism swept over the region. At the community level, black and Indian schoolchildren were required to sing "Rule Britannia" as part of their imperial education.

Blanshard was an American foreign policy adviser assigned to the British West Indies. He was not a part of the colonial system and experienced it as a relic in a region that should have benefited from the lessons of the American Revolution. He recognized, however, that the decision of his nation at the moment of its independence to build on the foundations of plantation slavery had much to do with what had survived in the West Indies. He also contemplated that with his country's occupation of Haiti, and the emergence of a local popular resistance front, racism in the West Indies was sustained by all nations with imperial ambitions.

---

8. Sydney Olivier, *The League of Nations and Primitive Peoples* (London: Oxford University Press, 1918); Sewell, *Ordeal of Free Labor*.

9. See Paul Rich, "The Baptism of a New Era: The 1911 Universal Races Congress and the Liberal Ideology of Race", *Ethnic and Racial Studies* 7, no. 4 (1984): 534–50; Michael Biddiss, "The Universal Races Congress of 1911", *Race* 13, no. 1 (1971): 37–46. W. Ormsby-Gore, "British West Indies", *United Empire* 13, no. 7, July (1922): 460–63.

Managing the West Indians, now called "natives," remained the core remit of Britain's imperialism. This was the principal task of the governor. Blanshard makes the following observation in respect of these imperial officers: "They never acquired the habit of living with the people whom they rule – they live above them. They come inevitably to regard all advocates of local democracy as agitators, and they acquire all the slick devices for keeping native malcontents quiet enough so that reverberations will not reach . . . London."[10] Some of them, he noted, "stood between the avarice and cruelty of a local white oligarchy and a hapless native population", but the majority were of the opinion that blacks, no matter how far removed from slavery, were not fit to run the affairs of the West Indies. They did not see it as their duty to bridge "the gap between slavery and the twentieth century" in order to create development, but rather to use the gap to further divide Westminster and the West Indies.[11]

In general, noted Blanshard, the British used their power in the West Indies "for a hundred years after emancipation" to promote their own narrow interest and "little to prepare the people for self-government". Illiteracy among the workers was the norm, and the few schools "are often nothing but education slums". He described British rule after a hundred years of emancipation as follows:

> The schools concentrate upon either elementary subjects or technical train-ing. High schools are few, and universities completely absent. The so-called "liberal-arts" are represented feebly if at all . . . and studies which would give the student perspective on the world and his country's place in it – are avoided; the brutal truth is that such subjects are deliberately avoided in order to hide from the native student their lowly status in comparison with free peoples and thus keep them from inevitable discontent and rebelliousness.[12]

These and suchlike policies were designed, noted Blanshard, so that the people are not "given a fair chance to learn democracy by practice".

At least 95 per cent of the colonial subjects in these British West Indies, Blanshard concluded, were excluded from voting by deliberately rigid property qualifications intended to disenfranchise the poor. In 1939, an official House of Commons sessional paper showed the voting population as minuscule, representing less than 7 per cent per colony.

---

10. Blanshard, *Democracy*, 16.
11. Ibid.
12. Ibid., 17.

Table 5.1. Per cent Franchise Holders in British West Indies, 1939

Country	Per cent
Barbados	3.4
British Guiana	2.9
Jamaica	5.5
Trinidad	6.5

Source: Blanshard, *Democracy*, 17.

Strategies of democratic exclusion were facilitated, Blanshard noted, by the few black and Indian elected representatives "becoming either sycophants in search of rewards which can be offered by a white aristocracy, or irresponsible racial agitators who are never in a position to make good on their promises" (table 5.1).[13]

Commenting on the effects of British domination, Blanshard stated that "a bitter struggle against restricted democracy has been in progress . . . for a generation". Also, "its leaders have been prosecuted and jailed by arbitrary governors" but many have emerged from prison "with enhanced prestige". This, he noted, had been the context at the turn of the twentieth century. Their nineteenth-century predecessors were generally hanged, shot or crushed to death by hard labour in prisons, as the legacy of Governor Eyre in Jamaica illustrates.[14]

Against this history of horrific anti-democratic repression in the early twentieth century, West Indian workers' demand for social justice, economic participation and development led Blanshard to conclude that across the West Indies, governors were "sitting on a political powder keg". He wrote, "The region is alive with revolt against British imperialist tradition and white control."[15]

The denial of this reality, Blanshard observed, was also a critical part of Britain's passion to persist in domination. White legislators in Jamaica, he pointed out, "were so afraid of black control [after Bogle's war in 1865] that they abdicated entirely and went back to personal control" from Britain. This was when "Governor Eyre had ordered the execution of 354 persons and the killing of 75 without trial".[16]

---

13. Ibid., 18.
14. Ibid.
15. Ibid., 20.
16. Ibid., 21.

An effective way to look at the West Indies in the 1930s, he wrote, was to consider it "a poorhouse, and nearly all the people are occupants of various wards in the institution". In it, he said, "the labouring population . . . lives at a level below human decency". The outward signs of poverty, he added, were particularly visible in Kingston: "ragged clothing, bare feet children with bloated bellies, shacks made of flattened cans, and lines of unemployed negro workers waiting at closed gates". Furthermore: "The black women who swing along the roads gracefully with their great baskets on their heads are probably better off than their grandmothers who did the same thing. These people came up out of slavery and continued to live in an economy in which ex-slaves were in the majority."[17] The West Indies, he concluded, were "primitive in industrial development" after three hundred years of British colonial rule. Their abject poverty, visible to the world, was made even starker because the colonies were publicly positioned "at the door of the richest nation in the world", and the people were "the wards of the wealthiest and the most advanced" nation in Europe.[18]

Between 1922 and 1942, West Indian workers experienced a reduction rather than an improvement in real wages. In Jamaica, for example, 52 per cent of employed males made less than $2.00 a week in cash income, and most women earned less than $1.20. These barometers of poverty, Blanshard commented, were most precisely revealed in the bloated "bodies of children" and the "appalling" infant mortality rate – ninety-eight per thousand as against fifty-three in England.[19]

Blanshard strikes at the heart of British policy in the West Indies with this statement he attributed to elite white men: "They are willing enough to discuss race in personal terms, and they are more than willing to dilate upon their hardships in extracting efficient labour from black employees, but when they are discussing racial issues in politics or business they emphasize the white man's burden or moral responsibility for backward masses, the white man's role as chief beneficiary in a system of racial exploitation."[20] Their typical mantra is that "black men are poor because they are lazy and incompetent, and that white men are wealthy because they have organizing ability and a sense of responsibility". For them, "racial status corresponds with economic

17. Ibid., 41.
18. Ibid., 42.
19. Ibid.
20. Ibid., 51.

status", a reality that, if true, is rooted in two centuries of slavery and nearly four centuries of colonialism. In the West Indies, he concludes, "Almost all the poorest people are black."[21]

R.W. Thompson's Black Caribbean

Whites in the West Indies expected the black descendants of the enslaved, still suffering great and brutal losses of life in their quest for social justice and economic inclusion, to grovel before them in households, on plantations and in urban streets. Reginald William Thompson arrived in Jamaica and found the black poor offering "broad friendly smiles" and "arms waving as they shouted greetings". Impressed with the "sheer simple effervescence of the natives" and the "vast melancholy of the negro", he settled down to observing the general characteristic behaviour of the black community.[22]

If Jamaica is indeed a "confounding" nation, as Orlando Patterson surmised, the narrative of its identity is scattered through the pages of Thompson's interwar travelogue. The blacks, he said, lived in homes best described as "hovels", yet their welcoming postures spoke to a warmth that emerged despite the hardship of their lives.[23]

He considered nothing more confounding than the subservience of the Maroons to British power despite their 150 years of anti-slavery mountainous flight and fight. He noted: "The head of the maroons, unassailable in their 'cockpits', had been an honorary colonel in the British Army, and was acknowledged a 'King', and received as an ally." The Maroon leader was welcomed into Kingston by the British governor, who acknowledged him as "king of the mountains" overlooking the city.[24]

The ambivalence of the poor in respect of the British was rooted in the fear and vulnerability they experienced as a consequence of British brutality. "If the people of the West Indies are any guide", he concluded, then they are "proud of their British nationality, and loyal to the ideal of Britain" as the weak worship

---

21. Ibid.

22. R.W. Thompson, *Black Caribbean* (London: MacDonald, 1946), 60, 62, 64, 215, 217, 262.

23. Orlando Patterson, *The Confounding Island: Jamaica and the Postcolonial Predicament* (Cambridge, MA: Harvard University Press, 2019); Thompson, *Black Caribbean*, 79.

24. Thompson, *Black Caribbean*, 69, 71.

the powerful. The problems in the West Indies "are our domestic problem", he wrote, "it is our house, and we shall put it in order . . . we shall never abandon Jamaica, either to its own Haitian shambles, or to anyone else".[25]

Behind these expressions of a tortured history, Thompson concluded, lay "the stirring of 'Black Democracy'", a force as inevitable as a "body awakening, and finding its voice". But Jamaica, he said, "is our child", and "we have ill-treated it, and it touches the heart". The Englishman's lament was as heartfelt as his racist adherence to the twentieth-century legacies of Carlyle's Quashee and Froude's Sambo.[26]

There was nothing the black woman desired more than the love of a white man, Thompson stated, to erase her self-hatred, end her yearning for freedom and to elevate her status with the birth of a brown child. He penned the "Cry of the Negress" thus:

> Oh lie with me, beloved,
> For your seed is white;
> Oh lie with me beloved:
> Lift me a little from the black pit,
> Lie with me, beloved,
> And give me a child.

The reality of emancipation, he said, lay in the black woman's dream of escape from brutality.

Thompson said, "For centuries these Negroes had sought freedom, as all men seek freedom, according to their knowledge and their natures", but they had not achieved their targets. Their "black, naked bodies shone with sweat against the white walls and strained at the sweeps of the galley", and yet, "there is a sort of kindness and tolerance on the face of a Negro that you seldom see on any other kind of face". He added, "If the Jamaicans don't kick now, then they haven't any guts."[27]

The governor's job, said Thompson, was to maintain the safety of Jamaica, and if the Negroes revolted, as it was generally assumed they would, then he would have no choice but to rein them in. "Democracy, if it can't and won't behave", he tells us, "must be controlled." It is a "dangerous business . . . in a

---

25. Ibid., 71.
26. Ibid., 70.
27. Ibid., 78, 79, 81.

dangerous world". Eyre called upon the pledged loyalty of Maroon militias to Her Majesty in 1865, and got it. Their descendants, seventy years later, were dined by the governor, Thompson said. "Democracy", he assessed, "is only possible in direct proportion to literacy", and "Jamaica was no more fit to govern itself, or for democracy, than is a month-old baby to change its own napkins".[28]

The deep wounds of war inflicted in the 1831 Sam Sharpe Rebellion remained unhealed a century later when Marcus Garvey emerged as the people's political hero. Yet blacks and whites, Thompson said, could be seen "arm in arm, and arms around necks". But the moment the sound of a gun was heard, he stated, it was followed by the white cry: "Da black nigger bastard!"

The success of British rule, Thompson concluded, was to be found in this phenomenon that enabled white elites to rule black majorities with black support, and the solid commitment of the mixed-race, coloured people. The two Jamaicas, so often identified as a social construct of slavery, remained resilient a century later. By the 1930s, white rulers were beginning to feel the volcanic heat beneath.[29]

Warning from the West Indies: William Miller Macmillan, 1936

In 1934–35, a middle-aged, middle-class Scottish intellectual with extensive experience in racially segregated colonial South Africa visited the West Indies. He brought with him considerable British cultural baggage and a Christian evangelical, progressive perspective. His impulse was to support racial integration and the idea of state support for the colonial poor.

He was not well known in Britain for his activism around these concepts in Southern Africa. Knowledge of his progressive race views did not precede him, and his arrival in and tour of the West Indies seemed uneventful. In 1936, his book about his tour was published, bearing the title *Warning from the West Indies: A Tract for Africa and the Empire.*[30]

Macmillan was a graduate in history from Oxford University, and like Anthony Froude before him, had a curious engagement with the British colonial frontier in Southern Africa. He was one of the first group of Rhodes Scholars

---

28. Ibid., 82.
29. Ibid., 83.
30. Macmillan, *Warning.*

in 1903, following the death of Cecil Rhodes the previous year. Coming from this academic lineage, he was well positioned to follow in the academic tradition of Carlyle and Froude and to defend and celebrate British colonialism. Like Carlyle and Froude, he had an attachment to religion and the profession of the clergy, which led him to study divinity at the University of Glasgow. Rather than turn to the political right, however, and follow Froude's racist route, Macmillan turned left, and in 1911, at twenty-six, joined the socialist Fabian Society.

The West Indies presented him with an opportunity to recite the clearest indictment of Britain colonialism by a scholar from a social-democratic civil rights perspective. His book was written in the academic discursive tradition of J.J. Thomas in that it called for a development vision from within the West Indies. Like many travel writers of the time, he commented on the ruthlessness of British imperial triumphalism, which bred both racial conceit among colonial whites and racial outrage within the anti-colonial community. He gave notice that West Indian workers, after centuries of the excesses of British brutality, were preparing to stand and fight against the empire.

Macmillan immediately got down to the task of recording the facts: that British colonization in the West Indies was built on the economics of wealth extraction, and that the system of labour exploitation could not be justified in human terms. But the empire, he said, "tells a tale of poverty so profound as to give little warrant for the assumption that colonies are a source of great profit to the possessing country". Critically, he commented, "the history of the West Indies would show that in the past quick profits may have killed the goose with the golden eggs and robbed the soil".[31]

Looking at the full spread of British colonial wealth, he concluded, "the most ruthless exploitation" had been inflicted upon the West Indies, and the time was long overdue for a development plan. He added, "Whatever the shade the people's skins, health services are needed, and more and better education." The region's progress could no longer be based upon the interest of "the immigrant planter" who had long been supported "to the detriment of progress with the essential task of development". It was the Caribbean amateur farmer who would save the region, he argued, not the white "gentleman farmer" of tradition.[32]

---

31. Ibid., 13.
32. Ibid., 15–16.

The West Indies was ready, Macmillan concluded, to move on and must no longer be curbed by backward colonial policies. Furthermore, he argued, "the continued perceptions of colonisers that blacks constitute no more than free or cheap labour, and should be considered as 'reserves' rather than producers", meant that West Indian "reconstruction therefore is blocked". It was this "fatal economic tradition" that doomed the West Indies.[33]

The crimes of the past, Macmillan showed, had caught up with the popular call for justice and repair. "Little effort was made", he stated, "to follow up Emancipation by some attempt to redress the wrong done to the slaves; it was as if the only injury was to their owners who could freely blame fate and Emancipation for their difficulties". The problems of production and ownership that now haunted the region were the result of the failure to address "the defects of the plantation system itself, its agricultural methods, its misuse of labour and, especially in later times, its whole financial and business organization".[34]

These and other such statements represent, however, a considerable degree of literary repetition. Macmillan's call for a new development paradigm for the West Indies, which begins with the abandonment of the "settler ideology" and the creation of "a new orientation", was not new and could be found in the 1897 Royal Commission's report. The "whites cannot, if they would, continue as they began, putting their own convenience before all else", and move to the adoption of "cooperative and constructive leadership". In the rehashed development model, he concluded, there "must be ample room for whites in their own enterprise, and in positions of management where their best hope lies in sharing the wealth and activity with a healthier, educated, and economically fitter black population".[35]

The book, he concluded, would serve its purpose if "by showing the state of our oldest colonies after centuries of British rule, it can at all shake this complacency and rise at once to a livelier sense of our responsibility to the old West Indies". But the problem was more than imperial complacency. It was a culture of racial entitlement and arrogance, embedded in a fascist mentality projected into the West Indies, illustrating the other, darker side of British democracy.[36]

---

33. Ibid., 16.
34. Ibid., 73.
35. Ibid., 19.
36. Ibid., 20.

Colonization was meant to produce no other outcome. The "sharing alternative" would have subverted the economic extraction model, both in terms of its economic integrity and its political practice. For this reason, then, Macmillan could conclude that "a social and economic study of the West Indies is therefore necessarily a study of poverty".[37]

Only a wealth-retention strategy could be the basis of a Caribbean development model, and Macmillan understood this. It would represent a radical turn of affairs which he hoped could be attained within an enlightened awakening at the heart of Empire. But he also understood that the arc of history did not tilt in this direction. Colonialism was inherently anti-egalitarian, and his attempt to be apologetic for parts of it failed and revealed the limits of his political imagination and economic concerns.

He was in public a socialist, but at heart a liberal, and Macmillan's plea for policy reform to integrate West Indian workers into the economy as peasant producers, and into the emerging middle class as political administrators, could not succeed. It would require abandoning two centuries of thinking about economic extraction from the West Indies. While his warning facilitated the validation of what was long known in the West Indies and London, that reform could not save the empire, his message was ultimately more a plea for justice than a plan to liberate the colonized.

There was nothing new in Macmillan's assertion that large "proportions of the population are very much where slavery left them". His conclusion that "the real work of reconstruction still lies ahead" was also as banal as his notion that "the efforts of modern officials to help them [angry blacks] and develop the country have to face unreasoning suspicion that their promoters are no more disinterested than earlier governments in the days of slave-owning". This, of course, was the eternal fear of the liberal, that gratitude is neither spontaneous nor assured.[38]

The condition of West Indian workers, Macmillan rightly said, was "deplorable" and the development crisis of the West Indies was rooted in the emancipation process that gave "Liberty without Equality". The British people, he hinted, ignored the depressing state of the region, and yet expected it to celebrate historic moments such as royal events. Also, they took pleasure in

---

37. Ibid., 37.
38. Ibid., 46–47.

describing the West Indies as "gems in the Imperial Crown". Yet the region's dependence on the British treasury, he surmised, generated contempt and yielded meagre support.[39]

But it was Macmillan's recommendations that laid in part the basis for a new development language about the West Indies. They stood in stark contrast to the long tradition of reform to colonial policy. He called for a partial ending of the extraction approach and argued instead for a reversal – development financing in addition to grant aid.

For centuries the West Indies had exported the bulk of its financial resources to fund Britain's economic development, leaving little behind for expenditure in the region. The region was now expected, he said, with no residual resources, to be financially self-sustaining and independent. Finally, his call for implementing the recommendations of the 1897 Royal Commission in respect of an official policy on peasant ownership warmed the heart of his Fabian mentor, Sir Sydney Olivier.[40]

Macmillan also called for the establishment of a West Indian university "to stimulate and focus intellectual life and bring an infiltration of fresh minds and new ideas". This was visionary, and echoed Garvey's call a decade earlier for a relevant, regional tertiary-level institution. He was not at all surprised, however, by the contempt with which the idea was received in elite colonial society. It was on this matter of creating an intellectual community in the region that the imperial government took the view that his "warning" from the West Indies should be ignored.

---

39. Ibid., 59, 61.
40. Ibid., 145–46.

Marcus Garvey, founder and leader of
the global black liberation movement

Clement Payne, Barbadian/Trinidadian
Garveyite organizer, and leader of the
Barbados anti-colonial rebellion, 1937

Henry Sylvester Williams, Trinidadian
anti-colonialist and organizer of
the first pan-African conference in
London, 1900

Mahatma Gandhi, leader of the
Indian anti-colonial movement

Winston Churchill, British prime minister, with a political life dedicated to imperial rule

Lord Sydney Olivier, British liberal colonial administrator

Lloyd George, British prime minister

Walter Guinness (Lord Moyne), British imperialist politician

CHAPTER 6

Garvey's Grassroots Guerrillas

It is true to say that the standard of living of workers in the colonies was generally low. This fact was inevitable and absolutely natural; it was even right in colonial conditions. In countries where the sun shone perpetually and nature was very bountiful and where the problems of life were comparatively few and simple, people could be content and happy with a comparatively simple manner of life and with simple standards. Indeed incursions of expensive ideas very often destroyed happiness.

—Malcolm McDonald, Secretary of State for the Colonies, *Daily Gleaner*, 20 November 1939

BY 1900, CRACKS HAD APPEARED IN the British Empire in the West Indies. Recurrent workers' protests against disenfranchisement generally – economic marginalization, political exclusion and social injustices specifically – had successfully breached the barricades. The order the British government gave to colonial governors was to use force against organized workers and their middle-class allies.

The political environment in the region, shaped by rising ideological consciousness, hunger and famine, was tense. Militia, police and soldiers stood ready to take on workers as they appropriated idle crown lands and raided plantations' food reserves. Sugar fields became killing fields. The starvelings resisted the system of plantation domination and were shot, imprisoned with hard labour and beaten down with batons.

The plantation system was defended to the end by the British government. In so doing, it ignored the moral crisis associated with widespread starvation, particularly in Barbados and the Windward Islands. The public outcry focused on the reforms recommended by the 1897 Royal Commission, particularly the call for a significant measure of land redistribution. While there was no consensus among the commissioners on this hotly contested issue, the general thinking in the region was that policy support was needed to facilitate black and Indian farming communities. The recommendation represented a radical break and gave hope to workers wishing to become farmers. The response, however, was glacial. Its rejection was what first pushed the poor towards revolt.

Unable to foresee how sugar producers could be saved from the competition of beet sugar farmers in Europe, the British government decided to reject any proposal that weakened its position in the West Indies. This required the suppression of land-ownership demands by black and Indian communities. The peasant-farmer option would not be a significant operation but a token gesture to ease the pressure.[1]

British land policy met with militant protest by workers in towns and villages. Also, the idea of the small farmer and peasant producer gained some traction amongst agro-technical experts. Barbados, for example, represented the colonial standard of white supremacy, but Parliament preferred a tentative step in favour of the "small man" in the rural sector.[2] Nonetheless, the resistance at the heart of Empire was consistent: no land for the small man.

Reformers insisted that it was "not impossible for the two systems, large estates, and peasant holdings, to exist side by side with mutual advantage". The 1897 commissioners opined that while securing the economic leadership of white elites, "a good prospect for the permanent welfare in the future of the West Indies" could reside in "the settlement of the labouring population on the land as small peasant proprietors". There was an impassioned plea to modify the plantation model. They ended the case thus: "a monopoly of the most accessible and fertile lands by a few persons who are unable any longer to make beneficial use of them cannot, in the general interest of the islands, be tolerated, and is a source of public danger".[3]

---

1. Glen Richards, "The Maddened Rabble: Labour Protest in St Kitts, 1896 and 1935" (unpublished paper, 1987); Glen Richards, "Order and Disorder in Colonial St Kitts: The Role of the Armed Forces in Maintaining Labour Discipline, 1896–1935" (unpublished paper, 1993); Beckles, *Great House Rules*; see also Eric Foner, *Nothing but Freedom: Emancipation and Its Legacy* (Baton Rouge: Louisiana State University Press, 1983); Walter Rodney, *A History of the Guyanese Working People, 1881–1905* (Baltimore: Johns Hopkins University Press, 1981).

2. Bolland, *Politics of Labour*, 127; WIRC, *Report*, 18–19.

3. Bolland, *Politics of Labour*; "To Enable Sugar Plantations to Be Cultured and Managed for a Limited Period", 9 August 1886, CO 28/220; Governor Hemmings to Joseph Chamberlain, 4 March 1897, CO 111/443; "Report of the Commissioner Appointed by the Governor to Enquire into the Origins of the Riot in the Town of Belize which Began on the Night of July 22nd, 1919", CO 123/296.

Sir Sydney Olivier believed that the spirit of slavery was still alive in the white community at the start of the twentieth century. The land-reform camp recommended the framework for a significant West Indian economic development agenda. The British government would have none of it. The fear of democracy and notions of development, in any form, shaped its thinking. Any progressive idea that emerged from the workers' movement that challenged white supremacy was rejected. The land-reform proposal died in the arid soil of British imperial policy.

By 1900, middle-class intellectuals and professionals were rising in support of grassroots organizations. Preachers, teachers, trade unionists, lawyers and local government officials were joining the workers' protests and laying the foundation for the transition from plantation reform to broad-based anti-colonialism and nationalism. The eruption was extraordinary, though not surprising.

In Jamaica, for example, J.H. Reid, a black intellectual, joined with black journalist and medical practitioner Dr Robert Love, editor of the pan-African newspaper *Jamaica Advocate*. The purpose was to build a bridge between professional advocacy and peasant philosophy. In Guiana, David Straughn, A.A. Thorne and Hubert Critchlow were publicly speaking and writing about the evils of Empire and calling for its end. Black, coloured and Indian radicals formed anti-colonial organizations that rolled out the road map to nationhood.[4]

The Trinidadian intellectual and anti-colonial organizer H. Sylvester Williams had already formed the African Association in 1897 in London. This network of nationalist activists and sympathizers solidified across the West Indies the determination to end British domination, replacing it with a participatory democracy.

The empire was now up against not just militant plantation workers and peasants, but a regional and global network of experienced, professional anti-

---

4. Bolland, *Politics of Labour*, 134, 135, 136. Diane Austin-Broos, "Redefining the Moral Order: Interpretations of Christianity in Post Emancipation Jamaica", in *The Meaning of Freedom: Economics, Politics, and Culture after Slavery*, ed. Frank McGlynn and Seymour Drescher (Pittsburgh: Pittsburgh University Press, 1992), 221–43. George Belle, "The Struggle for Political Democracy: The 1937 Riots", in *Emancipation III: Aspects of the Post-Slavery Experience of Barbados*, ed. Woodville Marshall (Bridgetown: National Cultural Foundation, 1988), 56–91; Nigel O. Bolland, "Systems of Domination after Slavery: The Control of Land and Labour in the British West Indies after 1838", *Comparative Studies in Society and History* 23 (1981): 591–619.

colonialists. Organizations sprang up in every colony under their leadership, demanding franchise reform, taxation amendments, mass educational access, civil and legal rights expansion and, in some instances, West Indian independence.[5]

This formidable alliance targeted the policy framework of the British government. While some British officials recognized the fast-moving fundamental change in the West Indies, most could not resist restating the Carlylian view that blacks were savages and usurpers. Chamberlain, secretary of state, recognized that his leadership was being challenged. He reacted aggressively: "local government falsely so-called is the curse of the West Indies. In many islands, it means only the rule of the local oligarchy of whites and half-breeds – always incapable and frequently corrupt. In other cases, it is the rule of the Negroes, totally unfit for representative institutions and the dupes of unscrupulous adventurers." He grudgingly agreed, nonetheless, that some reform of colonialism was necessary. But the idea of a West Indian development plan to promote a racially egalitarian society and economy was hardly to be considered.[6]

Professional women and men, such as the Trinidadian Arthur Andrew Cipriani, veteran of the First World War, Alma La Badie and Amy Ashwood Garvey of Jamaica, and Dr Charles Duncan O'Neal of Barbados (who had practised medicine in Britain) joined the labour movement. Their impact was immediately positive. But it was the intellectual energy and organizational genius of Marcus Mosiah Garvey that shattered the legitimacy of colonialism throughout the West Indies in the 1920s and early 1930s.[7]

Swithin Wilmot and Don Robotham, for instance, have shown that in the history of workers' protest in Jamaica, the young Garvey possessed a considerable political pedigree. His parents were known within the movement and his early profession as a journalist exposed him to the relevant political and historical literature. Furthermore, the black community in which he was born and bred was still reeling from Governor Eyre's 1865 mass murder of protesting peasants.

Garvey was born in St Ann's Bay, on the north coast of the island, nearly a hundred miles from the St Thomas scene of the Morant Bay slaughter. His

5. See Patrick Bryan, *The Jamaican People, 1880–1902: Race, Class and Social Control* (London: Macmillan, 1991); Gisela Eisner, *Jamaica, 1830–1930: A Study of Economic Growth* (Manchester: Manchester University Press, 1961); F.W. Elkins, "Black Power in the British West Indies: The Trinidad Longshoremen's Strike of 1919", *Science and Society* 33, no. 1 (1969): 71–75.

6. Bolland, *Politics of Labour*, 137–38.

7. Ibid., 167.

father, a mason by profession, Wilmot noted, was a seasoned activist in the campaign to popularize black identity politics. As a platform speaker in the movement, Garvey senior was, therefore, an important part of the anti-colonial, pan-African, progressive movement.[8]

Garvey brought the West Indies together with grassroots political advocacy. His focused rhetoric and reasoning rallied the middle classes and working-class agitators against Chamberlain's colonial policy. Bolland noted: "In 1907 Garvey was elected vice-president of the compositors' branch of a printers' union, affiliated with the African Federation of Labour. . . . In 1910 Garvey was elected assistant secretary of the National Club of Jamaica, an early anti-colonial organisation that called for self-government within the British Empire. . . . This became Garvey's life mission."[9]

The National Club published a fortnightly magazine entitled *Our Own*, and was guided editorially by its founder, S.A.G. Cox, a bold and respected black lawyer, whose writings inspired Garvey and other pan-Africanists. In one edition, Cox noted: "The coloured and black people of Jamaica can only hope to better their condition by uniting with the coloured and black people of the United States of America and with those of other West Indian islands, and indeed with all Negroes in all parts of the world."[10]

Between 1910 and 1912, Garvey began his first organizing travels across the Caribbean, laying the foundation for the final fight against the empire. From Barbados to Belize, Panama to Port of Spain, his voice rallied millions.

Branches of his organization, the Universal Negro Improvement Association (UNIA), sprang up everywhere. Its members were mostly women and men

---

8. Ibid., 167–68. See Don Robotham, *The Notorious Riot: The Socio-Economic and Political Bases of Paul Bogle's Revolt*, Working Paper no. 28 (Kingston: Institute of Social and Economic Research, University of the West Indies, 1981); Swithin Wilmot, "Emancipation in Action: Workers and Wage Conflict in Jamaica, 1838–1840", *Jamaica Journal* 19 (1986): 55–62; Swithin Wilmot, "The Growth of Political Activity in Post-Emancipation Jamaica", in *Garvey: His Work and Impact,* ed. Rupert Lewis and Patrick Bryan (Trenton, NJ: Africa World Press, 1991).

9. Bolland, *Politics of Labour*, 169. See also Rupert Lewis, *Marcus Garvey: Anti-Colonial Champion* (London: Karia, 1987); O.W. Phelps, "The Rise of the Labour Movement in Jamaica", *Social and Economic Studies* 9, no. 4 (1960): 417–68; Ken Post, "The Politics of Protest in Jamaica, 1938", *Social and Economic Studies* 18, no. 4 (1969): 374–90; Ken Post, *Arise Ye Starvelings: The Jamaican Labour Rebellion and Its Aftermath* (The Hague: Martinus Nijhoff, 1978).

10. Bolland, *Politics of Labour*, 169.

committed to the overthrow of the British colonial yoke. Garvey's initial organization, the People's Political Party, and his first monthly magazine, *Blackman*,
"had changed the regional landscape in terms of their visionary focus on West
Indian unity, workers' solidarity, and nationalism for development."[11]

But nothing consolidated and sustained the power of Garveyism like the
determination to defeat colonialism in the minds and hearts of millions of West
Indians. His flagship publication, *New World*, was to be found throughout
the region. It was Garvey who inspired the broad-based alliance between the
Universal Negro Improvement Association, professional and business communities, and trade unions.

Despite the challenges Garvey faced from the British and American political
and judicial systems during the 1920s, a decade later the backbone of British
colonialism in the West Indies was broken. The empire entered its final phase,
crippled and awaiting its demise.[12]

Migration

The final flurry of British rule was the promotion of labour emigration as a
counter-strategy to the Caribbean demand for economic development. The
British considered migration as "letting off steam" a winning strategy. Black
and Indian communities pressed for civil rights beyond land redistribution,
into the arenas of democracy and industrial development. Colonial officials
resisted and found a holding pattern in the notion of disposing of stress-
enhancing surplus labour. The workers' movement was supportive. Repressive
British policy was given an opportunity to appear ameliorative, since it was a
better option than violence and killing.

But in the first quarter of the twentieth century, in which workers' protest
grew and populations rose significantly, intensified pressure on colonialism
remained the norm (table 6.1). Open doors to non-British regional colonies
and the United States presented workers with the opportunity to vote with
their feet against Empire. Many migrants understood, however, that both the
frying pan of British colonialism and the fire of American imperialism were
the result of white supremacy.

---

11. Ibid., 170.
12. Ibid., 171.

Table 6.1. Populations of the British West Indies, 1891–1921

Country	Year		
	1891	1911	1921
Barbados	182,867	172,337	156,774
Belize	31,471	40,458	45,317
Guiana	270,865	289,140	228,541
Jamaica	639,491	831,383	858,118
Antigua	36,819	32,269	29,767
Montserrat	11,762	12,196	12,120
St Kitts and Nevis	47,662	43,303	38,214
Virgin Islands	4,639	5,562	5,082
Trinidad and Tobago	218,381	333,552	365,913
Dominica	26,841	33,863	37,059
Grenada	53,209	66,750	66,302
St Lucia	42,220	48,637	51,505
St Vincent	41,054	41,877	–
Total	1,607,218	1,951,327	1,999,159

Source: Bolland, *Politics of Labour*, 157.

Estimates of fifty thousand people, mostly from Jamaica and Barbados, heading to Panama to work on the canal were in widespread circulation. Bolland notes:

> In the disease-ridden environment [the canal zone], thousands of workers succumbed to malaria, yellow fever, and the bubonic plague, but thousands sent home Panama money, which encouraged others to follow them. Between 1905 and 1913, US labour recruiters in Barbados shipped 20,000 Barbadian male contract workers and hundreds of others from neighbouring islands for construction work in the Canal Zone. Perhaps 40,000 other Barbadians and between 80,000 and 90,000 Jamaicans travelled informally to work on the canal. It is estimated that over 15,000 British West Indian workers, or about 10% of the total, died from disease, exhaustion, and accidents in this enterprise.[13]

---

13. Ibid., 158. See also Velma Newton, *The Silver Men: West Indian Labour Migration to Panama, 1850–1914* (Kingston: Institute of Social and Economic Research, University of the West Indies, 1984); Elizabeth Petras, *Jamaican Labor Migration: White Capital and Black Labor, 1850–1930* (Boulder: Westview Press, 1988); Jesse Proctor, "British West Indian Society and

Thousands of others were absorbed subsequently into the sugar and banana plantations of Cuba, the Dominican Republic and Costa Rica, where American corporations were investing in large-scale production.

Wages were considerably higher beyond the empire, and the opportunity to return home on a seasonal rotation was attractive to many migrants. The United States also recruited over ten thousand workers in 1924, a bumper batch, who were distributed across the industrial, hospitality service and agricultural sectors. Technology-work opportunities also opened in the Dutch West Indies, where oil refineries were being constructed in Aruba and Curaçao, in conjunction with Venezuelan oil exploration and exports.[14]

According to Bolland, "The movement of these workers both reflected and contributed to the underdevelopment of the British Caribbean." Jamaica, he said, experienced a net loss of "69,000 people between 1881 and 1911, and of 77,100 between 1911 and 1921, 63% of whom were female". During these forty years, he suggested, 46,000 workers went to the United States, 45,000 to Panama, and at least 22,000 to Cuba. Thousands more migrated to Costa Rica and other Latin American countries. The loss of these mostly young, energetic citizens adversely affected the capacity for development by absorbing their creativity in non-sugar-related activity.[15]

Governance: Dictatorship of the Proletariat

The British governance of the region, therefore, was keen to promote migration rather than the economic empowerment of workers. This was consistent with the policy of military dictatorship over the West Indian proletariat that underpinned the post-slavery paradigm. Equipped with the full backing of professional soldiers and local militias, colonial governors and their staff ruled with an iron fist. Murder and mayhem were unleashed upon protesters and their families. With or without legal trials, the results were the same.

Whether governors used the constitutional provision of direct rule, Crown colony, or conducted their affairs with the assistance of carefully selected locals who served on legislative councils and elected assemblies, the exercise of imperial power was fierce and ruthless. The reluctance of blacks to publicly celebrate

---

Government in Transition, 1920–1960", *Social and Economic Studies* 2, no. 4 (1962): 273–304.
  14. Bolland, *Politics of Labour*, 160.
  15. Ibid.

their freedom was an outcome of the fear governors were expected to instil. This circumstance remained the norm into the 1930s and beyond, despite adult suffrage and other democratic rights. Black self-government was imprinted into some black minds as "Haitianization", the term used by the British to denigrate the idea of West Indian development.

The most liberal of governors was Sir Sydney Olivier. He served in Jamaica, and was known as a socialist advocate. But even he could not come to terms with the notion of popular black economic empowerment in the West Indies. His allies in the workers' movement did not expect him to argue, as he did in his 1936 book, that the social majority was not mature enough to participate in or administer a democracy.[16] But they understood why he would make the suggestion.

The failure of white socialists in the anti-colonial discourse to advocate democracy and Caribbean development was in alignment with conservative caucuses as anti-colonial protest became the norm. As cracks appeared in the colonial wall, they called for meaningful reform rather than full-scale demolition. Socialists, liberals and conservatives were united against black anti-colonial discourse.

Governors on the ground were expected to hold a firm military grip until otherwise instructed. Teaching the "natives" by example of harsh responses remained the policy. By the 1930s, it was clear, noted Bolland, that the "battle of the West Indian people . . . could only be won in the West Indies, not in Church Street or Downing Street".[17]

Some governors, noted Morley, "were not pure autocrats but benevolent despots". His excellency the governor was "very much the monarch of his little kingdom". He was, according to Hewan Craig, "at the same time the [royal] representative, the prime minister, agent of the imperial". Governors were chosen to manage the colonial administration in any way but a democratic one. The 1920s was the first time in three hundred years that they glimpsed the credible possibility of a "rising tide of demand for democratisation". They were instructed to defend the imperial order and to cede no constitutional benefits to the blacks.[18]

---

16. Ibid., 104.
17. Ibid., 107.
18. Morley Ayearst, *The British West Indies: The Search for Self-Government* (London: Allen and Unwin, 1960), 41, 70, 141.

West Indians, then, entered the 1930s in the full knowledge that the democracy at the heart of their agitation had neither support nor sympathy among the British government. Progressive forces faced governors as enemies and obstructionists. Nothing of significance had changed constitutionally in the century since the emancipation reforms of the 1830s. The workers' movement had come to terms with imperial resistance, and resolved that only the revolutionary option could pry democracy from the iron rule of the British.

No liberal tradition existed in the West Indies that offered hope to the majority populace in respect of democratic governance. They would have to start from scratch and consider how best to develop their society from autocratic militarism to a culture of social and economic justice. This was the legacy of British rule a century after slavery. Those conscious of this centenary were also calling for an appropriate response to mark the moment.

Political power was not meant to serve social groups other than white elites. Only the governor could dispense economic benefits and social status; hence the reverence he attracted. The region, then, was politically gridlocked at the outset of the 1930s as workers proposed governance models to promote economic development and social transformation. The dictator on the ground was one man, the governor. On all matters relevant to social inclusion and economic openness, he stood in the way.

Adopting a servile posture in the presence of the governor was the norm in colonial culture. Fear and subservience went hand in glove. For blacks, Indians and coloureds to bow physically and mentally before His Excellency was also the pattern in middle-class progressive political circles. It enabled workers to observe the mendicancy of the professional classes. A visit to Government House was high on the social scale, and was a public marker of one's favour with the empire.

Likewise, to be ostracized by the empire was to be ignored and therefore punished by the governor. Crafting one's behaviour to accommodate the thinking and policy of the governor was a practice of the conservative local middle class that also served to undermine the effectiveness of the anti-colonial movement. Betrayal was best seen on display on the balconies of governors' mansions.

No to Industrialism in the West Indies

"Not a nail, not a horseshoe", British prime minister William Pitt the Elder instructed, was to be manufactured in the West Indies. The man who served as an architect of Empire during the Seven Years War, 1756–63, and which he expanded with his defeat of the French, made Britain the leading imperial power. Pitt was known for his aggressive British nationalism and colonial domination in the Caribbean. His publicly declared imperial philosophy was based on a hundred years in which West Indian colonies were kept for the mother country's enrichment and national pride.[19]

The mercantile commercial order, structured by the trade laws of the seventeenth century, defined the unequal commercial exchange objectives between Britain and the West Indies. The role of West Indian production was to make available the exports of raw materials and commodities to facilitate manufacturing in Britain. The West Indies, therefore, would import and not produce manufactured goods. The "nail and horseshoe" metaphor denoted West Indian subservience to British political and military power.

The West Indies, therefore, were stripped of their potential for significant industrialization, while Britain was transformed into the first industrial nation. "Made in England" became a global stamp on manufactured goods that were consumed in the West Indies and far beyond. Nothing was allowed to carry the stamp "Made in the West Indies".

It was this exploitative business model that Britain, in Pitt's lifetime, was to lose in its American colonies, which developed the military strength to defend their right to manufacture and implemented a Caribbean industrialization policy. American colonists took umbrage at the economic extraction, broke ranks with Britain and promoted industrialization as an illustration of their economic freedom, the precursor to political independence.[20]

Efforts to promote industrialization were part of the anti-plantation, anti-colonial reform, and were stonewalled by governors. Policies that appealed to the governor were allowed; those he abhorred were rejected. Government House was the graveyard of progressive ideas, especially those emanating from the labour movement. Only in Barbados was the governor subject to a measure

---

19. E. Williams, *Capitalism and Slavery*, 56.
20. Ibid., 55.

of constitutional restriction: by the 1940s, some members of the legislative council were elected. This, however, gave sugar planters and the governor an opportunity to manage the parliamentary containment of black politicians.

Nowhere were governors given the green light to promote industrial development in an attempt to generate employment and produce economic diversification. The promotion of cottage industries, considered a creative evolution of craft, was allowed in some colonies as part of an effort to promote the artisan sector.

Richard Bernal has illustrated the effectiveness of anti-industrialization policy. Using data from Jamaica in the 1930s, he showed how Latin American countries were transformed as industrializing economies while Jamaica stayed static, and in many instances, regressed. The "virtual absence of locally produced manufactured goods" made Jamaicans "almost entirely dependent on imports for their manufactures". Three primary products accounted for 74.5 per cent of total exports in 1930: "Exports consisted of primary products, with bananas alone accounting for 57.3 percent of total exports." This pattern, he concluded, continued up to independence in 1962.[21]

The years of the Great Depression, however, did produce some manufacturing in Jamaica and across the region, but it was restricted to items such as soaps, oil and fats, with spasmodic production of simple textiles and furniture. Making comparisons with the rise and expansion of manufacturing in Latin America, Bernal concluded that "the main difference was that Latin America was free to formulate and implement policies to promote industrialization but Jamaican efforts were retarded by the British colonial policy designed to discourage industrialisation".[22]

British rejection of industrialization in the West Indies was criticized in predictable places. The manifesto of Garvey's People's Political Party, for example, called for the "encouragement of local industries" and a law to facilitate the promotion of manufacturing. Progressive forces in the region confronted the anti-manufacturing legacy and insisted that manufacuring offered the only "hope of permanent success".[23]

The 1929 Colonial Development Act was conceived in traditional terms,

---

21. Richard L. Bernal, "The Great Depression, Colonial Policy, and Industrialisation in Jamaica", *Social and Economic Studies* 37, nos. 1–2 (1988): 36–37.
22. Ibid., 40.
23. Ibid., 41.

to provide opportunities for the export of British goods. Creating a colonial market for British manufacturers, Parliament maintained, required an aid package for the region, rather than support for its industrialization. This was antithetical to what Garvey's grassroots organizations and the labour movement were calling for.

The persistence of support for sugar plantation hegemony into the 1930s accounted for regional underdevelopment and technological backwardness. Three hundred years of enforcing the plantation extraction model shaped the structure of the economy both in terms of the absence of diversity and density of economic activity, and the endemic entrepreneurial fear of non-sugar competition.

As a result, the West Indies were required to contain public expenditure in the face of rising poverty, social decay and popular protest, and to do their utmost to project Britain as a "benevolent colonial power". If a colony wished to sponsor social services in order to ameliorate its humanitarian crisis, it was expected to fund them from domestic revenue.[24]

The act of 1929 provided small grants and loans, but these were insignificant and rarely taken up by sponsors of industrial projects. When pursued, the condition was that direct benefits would accrue directly to the British economy.[25] Consistently, then, the British government denied and ignored West Indian claims for economic development and social alleviation. It maintained the position into the 1930s that any financial or capital support for the region should place no "new burdens on the Exchequer".[26]

The 1930s: The Colonial Mess in the West Indies

After two hundred years of enslaving black people in the West Indies, followed by one hundred years of post-slavery apartheid, including seventy-five years of deceptive indenture in respect of thousands of Indians, Britain's policy of white supremacy in the 1930s had driven the majority of West Indians into

---

24. Howard Johnson, "The Political Uses of Commissions of Enquiry (1): The Imperial-Colonial West Indian Context: The Forster and Moyne Commissions", *Social and Economic Studies* 27, no. 3 (1979): 268.

25. Ibid.

26. Ibid., 269.

desperation and destitution. Indicators of wellbeing pointed to deepening poverty among the working classes.

Everywhere in the region the social and economic results were generally the same. Trapped in poverty, workers realized that Britain's intent was to deny them both democratic political rights and an economic development plan that included non-plantation employment and racial equality. They looked back and, in imagining the future, saw more of the same – a general indifference to their interest, and a life as "hewers of wood and drawers of water" for Britain.

The evidentiary basis of their conclusion can be found in literary and political narratives, the footprint of mass migrations, the intellectual discourse rooted in the rejection of white supremacy, popular demands for democracy and everyday protest and rebellion. The broad-based embrace of Garveyism as the ideological and political infrastructure in black grassroots communities, supported by middle-class professional activists, created a new intensity in anti-colonial engagement.

Lord Harris was correct a century earlier when he proclaimed in 1838 that emancipation had ended the slavery element of the plantation system without producing a new, free society. A century later, the records of British colonialism confirmed the persistence of social and economic servitude as the norm for black and Indian workers.

There was an endless stream of royal and parliamentary reports on workers' wellbeing – or rather, mass hunger and housing horrors. The 1939 official report by Major Orde-Browne, for instance, on "Labour Conditions in the West Indies", provided proof of white colonial contempt for blacks and Indians. It reflected imperial commitment to keeping them in a slave-like condition for as long as possible. This was also reflected in the Olivier-Semple report of 1929–30.[27]

The British government, now confronted with workers' uprisings against this imperial model, was gearing up for the long haul. The idea that rebellions constituted evidence of a system in crisis was rejected. Such actions by peasants and proletariat were considered mere surface fissures that would be confronted with arms and suppressed. The truth, as the British government saw it in 1930, was that the fundamentals of Empire in the West Indies were sound and the future assured (despite the experiences of white colonials indicating otherwise).

---

27. Gordon Lewis, *The Growth of the Modern West Indies* (London: MacGibbon and Kee, 1968), 77.

Critics of Empire, however, continued to argue that the West Indies were "practically devoid of all the multifarious institutions, official and unofficial, which characterised British public life". Also, that "the wage level had barely advanced beyond the daily shilling rate introduced after Emancipation". It was easy for the British government to ignore these criticisms. It had no intention of promoting and developing the West Indies as a place of organized cultural life that constituted a recognized civilization. The region remained a site of wealth extraction, and even if philistine by nature and in conduct, it served the primary purpose of supporting the empire.[28] To moralize about the material degradation of the worker, therefore, would convey the false impression that something was broken and needed to be fixed.

Investigative reports highlighted the "gross malnutrition and chronic sickness in the people", but were comfortably set aside. Gordon Lewis noted how this social condition was "made worse by a general medical education of exclusively overseas character, which emphasised curative rather than preventative medicine, with the result that bitter resentment against the medical profession was evident in many of the colonies".[29]

The derelict housing stock of the working classes stood out in the physical ecosystem of racial domination and entrapment. The plantation hut, as a house, was intended to hold the worker hostage. The author of a 1930s report offered descriptions reminiscent of slave housing in the 1830s, making reference to "a picture characterised by decrepit, verminous, and insanitary houses". He was describing the accommodation of Guianese East Indian estate workers. Families, he said, were huddled in huts and "unlighted hovels"; "women and children" were the "most exploited of all West Indian persons".[30]

Child labour was targeted for complete eradication by the labour movement. There was some success, but adult migration to Panama and other places created a reason for retaining children in sugar production. By 1930, the use of child labour was trending through the region, creating moral and material flashbacks to slavery.

The West Indies, then, was reflecting its reputation as the "slums of Empire", as the poor lived in fear of returning to a state of actual slavery. Official reports

28. Ibid., 78.
29. Ibid.
30. Ibid.

on workers' conditions, rather than validating ideas of freedom, development and democracy, typically made tentative ameliorative recommendations. Much more strident and fulsome in these reports were racist cultural and moral condemnations of black and Indian communities. A favourite social feature of writers and commissioners was the alleged moral degradation of family relations and domestic structures.

From the 1833 Emancipation Act to Lord Moyne in 1938, the economic and political assault on black and Indian communities was intense. Moyne, in his guise as a missionary, sustained the critical attitude of Carlyle into the mid-twentieth century. White men as colonial administrators held firmly to the myth of their right to rule. Whether liberal or conservative, their narrative of the black condition was infused with references to black inferiority.

The first impressive critique of this perspective came from T.S. Simey, and was found in his 1930s social surveys and 1940s economic planning recommendations. The "most striking fact about West Indian peoples", he wrote, "that is exemplified in their housing, is their poverty". He noted that "their wages are low", and "the usual clothing of the men is ragged and dirty". This is reflected in their "poor physique", the "prevalence of pellagra" and tuberculosis, and their "low resistance to infectious diseases".[31]

In many parts of the region, Simey lamented, "poverty, ignorance, over-crowding, unemployment, illness, discontent, and even despair may be so overwhelming as to touch the emotions of the most dispassionate or 'scientific' of observers". In general, he said, most workers might not be starving, but they "subsist on chronically insufficient diets", and spend much of their time "working to find [the] next meal and craving for the sensation of a full stomach".[32] Poverty breeds sickness and disease, which in turn drives discontent and the impulse to protest. He believed that "much of the ill health arose from poverty of the individual, and of the governments. Every condition tending to produce disease was to be found in decrepit homes in both town and country."[33]

Simey's description of the neo-enslavement of West Indian workers confirmed the success of colonial policy to keep them in destitution in order to "promote their industry", which was an explicit anticipated outcome of the Abolition of Slavery Act. He asserts that "the aftermath of slavery is still present in the

---

31. T.S. Simey, *Welfare and Planning in the West Indies* (Oxford: Clarendon, 1946), 11, 126.
32. Ibid., 14, 126.
33. Ibid.

West Indies", and the masses are aware that they are "unjustly treated", and that "balance requires redressing today".[34] There is no doubt, Simey asserts, that "the black masses are still exploited by the white employer".

The workers resolved to act in their own best interests. Simey concludes, "It may be strongly doubted in any event whether the West Indian was really more contented in the nineteenth century than he is in the twentieth. The significant difference is that he is no longer willing to accept an inferior position for himself." He diagnosed that "hunger or the fear of hunger" serves to create "a large accommodation of explosive matter" that is endemic in the region.[35]

The significance of Simey's social and economic survey, and the plea for reform that characterized his recommendations, stand within the discursive tradition of Macmillan's 1936 *Warning from the West Indies*. The theoretical tendency of both observers was to see blacks as equals with a unique and peculiar history, but representing a "colonial problem" to be resolved. The subtle critique of blacks' cultural capabilities, for example, and their praise of the benefits of colonialism, illustrated their subliminal white-supremacist attitudes, if not an embrace of Empire. Garveyite pan-Africanism rejected much of their thinking and became the basis of the region's preparation for a civil war to bring about democracy.[36]

The 1930s, then, witnessed widespread preparation for "the final battle in that social contest between planter and peasant". The maturity of the conflict was recognized at multiple levels of political exchange and engagement. From the cultural to the material and economic levels of the extraction model, the conflict had simmered for decades, and the outcome was now to be determined.

The commissioners of 1897 and 1938 gave the workers a mitigating message while undermining their determined efforts. They tried to disguise the weapon of white supremacy in rhetorical morality. But the intellectual agility of working-class activists, progressives and trade union organizers assured the disclosure and defeat of the strategy.

Imperial unwillingness to implement recommendations such as industrialization for job creation, a West Indian university for those who escaped the plantation and full democracy based on adult suffrage was sufficiently powerful that in the 1930s Britain was ready to defend colonialism by force of arms.

---

34. Ibid., 19.
35. Ibid., 30.
36. Ibid., 26.

Ending Colonial Fascism

By the end of the 1930s, West Indians emerged as an ideological nation, even if a politically fragmented one. British policies of prior centuries had bonded a generation of grieving workers and peasants and discontented professionals. Each colony nursed its wounds as popular rebellion became the norm. Worker emigration across the region fanned the flame. The common cause, and commitment to a one-Caribbean solution, saw to it that the labour movement appeared united as a regional force.

The Panama Canal zone was the first major melting pot where thousands of the region's youngest, bravest and most determined worked in gangs, played cricket, created families – and died in large numbers. The first sporting hero of the "nation" was cricketer George Headley, who was the Panama-born son of a Barbadian father and Jamaican mother who had met and worked on the canal. His parents took him to Cuba before he settled as a teenager in Jamaica. By the early 1930s, the region had deemed him its hero, the best batsman in the world. From Jamaica to the Leeward and Windward Islands, to Barbados, Trinidad and Tobago, and Guiana, he was a sports icon.

Making this possible were the regional grassroots movement and message of Marcus Garvey. The migration of the peasantry, mostly landless and hungry for change, extended throughout the region. The migration also found organizational form in the United States, and in New York in particular, where the diaspora was determined in one way or another to facilitate the Caribbean revolution. Garvey and other inspirational leaders built the community base with branches dedicated to pan-Africanist liberation in towns and villages. Garvey emerged as the West Indian "Moses".

Political circumstances in the region gave the lie to the British government refrain that there was "nothing to be called an anti-colonial movement" in the West Indies. Lewis was calling for an industrialization policy in addition to agricultural reform. The Garvey movement had been doing the same a decade earlier. There was considerable evidence of the maturity of the anti-colonial movement as a holistic, democratic and revolutionary process.[37]

The revolution was not simply a "response to the economic distress" of the 1920s depression. The environment that matured political consciousness was

---

37. Bolland, *Politics of Labour*, 212.

populated with sophisticated professional activists. Many lived in communities far removed from the peasantry and urban proletariat. The awareness that integrated their politics transcended the hunger in the belly and was connected more to the fire in the mind.[38]

Clement Payne, for example, veteran Garveyite campaigner of the pan-African movement in Trinidad, travelled to his parents' home in Barbados, and there articulated one of the most eloquent anti-colonial narratives of the twentieth century. In so doing, he rallied in 1937 the revolutionary coalition of the radical black middle class, the urban poor and the rural dispossessed.[39]

The concept of anti-colonial revolution refers to the process that sought to make an irretrievable break with the past. When the workers' movement rose against colonialism, imperial authority could not reverse the tide. There was no going back. The regional community gave a widespread dimension to the revolution as the imperial assault on rebels in one colony triggered the onslaught against colonialism in another. The effective communication strategies of Garvey's guerrillas across the region assured the effectiveness of the rising. That regional coalition held its shape for nearly five years. Shootings, beatings and imprisonments of workers served to postpone temporarily the inevitable – the fall of Empire in the West Indies.

The internal movement and logistics of the revolution have been carefully mapped, including the following events: "The February, 1934, labour agitation in British Honduras (Belize) ended in a riot; May–July, 1934, sugar estate disturbance on Trinidad, which broke out on several estates in the central sugar belt, involved over 15,000 Indian estate labourers; the January, 1935, St Kitts sugar strike . . . turned into a general strike of agricultural labourers. [Then] came a March strike in Trinidad's oilfields and a hunger march to Port of Spain." In Jamaica, labour protest broke out in May 1934 on the northern coast. Rioting among banana workers in the town of Oracabessa was succeeded by a strike of dockworkers in the small town of Falmouth, which ended in violence. Furthermore, "In September and October there were riots on various sugar estates in British Guiana; there had been strikes the previous September on the five estates on the west coast of Demerara. In October, rioting also took place on

---

38. Ibid., 213.
39. See Hilary McD. Beckles, *Chattel House Blues: Making of a Democratic Society in Barbados – From Clement Payne to Owen Arthur* (Kingston: Ian Randle, 2004).

St Vincent in Kingstown and Camden Park. . . . After a relatively tranquil year in 1936, there was widespread unrest in Trinidad which saw unprecedented cooperation between Indo-Trinidadian and Afro-Trinidadian labourers."[40]

The 1937–38 rebellions were of greater magnitude than those of 1934–35, which had been more localized. In Trinidad, for example, the protest began in the oilfields but eventually spread to the sugar belt and towns. In Barbados, the rebellion that started in Bridgetown spread to the rural areas. In Jamaica most parts of the island experienced serious strikes and rebellions.[41]

West Indian workers, once again, paid dearly with the loss of life. They confronted professional regiments and militias. The sugar workers, in Kingston, for example, lost forty-six lives in two days. More than fout hundred were seriously injured, and thousands were detained and prosecuted. Many of these were women, who provided vangard organizational leadership as well as rank-and-file support in battle. In Barbados, fourteen black people were killed, forty-seven injured and over five hundred arrested. Many were tried, convicted and imprisoned after receiving severe beatings from police and special constables. Reports suggest that across the region over a hundred people were killed, and more than five hundred severely injured.[42]

Blanshard noted that as "revelations of social discontent and advertisement of social injustice, the events were the most successful demonstrations in Caribbean history". The police used rifles to beat back the blacks in St Kitts, resulting in several killings. In Barbados, he noted, the grievances of workers "were apparently no worse in 1937 than they had been for a generation", yet they threw in their lot with their regional comrades. In Jamaica, in 1937, he noted, where the "rank and file" of policemen "are coal-black", they put down a demonstration of workers in Kingston with batons, demonstrating the aggressive rage that typified the colonial response. The waterfront workers' strike in May 1938 resulted in eight people being shot dead, 171 wounded, and over seven hundred arrested.[43]

---

40. See "British West Indian Labour Unrest of 1934–1939", Wikipedia, https://en.wikipedia .org/wiki/British_West_Indian_labour_unrest_of_1934%E2%80%931939; Hart, *Labour Rebellions*; Cecilia Green, "Caribbean Politics and the 1930s Revolt", *Against the Current* 70 (September–October 1997), https://www.marxists.org/history/etol/newspape/atc/1992.html.
41. Ibid.
42. See Beckles, *Chattel House*, 19; Blanshard, *Democracy*, 22.
43. Blanshard, *Democracy*, 22, 23, 26.

By the end of the 1930s, West Indians had confronted colonial dictatorship, setting an example for colonized Africans and Asians. The democracy movement now sought institutionalization and its rooting in an economic development strategy. West Indians were now in common control of their collective future.

The refusal of the imperial government to concede basic democratic rights had resulted in workers directly taking on the colonial forces. The Barbados governor's commission of enquiry reported this truth:

> After a careful review of all the facts connected with wages we feel it our duty to state emphatically that in our opinion there can be no justification short of bankruptcy of trade and industry for the maintenance of a low standard of wages. . . . We have been impressed by the high dividends earned by many trading concerns in the island and the comfortable salaries and bonuses paid to the higher grades of employees in business and agriculture. . . . A fundamental change in the division of earnings between employer and his employee is essential if hatred and bitterness are to be removed from the minds of the majority of employees.[44]

The colonial context, of course, was but a microcosm of the empire. The extractive economy of the Caribbean that impoverished and embittered workers in individual enterprises were units of the grand imperial order.

West Indians, finally, after three centuries, had taken charge of important aspects of their destiny and prepared to dismantle the edifices of Empire within the context of labour politics. For the first time, also, an economic development paradigm was being formulated within the workers' movement. The imperial focus on social welfare and aid was dismantled and replaced by a balanced social and economic strategy. The dying colonialism was about to yield that which had been long denied, a West Indian nation that was forward-looking.

---

44. Ibid., 26.

CHAPTER 7

Ending Empire
The 1930s Revolution

While the United Kingdom must play an important part in the improvement
of conditions by providing financial assistance for social services and markets
to foster West Indian economy, it is equally important that an emergence of a
spirit of self-help, thrift and independence should come about among the West
Indian people themselves . . . some small increase in industrial employment may
be afforded by the development of secondary industries; but these can at best be
dependent for their prosperity on that of the main industry of the whole area,
namely agriculture. A new economic policy for the West Indies must therefore
be an agricultural policy.

—*Report of the West India Royal Commission,* 1945

BY 1940, THE LABOUR MOVEMENT HAD completed phase one of the revolution to
overthrow the British Empire in the West Indies. In the prior decade, imperial
forces had resorted to the use of arms in order to crush popular anti-colonial
rebellion. Colonial governors were instructed to use maximum military power
to repress the movement and to dispose of the leadership that posed the threat.
Imperial thinking was that democracy was unsuited to the masses. As a consequence, the British government moved to consolidate colonialism deep into
the twentieth century.[1]

Arthur Lewis, a participant in the labour movement, argued that the workers'
actions constituted "nothing short of a revolution".[2] But the British government,

---

1. Post, *Arise,* 307–50; Paget Henry, *Peripheral Capitalism and Underdevelopment in Antigua*
(New Brunswick, NJ: Transaction Books, 1985), 71–99; Beckles, *Chattel House,* 25–41; F.A.
Hoyos, *Grantley Adams and the Social Revolution* (London: Macmillan, 1974); Knight,
Caribbean; G. Lewis, *Growth.*

2. W. Arthur Lewis, *Labour in the West Indies: The Birth of a Workers' Movement* (London:
Victor Gollancz; the Fabian Society, 1939), 34.

he said, with its back against the wall, was determined to hold on to the region and its people. It continued to resist reforms in land redistribution, public education, wage increases, civil rights and extending the franchise.

For the first time since the legal ending of enslavement and of indentureship in 1917, workers had become organized politically and their interests "forced into the foreground". From this moment the leadership of the workers' movement would determine the general direction of regional politics. The political crafting of West Indian nationhood was now in the hands and imagination of a regional network of labour leaders working to achieve a common objective. According to Lewis, the "full significance of this revolution" resided in the politics of constitutional democracy, which was rapidly unfolding.[3]

In addition to critical political developments forged in the Panama migration, there was the exposure that West Indian soldiers gained in the First World War. Many of them understood the war for what it was, a competitive imperial struggle to colonize and partition Africa, and by extension consolidate a new global colonial policy, and they resented it. They were dismayed to discover that Britain was planning a major operation to subjugate all black people, specifically under an apartheid system, rather than opening doors for democratization. This was what radically altered the mindset of men like Captain Cipriani in Trinidad, leaving him passionately committed to freeing the West Indies from British rule.

An important consequence of this development was the consolidation of the strategic alliance between workers and progressive elements in the black, Indian and coloured professional middle class. The forging of a stronger ideological bond facilitated greater demands for democratic reforms. In Trinidad and Tobago, for example, and in Grenada, Workingmen's Associations took the lead in a coalition that pressed for specific workers' compensation benefits. They rolled out an agenda of issues such as mass access to basic education, slum clearance and specific political reforms intended to elect their representatives to legislative assemblies.

The attempt by the British government to contain the advance of this agenda prompted Lord Halifax's tour of the region. Representing the Colonial Office, he made recommendations on his return with limited concessions to the workers' movement. One concession nonetheless enabled a few candidates from the

---

3. Ibid.

black, Indian and coloured professional classes to be selected to governors' legislative councils. But his recommendation was read in the region as an attempt to frustrate the liberalization of the franchise and derail the constitutional aspects of the revolution. It was therefore rejected, particularly in Trinidad and the Windward Islands, where the strategy was most publicly ventilated.

It was obvious that the British government was deploying its traditional divide-and-rule approach, and that a counter-strategy was required to advance the nation-building project. The immediate realization was that more advanced action was required to coordinate the labour movement. It was this development, driven by a combination of proposals from the Garvey movement and workingmen's associations, that produced the Dominica Conference in 1932.[4]

The gathering revealed both the progressive and conservative elements of the labour movement. Organizers sought to discuss issues that were resonating at the grassroots level and within left-leaning cadres of the intellectual and professional classes. Universal adult suffrage – the core of the demand for democracy – was given top priority as the strategy to topple colonialism. Alongside this was the call for a federation as the framework to achieve and sustain results on a regional rather than insular basis. Ironically, the recognition that colonialism operated effectively at both levels focused attention on the specific circumstances in each colony.

The two political planks of the conference seemed comfortable with each other until Trinidad and Tobago pushed for unanimous agreement on both adult suffrage and political federation. Barbados did not accept the full adult suffrage recommendation, on the basis that the local labour movement was insufficiently organized to implement it. The federation proposal, however, was accepted, and delegates left Dominica resolved on this quest.

The splinter on adult suffrage signalled the extent to which middle-class professional leadership and the working men's movement were out of step. The lessons arising from this development focused greater attention on the degree to which anti-colonialism and pro-democracy nation-building could be a cohesive process.

The triumph of workingmen's associations and Garvey's pan-African approach considerably suppressed the division over adult suffrage in the next few years. This was particularly evident as anti-worker violence by the colonial government

---

4. Ibid., 35.

in Belize and St Kitts revealed that no significant constitutional concessions were forthcoming from Britain. But the workers were adamant in their advocacy of the twin pillars. By 1940, the demand for universal adult suffrage and federation were the two undisputed objectives that West Indians had agreed would be the anchors of the free West Indian nation.

The Italian military assault upon Ethiopia, in particular, closed the lid on any belief that Britain was prepared to make a commitment to multiculturalism in the empire over the policy of white supremacy. Since the 1890s, Italy had made unsuccessful attempts to invade and colonize Ethiopia. By the time of the West Indian revolution, Ethiopia was arguably the only African kingdom that had not fallen into Europe's imperial clutches. It became, furthermore, a symbol of the emerging pan-African movement, long headquartered in the West Indian theatre of resistance, from Toussaint L'Ouverture to Marcus Garvey.

Serving as an icon for black freedom, Ethiopia, and its young black king, Haile Selassie, in particular, occupied an elevated place in the pantheon of West Indian anti-colonialism. Named Ras Tafari Makonnen, he was branded with a new identity in 1916, Crown Prince Haile Selassie I, regent of the Ethiopian Empire. He was crowned king in 1928 and emperor in 1930 – Negusa Negast, King of Kings, offspring of King Solomon and the Queen of Sheba, lineage to Menelik I. West Indian pan-Africanists drew inspiration from the young king as a voice of black sovereignty and dignity. He embodied their hope for democratic freedom in both the West Indies and in Africa.

On 3 October 1935, the Italian army, which had been defeated by the Ethiopian army in the Battle of Adwa in 1896, invaded the kingdom. It conquered Adwa three days later, and Aksum within two weeks. Italy's fascist regime, led by Prime Minister Benito Mussolini, finally annexed Ethiopia on 7 May 1936 and declared King Victor Emmanuel III its new emperor. Haile Selassie had escaped into exile on 2 May, three days before the fall of Addis Ababa.[5]

News of these developments was devastating for pan-Africanists everywhere, particularly in the West Indies. Large numbers of men and women of all social strata joined up as soldiers to defend Ethiopia and its legitimate emperor. The battle for the soul of the African race was considered tied to the outcome in Ethiopia, where sovereignty was finally lost. This was the high moment for the

---

5. Winston James, *Holding Aloft the Banner of Ethiopia: Caribbean Radicalism in Early Twentieth-Century America* (London, Verso, 1998).

Garvey movement, which intensified its global mobilization to defend the sacred nation and its monarchy against the wave of racist, fascist terror in Europe.

Two critical events in Ethiopia focused West Indian attention on Britain's attitude and policy on the future of colonialism. First, it became obvious that despite the rhetoric to the contrary, Britain had no intention of defending Ethiopia against Italy's invasion. Mussolini read the mind of the British secretary of state most precisely in recognizing that there would be no military support for the Africans and that his march on Addis Abba would meet no British resistance. Second, West Indians understood this situation as yet another example of British diplomatic duplicity that led to the betrayal of Ethiopia and the entire black world. European ethnic solidarity was uppermost in British thinking.

Meanwhile, Britain was pressing ahead with its plans to tighten its colonial grip on Southern Africa and to establish an apartheid regime there as the twentieth-century expression of a new empire. Betrayal in northeast Africa, then, and humiliation in South Africa, led West Indians to understand more clearly that the British government would deal with them in a similar fashion.

The cry of "shame on Britain" across the West Indies resonated in particular in Jamaica, where a group that dedicated its existence to the legacy of Ethiopia's emperor, and carrying his name, Ras Tafari, sprang into action to resist the criminal violation of Africa. The Ras Tafarians grew in large numbers and influence within Garvey's movement. By 1937, they were a significant advocacy group in organizations dedicated to African liberation. They added considerable energy and ideological focus to anti-colonialism, and provided creative commitment to the liberation movements of Africans everywhere.

Solidarity from Africa and Asia strengthened West Indian demands for federation and nationhood. The insistence that the plantation economy be reformed to accommodate a small-farmer cooperative culture highlighted the following objectives: that urban slum clearance should be funded as a reparatory justice programme; a meaningful social welfare investment strategy should be implemented to promote community development; and an industrialization programme should be rolled out to provide jobs for skilled workers. These proposals reflected the advanced thinking of the regional labour movement. The workers' revolution, then, had conceptually broken the back of Empire and its agenda would lay the foundation for political integration and nation-building.[6]

---

6. W.A. Lewis, *Labour*, 35.

Long before Arthur Creech Jones, member of Parliament for Shipley in the United Kingdom, stood in the House of Commons on 28 June 1938 and demanded of William Ormsby-Gore, secretary of state for the colonies, an "independent and searching enquiring" into the workers' revolution, popular opinion in the region was supportive of the actions of labour leaders. It was just a matter of negotiating the closing chapter of Empire.[7]

Colonial governments were already conducting their own investigations into the mass rebellion. In Trinidad and Tobago, the Forster Commission was established in 1937, and likewise in Barbados, the Dean Commission. Both commissions reported on the causes of uprisings. Recommendations were intended to defuse the local situation by focusing on economic and social hardship rather than rising anti-colonial consciousness.

In Barbados, the Dean Commission held thirty-one meetings across the island, and received testimony from 135 witnesses and civil-society experts. It concluded that the decade of discontent found a growing body of "explosive matter in the island", and that the governor's decision to deport Clement Payne, the charismatic Garveyite leader, "only served as a detonator". The three-man commission, however, denied the peculiar significance of mature political organization and anti-colonial sentiments in communities and concluded that the "root cause" of the revolution was the hunger and suffering of the masses resulting from overpopulation and the global recession.[8]

The British government was less concerned, however, with the reason for rebellion in Trinidad, and more with its containment and suppression. The oilfields in the south of the colony were of critical value to the British war effort. Barbados's sugar might have been disposable; Trinidad's oil was indispensable.

The Forster Commission, in the face of workers' complaints about institutional racism in the management of the oil industry, and anger at the Italian invasion of Abyssinia, focused instead on appeasement strategies. This involved granting concessions to "moderate" and "authorized" trade unions and creating a modern industrial relations infrastructure to negotiate and settle the legitimate grievances the governor believed to exist. The British government

---

7. Johnson, "Political Uses", 257.

8. Henderson Carter, *Labour Pains: Resistance and Protest in Barbados, 1838–1904* (Kingston: Ian Randle, 2012). See also Green, "Caribbean Politics"; David Abdulah, "Caribbean Movements Then and Now: A Labor View", NACLA, 25 September 2007, https://nacla.org /article/caribbean-movements-then-and-now-labor-view.

was also aware that Trinidad was considered an intellectual and organizational epicentre of the regional revolution and that further military repression would not serve the imperial end.[9]

West Indian commissions, then, were precursors to the Royal Commission that arrived in the region in 1938. Its royal imprimatur originated in a remit from Parliament. Such a commission, and no other, was required to intervene and prepare a policy report to appease West Indians. Its recommendations had to excite labour leaders while assuring the British government that nothing would be done to hasten the advance of democracy and economic transformation.

The report had to be a masterpiece of imperial craftsmanship that could satisfy West Indian expectations. Protecting and preserving the empire in the West Indies was the principal mandate of both the local and imperial commissions. There was no sense of panic in the British government about the arrival of the commission, because it was assured that West Indians were in the mood to negotiate. The immediate objective was to find the tone and texture for general discussion, specific negotiations and possible constitutional reform.

Protecting the oppressive sugar sector was the prime remit of the commission. Sugar planters wanted a better trade deal for themselves. The blacks and Indians had brought the colonial order to its knees with their protests and wanted from the Royal Commission a road map to sovereignty with signposts such as racial justice, economic empowerment and universal adult suffrage. Balancing the needs of sugar and sovereignty would not be a simple task for the commission.

A concern of the British government, however, was that the commission might lean in favour of reforms and recommend measures which the State would be unwilling to accept or finance. It was well briefed before leaving London. Members understood that the government "would not entertain any proposal for increased financial assistance to the West Indian colonies".[10]

Sir Henry Moore noted that from the British government's perspective, the "immediate advantage would be the beneficial political effect it would have both in the West Indies and at home in assuring the public that His Majesty's Government was prepared to take a hand in West Indian problems on a long range basis".[11]

---

9. Johnson, "Political Uses", 259, 263.
10. Ibid., 266, 267.
11. Ibid., 268.

A Royal Commission was designed and established to contain and corrode a workers' revolution. According to Johnson, "It was recognized that the British Government would have to assume some financial responsibility" for a higher level of social commitment, since "most colonies would be unable to finance them from revenue". The Colonial Office response to the political crisis, he added, "may be described as channelling revolution along paths of peaceful reform by providing cash". This is where the discourse had reached in the summer of 1938 when the commission was established.

From this perspective it was a commission like no other in the history of the region. It was created on the assumption that the West Indies crisis could not be answered by confronting communities with more arms, nor by "large-scale financial assistance". The commission was made up of politicians, academics and professionals from the private and public sectors. Lord Moyne, the chairman, was a prominent participant in the domestic arena, having served successive governments as a parliamentarian for over two decades. He was a minister of agriculture and fisheries for four years (1925–29) before receiving a peerage in 1932.[12] He also served as chair of the financial enquiry into the colonial administration in Kenya.

Fear of Reparations

Official arguments for the establishment of the commission point to one overwhelming conclusion – that the British government feared having to pay a large sum of money to create and sustain social stability and promote economic development in the West Indies.

They were aware that the West Indian spirit could not be caged again. But officials were faced with two disturbing challenges: giving serious account of the social effect of three hundred years of draining economic extraction; and recognizing that the social consequences of this exploitation constituted the evidentiary basis of the judgement that the West Indies were the "slums of Empire". The British government hoped that superficial ameliorative reforms would cost no more than a modest sum.

Fear of funding economic repair in the West Indies, and the popular resent-

---

12. Ibid., 270.

ment it would entail in England, determined how the commission was constituted and politically oriented. The government knew that a progressive report was necessary to appease the liberal core in the cabinet, and parts of the national community. But the expectation was that its recommendations would be economically reasonable and that the West Indians themselves would ultimately agree to bear the burden of cleaning up the colonial mess.

The minimalist attitude inherent in this policy was not unexpected. The British were not prepared to contemplate a moment in which the West Indian colonies would be a net retainer of economic value. To imagine a position in which a meaningful portion of the wealth extracted could be reinjected, or left behind to promote economic development, was just too much. In the heart of the British government, Whitehall and Downing Street, West Indians were considered undeserving of economic inclusion and capital-development reparations.

As a consequence, no West Indian was appointed to the Moyne Commission. This was no coincidence. Generations of writers have since apologized for this blatant rejection of the West Indian voice. There was instead the racist assumption that British people with experience in the West Indies would represent the consciousness of the region, and this was consistently expressed. In 1938, this thinking was intended to delegitimize the workers' leadership and popular support for the revolution.

Arthur Lewis, despite being a perfect example of an excluded commissioner, was excessively generous in his assertion that the all-white commission could be explained in other terms: "Colonial Office officials were more deliberately catering to the prejudices of the colonial population who were more likely to accept the recommendations of a commission comprised of men of status in British society rather than one including local representatives."[13] Johnson, even more generously, suggested that "it is possible to argue that this Commission was aimed primarily at convincing the British public of the wisdom of a potentially expensive solution to West Indian problems and was thus composed of persons known to them". In every instance the twisted thinking that determined West Indian exclusion turned on the one important matter: anxiety about making a reparatory justice investment in the development of the West Indian economy.[14]

13. Ibid., 273.
14. Ibid.

To understand the nature of this concern it is necessary to return to the scene of every seminal moment in the previous hundred years in which the British government effectively rejected the call from the black community for economic and social repair. The emancipation reforms in the 1830s ignored black demands and adjustments in the sugar sector in the 1840s were intended to secure the plantations as control centres for rebellious workers. From the 1840s to the 1897 Royal Commission, the British focus on governance was about the maintenance of robust cost containment and enhanced wealth extraction.

Gordon Lewis, British political historian of the Caribbean, was therefore off target when he noted that the "weakness" of the Moyne Report "was the general timidity of its recommendations". This was its raison d'etre. What Lewis described as "the bias in favour of social welfare" was consistent with British opposition to economic reform. The leaning towards social welfare was structurally positioned so as to block access to economic participation. The commissioners were particularly clear on the latter, reflecting the instructions received in London about the need to support hegemonic plantation interests.[15]

Where Lewis was correct, however, was in noting the persistent moral and cultural condemnation of blacks throughout the report. The British obsession with the idea of morally rehabilitating blacks, as opposed to materially liberating them, was palpable. Focus on building a moral black society transcended interest in developing a black economy. As a result, recommendations were costed around social welfare rather than economic empowerment. Lewis concludes: "Since the underlying economic assumption of British colonial rule was that the colonies were best suited for producing agricultural products, it was perhaps inevitable that the Commission's sole reference to the possibilities of West Indian industrial development should have been disparaging in tone; but the prejudice was noted by West Indian commentators at the time."[16]

There was, therefore, nothing special nor peculiar about Moyne's leadership, other than his presiding over the funeral of the empire. His recommendations constituted a civic burial ceremony on a low budget. Neither was it surprising that his report, completed in 1939, did not see the light of day until 1945, after the war, even though recommendations were publicly known as early as 1940.

---

15. G. Lewis, *Growth*, 85.
16. Ibid., 85–86.

The British government did not give as its reason for withholding the report the fact that it had recruited thousands of black West Indians to fight an ethnic, narcissistic battle against the Nazis. The irony was not lost on West Indian soldiers that they were fighting to save an empire that had long been in the business of killing and brutalizing them as a race. Neither were they unaware that fighting for the empire was an opportunity to take the battle one further step, beyond Britain, to the Nazis, whose white-supremacist system was arguably more evil than the one they were familiar with back home.

With the war against the Nazis won, helped by thousands of West Indians, and the Moyne Report finally released, Britain returned to the question of how best to deal with the rebellious region. Officials considered the report a masterstroke in the colonial management of a people who had gone rogue.

Moyne admitted that Britain had created in the region a humanitarian mess and that the time had come to begin a clean-up operation with social rather than economic policies. "There is a pressing need", his report stated, "for a large expenditure on social services and development which not even the least poor of the West Indian colonies can hope to undertake from their own resources."

The concept of a "large expenditure" resonated differently among the membership of the commission. "Large" in British expenses meant "little" in West Indian experience. The imperial tradition of not giving back was a metaphor for black misery. The report recommended the British government pay a grant of £1 million per year for twenty years to support the West Indies. It would go a long way, Moyne wrote, "to finance social and economic development in the colonies".[17] Arthur Lewis had called for a repayment of the debt resulting from two hundred years of free labour. His argument was rejected in favour of a fund to finance petty projects.

Moyne's Petty Reparations Fund

When news of the recommended £1 million annual fund reached the West Indies, the organizational structures of the political revolution were already visible and objectives for mass action outlined. Workingmen's associations that held together the still-outlawed trade unions were robust in their anti-colonial

---

17. Johnson, "Political Uses", 274.

advocacy and had formulated a negotiation strategy to end colonialism. There was reduced interest in Moyne's message. If anything, the sum of £1 million was considered minor in the grand scheme of decolonization.

In Barbados, the Progressive League was created in 1938, with Grantley Adams at the helm. He had little choice but to advance the ideas that won popular support during Clement Payne's rebellion in 1937. In Jamaica, Norman Manley's People's National Party (PNP) came into being in 1938, bringing a significant middle-class professional radicalism to the anti-colonial leadership. Collectively, they consolidated the class alliance that had been a part of the 1930s revolution.

Adams's leadership established a framework for social welfare legislation in Barbados, including a significantly expanded franchise. This evolving electoral structure was rooted in the labour movement. In 1941, the league had evolved into the Barbados Workers' Union. The following year, Adams was invited by the governor to sit on the executive committee.

In Trinidad, Tubal Uriah "Buzz" Butler had organized the 1937 general strike of oil workers. Butler was recognized as a democratic socialist. He was an ally of Captain Cipriani, and together their anti-colonial politics took centre stage. But by 1938, Butler had eclipsed Cipriani as the leader of the labour movement, becoming the "first effective negro leader to emerge in Trinidad". He was arrested and imprisoned by the colonial government. There was no trial and he was not charged. The high-handed attitude of the governor served to intensify anti-colonial mobilization. Butler was replaced as labour leader by the charismatic Indian intellectual Adrian Cola Rienzi, a socialist barrister.[18]

The 1937 oil workers' strike and the 1938 formation of the All Trinidad Sugar Estates and Factory Workers' Union, along with the Negro Welfare and Cultural Association, were critical in establishing the Seamen and Waterfront Workers' Union and the Public Works and Public Service Workers' Trade Union. The union movement in Trinidad, therefore, provided the basis of the new anti-colonial culture of the regional workers' movement. It had a highly sophisticated infrastructure, with leadership skilled in negotiations. But significantly, its radicalism informed the movement to end the empire by moving ahead with nation-building.

---

18. Elisabeth Wallace, *The British Caribbean: From the Decline of Colonialism to the End of the Federation* (Toronto: University of Toronto Press, 1977), 35.

By 1939, Bustamante was undoubtedly the leader of the Jamaica labour movement, having established institutional control over working men's politics. He informed the governor that he "had 100,000 people behind him", and "if there is going to be a master in Jamaica then I am going to be that master". Like Butler in Trinidad, he was arrested and imprisoned by the governor. He was found guilty of the charge of sedition. While in prison Bustamante grew in stature as the people's hero. On his release, he became president for life of the Bustamante Industrial Trade Union – a general union of all workers, skilled and unskilled, in all sectors of the economy.[19]

Bustamante became a larger-than-life figure in Jamaica, with a determination to rip his country out of Britain's grip by championing the popular desire to uproot the empire. When accused by a conservative journalist of being a dictator, like the colonial governor whose power he wanted to usurp, he replied:

> Yes, I want power, sufficient power to be able to defend those weaker than I am; those less fortunate, and that's what I have today – Power. . . . It has been stated that I want to be a dictator. Yes, I do want to dictate the policy of the unions, in the interests of the people I represent, and the only ones who are giving results today are the dictators. . . . The voice of labour must be heard and it shall be heard through me.[20]

When his union moved to establish the Jamaica Labour Party in 1943, he was atop the "black mountain" of anti-colonial resentment on the island, and was poised to bring the empire to its knees.

The workers' movement, then, long before Moyne's report was published in 1945, was part of a solid system of trade unions, political parties and professional bodies that understood the history and functioning of Empire and was committed to its demolition through intensive, focused negotiations.

The dialogue was informed by an acute understanding of, and resentment for, colonial economic extraction, which was understood to be the basis of mass poverty, racial degradation and psychological terrorism. West Indian political leaders commonly argued, noted Wallace, "that white ruling groups in the islands were mainly interested in extracting profits from neglected and poverty-stricken people". The line was drawn at the dawn of the 1940s.[21]

---

19. Ibid., 37.
20. Ibid., 39.
21. Ibid., 35.

Cleaning up the Colonial Mess

Moyne, then, was primarily concerned with focusing attention on remedying the social effects of colonialism. The social decay, he admitted, had intensified since emancipation reform in the 1830s and was now an embarrassment to British colonialism. He could not see a way, however, with Arthur Lewis, to formulate and recommend a new economic development policy for the region. Had he done so it would have validated not only Lewis, whom he criticized, but the thinking and vision of the labour movement.

The offer of an annual £1 million bandage for twenty years would allow the British government, the report stated, "to undertake greater responsibility for the wellbeing of colonial peoples". That is, they would remain colonized and poor while being socially assisted. The grant would be administered through a "West Indian Welfare Fund" to be financed by the "Imperial Exchequer".[22] The report noted: "The object of the Fund should be to finance schemes for the general improvement of education, and the health services, housing and slum clearance, the creation of labour departments, the provision of social welfare facilities, and land settlement, apart from the cost of purchase of land."[23] No one, on either side, pretended the fund would be a panacea. It was considered a typical British penny-pinching plan for the colonized poor.

Moyne was forced by criticism to admit that the sum was small, but insisted it was a useful step. The report stated:

> most of the main social and economic defects of the West Indies have, in broad outline, been known and deplored for many years. They have been the subject of numerous enquiries both by local committees and by investigators or commissioners sent out from Great Britain. . . . Nevertheless, the problems have remained, and the efforts . . . have failed to make for radical reform. We therefore conclude that the means do not exist for effecting improvement on an adequate scale.[24]

This was the only conclusion to be drawn and represented the explicit thinking of the British government. It was not the cash that was lacking, but the mentality to care. There was no inclination or desire to reverse or abandon the

---

22. *The Moyne Report: Report of the West India Royal Commission*, intr. Denis Benn (reprint, Kingston: Ian Randle, 2011), 429.
23. Ibid., 428.
24. Ibid.

imperial economic-extraction policy. The allocation of the £20 million grant was to address the social collateral damage of economic extraction. It was given "in regard to the more recent developments of social welfare, public health policy and labour organisations and legislation".[25] Moyne was conscious of the expectation in Britain that he should put Arthur Lewis in a diminished space rather than legitimize him with discussions of economic development in the West Indies. Lewis understood that Moyne was putting him to the sword over his call for reparation payment to fund economic development.

West Indian labour leaders, with the Moyne Report in hand, doubted the sincerity and resolve of the British government. They read, very accurately, the motive and mission of the Moyne Commission. They understood that efforts on the social welfare front, including the £1 million-per-year gift as window dressing, were totally inadequate.

In effect, labour leaders experienced Moyne's mission as another attempt by Britain to distance itself from the real business of economic reform. The traditional style and diplomatic skill of colonial crisis management, including the use of reports from committees and commissions, gave the British government the confidence to defuse and contain anti-colonial agitation, and to use the injustice system to detain rebel leaders. But the West Indian labour movement was far from impressed.

Moyne's report, then, reflected no mystery in the management of the colonized. The commission had set out to accomplish a task for the British government in the West Indies, and to do so persuasively and with panache. Some in the labour leadership saw Moyne as another employee of the British government who was an imperial apologist and racist.

Once again, another commission had come out from London, leaving behind eloquent, insincere words intended to soothe centuries of pain. Two Royal Commissions in forty years, 1897 and 1838, provided Britain's governments and people with a "feel-good" effect emanating from reasonable recommendations, though they were designed to enable evading financial responsibility for colonial victims.

Transformational ideas were recommended in each instance. But at the end of the day, West Indians were left to carry the costs of the imperial retreat from reparations. Britain, the greatest economic extractor from the West Indies,

---

25. Ibid.

had again refused to inject anything like an adequate sum of cash. This was how Britain actively underdeveloped the West Indian economy. But, finally, a cadre of Caribbean nation-builders exposed the imperial ploy to public display, while West Indians pushed forward with plans for sovereignty without imperial support for economic development.

The sum of £20 million over twenty years, then, was not intended to confront or clean up the colonial mess. This much West Indian leaders understood. The region had exposed the inner objectives of Britain's colonial policy.

With the West Indies rising against Empire, it was only a matter of months before African and Asian colonies followed. The region ignited this flame. British policy then turned to punishing it for its audacity. It was the West Indies' finest hour, for which they would pay a great price in the coming decades.

In Jamaica, the PNP was first out of the blocks with a castigation of Moyne's strategy to deceive West Indians. The British government's decision not to put its money where Moyne's mouth had been was foreseen. This angered West Indians, who believed they had a right to reparatory economic justice funded by the imperial government. In one of the PNP's news releases, it rejected the British ploy and noted that "it was a futile effort" to substitute social services for significant political and economic reform.[26]

Moyne's social welfare scheme was intended to reflect the British plan to reject the West Indian demand for economic development within a framework of reparation. Evidence of the intention to prolong the empire, and to do nothing to encourage economic transformation and development, could be found in the objective of every recommendation within the report. It was therefore received by West Indian nationalists as an enemy report. While it might have appeased the conservative wing of the labour movement, as a token gesture rather than a reparatory "give back" programme, the general reception was at best lukewarm.

Manley rejected the British idea that the West Indies was not ready for economic reform and industrial development. This, he said, was "a colonial idea, carefully given to us by our colonial masters, and to be totally repudiated by us". But the British government, in accepting Moyne's recommendation, insisted on its plan to build the welfare aspects on the infrastructure initially established by the 1929 Colonial Development Act, which had failed.[27]

---

26. Ibid.
27. Wallace, *West Indies*, 47.

This strategy was seen by labour leaders as an indication that deception rather than development was informing British government policy. The funds made available for social welfare, with over a million people trapped in the slums of colonial towns with no amenities, were minuscule. The grants allocated for start-up projects constituted a token gesture rather than an effort at promoting serious economic activity.

The decision to bring to Parliament in 1940 a new Colonial Development and Welfare Act to cater for the entire empire, with a budget of £50 million annually over ten years, provided only £5 million for the West Indies. Again, while verbal tribute was paid to the development vision of the West Indian labour movement, the supporting financial resources fell disgracefully short of reasonable expectations.[28]

West Indian governments, still in the hands of white elites, did not approve of measures to draw down on grants when projects were considered supportive of democracy and popular economic enfranchisement. In the Bahamas, for example, the colonial government rejected welfare grants on the grounds that access to them required the legalization of trade unions.

Between 1945 and 1955 another £140 million was added to the Colonial Development and Welfare Fund. This time the paltry sum of £15.5 million was allocated to the West Indies. These funds, Wallace showed, would only scratch the surface of the need for "better roads, streets, and bridges . . . modern water supplies and sanitation facilities".[29]

The results, not surprisingly, were inadequate, reflecting both the magnitude of the task of cleaning up the colonial mess and the "meagre money" allocated for the purpose. By 1945, noted Wallace, "giant strides were still required to raise social services and living conditions . . . to an adequate standard. Education, health, and housing in particular, remained conspicuously deficient, while modest wage increases were largely cancelled by rising costs."[30]

The projects financed by the Colonial Development and Welfare Fund were described as mostly "small, pilot, ad hoc schemes which scarcely touched the fringe of the British Caribbean problems". Furthermore, "least attention was given to the urgent need for planned economic development". The British

---

28. Ibid.
29. Ibid., 50.
30. Ibid., 49–50.

government acknowledged their failure to have an impact on the West Indies but endorsed statements from its colonial officers that insularity in the region, fuelled by intercolonial jealousy, made a "broad regional approach . . . hard to achieve". West Indians, they implied, "suspected white officials, even when well-meaning, of condescension" with little real interest in the economic and social development of the people.[31]

The result, then, was the failure of the Moyne Commission from the perspective of social transformation and economic development in the region. The failures of specific recommendations were embedded in the long traditions of imperial policy on the West Indies that defined the region as a zone for extreme economic extraction that also required social and political suppression and tight administrative management. The radical anti-colonial West Indian leadership of the 1930s expected no more from the British government when it unleashed its troops upon the starving poor and used its criminal injustice system to imprison Caribbean leaders.

By 1945, British colonialism in the West Indies was in an endemic credibility crisis, leading to the popular view that it was best to formally end imperialism and aspire to economic development alone. It was clear that Britain had no intention of returning any reasonable portion of the wealth it had taken from the West Indies over three centuries to promote its own economic development. This understanding was based, finally, upon the government's refusal to fund even the social recommendations in the Moyne Report and its assertion that colonies should look to their own resources to fund local development. This hardened stance was the straw that broke the back of West Indian patience.

31. Ibid., 50.

CHAPTER 8

Arthur Lewis

Reparations for Economic Development

The Colonial governing classes are different in race from these whom they govern, and are on the whole rather snobbish and exclusive; they spend their spare time in the company of commercial men of their own race, they sit on executive and legislative councils to which such people are nominated and from which natives have been either excluded altogether or admitted only in small numbers, in the past; and so it is not surprising that the people of the colonies have suspected that their own interests were not adequately represented at the seat of power . . . the legacy of suspicion will remain with us for a very long time.

—W. Arthur Lewis, "Colonial Development"

THE POLITICAL REVOLUTION OF THE 1930S threw up a formidable anti-colonial, democratic political leadership in West Indian society. It was an alliance of labour leaders, professional groups and progressive intellectuals. Governance restructuring was its primary concern, followed by production diversification and economic development. It was resentful of the British white-supremacist policy that bankrolled elite plantation families, who dominated local legislatures in partnership with colonial governors. Critically, in rejecting the main recommendations of the Moyne Commission, it called for the beginning of an industrialization agenda, rupturing the extractive mercantile system.

Rising to the leadership of the movement was the young St Lucian economist Arthur Lewis. Lewis was based in London during the early 1930s, but kept in touch with labour leaders, becoming a prominent voice in the academic resistance. He was first to brand the politics of the labour movement "revolution". He was impressed that some labour leaders had articulated an economic development vision for the region and were insisting that imperial policy should shift in this direction.

When the Moyne Commission entered the region, and began hearings on 3 November 1938, labour leaders had already met in British Guiana, where they framed the region's economic development agenda. Arising from this summit was the establishment of the British Guiana and West Indian Labour Congress, which called for a regional economic development plan built around an industrialization programme and the political federation of the region. The congress was ready to engage the commission and to present a Caribbean strategy to take the region beyond colonialism to national development.[1]

The Garvey Black Business Model

As early as 1918, Garvey was politicizing West Indians about the need to break out of the colonial cocoon and prepare for commercial and industrial development. He urged communities to look beyond imperial oppression and the plantation principle, and prepare for the world beyond the empire. He was outraged by Britain's persistent racism against the region and knew its end was near. In October 1919, while promoting the financing of the Black Star Line, he said: "I want you to understand that opportunity is now knocking at your door. . . . The Black Star Line is the biggest industrial and commercial undertaking of the Negro of the Twentieth Century. The Black Star Line opens up the industrial and commercial avenues that were hitherto closed to Negroes."[2] In this and other ways he consciously juxtaposed the regressive plantation culture of black oppression with the progressive democratizing, liberating effect of Caribbean commerce and industry. His campaign was courageous and radical.

Why, Garvey asked, should West Indians not reject the old system and embrace their own growth agenda? He sought to show the feasability of embracing big commerce within communities: "We organised the Black Star Steamship Corporation three months ago for $500,000 and it will be a capitalised

---

1. John Mordecai, *The West Indies: The Federal Negotiations* (London: Allen and Unwin, 1968), 28–29; Report of the Hon. E.F.L. Wood, West Indies and Guiana, 1921–22, PP 1679; Report of the West Indies Guiana Commission, 1930, PP 1679; Report of the Closer Union Commission, 1932–33, PP 49, PP Cmnd. 4384; Report on Labour Conditions in the West Indies, PP Cmnd. 6070, 1938–39; WIRC, 1938/39, Recommendation, PP Cmnd. 6174.

2. Robert A. Hill, ed., *The Marcus Garvey and Universal Negro Improvement Association Papers*, vol. 2: *August 1919 to August 1920* (Berkeley: University of California Press, 1983), 120; Report of the Commission Appointed into the Disturbances: Barbados (Dean Report), 2 November 1937, CO 28/319/8; Hilton Vaughn's evidence, 16 August 1937, 28/319/9; Governor E. Denhamn to Cunliffe-Lister, 30 May 1935, CO 137/806/68557.

corporation of ten million dollars."[3] Two months later, in December 1919, he wrote:

> There is a world of opportunity awaiting us, and it is for us, through unity and will and of purpose, to say we shall and we will play our part upon the great human stage of activity. We shall start steamship lines, factories and banks . . . we shall cause men to regard us as equals in achievements, in industry, in commerce, in politics, in science, art and education. We shall make Ethiopia a mighty nation and we of this generation shall cause our children to call us blessed.[4]

Not surprisingly, the British government instructed governors in the region, and throughout the empire, to silence Garvey's voice and vision by outlawing his newspaper, *Negro World*, and related publications. But it was far too late in the day of anti-colonialism to exclude the literature of black enlightenment. Garvey wrote, "Negroes should refuse to listen to any other voice than that of liberty and true democracy. Give us that liberty and democracy first and then we will listen to you after, but so long as white men are going to rule and brutalize black men just so long must we continue to prepare for the greatest war in the history of the human race."[5]

Such democratizing language became normal in the West Indies. Garvey, more than any other anti-colonial leader, was laying the foundation for West Indian solidarity in preparation for a free democratic region. Speaking in April 1921 in what later became Belize, he said:

> You will remember that British Honduras was the first British Colony that moved, through its Legislative Assembly, to place a ban on the Negro World, to suppress it and prevent circulation in that country. At that time, we had but a circulation of 200 copies weekly in British Honduras, and a branch of the Association [UNIA] was not yet organized there. . . . I have just received a cable from the President of the Belize branch of the association, saying that his branch is now 8,003 members strong . . . and the Negro population . . . I believe, is not more than twelve thousand; and if we can have eight thousand in the UNIA you might see that we own Belize.[6]

---

3. Hill, *Marcus Garvey*, 133.
4. Ibid., 156.
5. Ibid., 187.
6. Ibid., 293; see also Report of the Commission of Enquiry into the 1935 Disturbances, 24 August 1936, CO 111/732/60036.

Furthermore, addressing the matter of British suppression of the black voice, he stated:

> What is true of Belize . . . is also true of the other British colonies in the West Indies; and I think the British Government made a great mistake when they suppressed the Negro World, because they only opened the eyes of those sleeping West Indian Negroes to a realisation that the government was trying to keep something from them, to keep them in darkness about the great progress of Negroes of the outer world.[7]

In many other places he spoke of the moment in which the masses of people would "build their own enterprises".[8]

Garvey was repetitive on the theme of economic self-empowerment in addressing West Indian and African American communities. It was time, he said, for blacks to end their habit of "begging white men to give us jobs in their factories, on their plantations, on their farms, and in their mills. But the UNIA has taken a farther step when it said that the Negro must build his own banks, his own department stores, his own mills and factories, and steamship lines. And when the Negro does this, he will get on an economic foundation which will give him real independence."[9] His advocacy was anathema to the British government. His message of economic development, commercial engagement and political independence from white domination singled him out as the primary West Indian enemy of Empire.

The polarity in policy – white empire versus black independence – had matured two decades before Moyne had arrived in Jamaica. Lewis wasted no time in publishing the findings of his research on the origins, implications and impact of the workers' revolution. Appearing as a pamphlet in 1938, and in 1939, ahead of the Moyne Report by six years, *Labour in the West Indies: The Birth of a Workers' Movement* captured the anti-imperial imagination of West Indians. It became the political and academic benchmark against which the Moyne Report was assessed and found wanting.

Publishing this work was a calculated move by the young academic, who saw the urgency of intervening in the post-rebellion environment and framing

---

7. Hill, *Marcus Garvey*, 293.
8. Ibid.
9. Ibid., 306; see also "West Indies: Proposal for an increase in the Garrison Force", March 1948, CO 318/419/1, no. 4.

the economic development dialogue before British imperial perspectives and propaganda could take root and dominate the discursive space.

By presenting the progressive vision of West Indian leaders, Lewis's writing anticipated and highlighted the inevitable British rejection of reform and their intention of restoring the status quo with meagre social appeasement measures. He got ahead of the British government and anchored West Indian economic development thinking. His recommendations, therefore, became the region's official position, rather than those of the Moyne Report.

Having stolen the imperial thunder of Lord Moyne, Lewis provided the region with a seminal intellectual rejection of colonialism. The extent of its impact was unmatched since J.J. Thomas had punctured colonialism with his critique of the pro-plantation postures of Anthony Froude sixty years earlier.

Labour in the West Indies represented the manifesto of the workers' revolution and constituted the principles of West Indian nationhood. This Lewis did consciously, using his intimacy with the region and the liberal support of the Fabian Society in London, which had sponsored the publication. Everywhere in the West Indies, politically aware people were reading his work.

A new labour movement, Lewis argued, had emerged in the 1940s from the anti-colonial class alliance of the 1930s revolution. He wrote: "The general aims are to raise the economic and cultural standards of the masses, and to secure for them conditions of freedom and equality." In the first instance, he added, "the total income of the West Indies must be considerably increased", and in "the second place it must be more equitably distributed". It would be, he added, "a mistake to ignore either of these two aspects" of the movement's programme.[10]

What can be done, Lewis asked, to raise the West Indian masses out of poverty and destitution? What should be the economic policy that pulls them to a higher, sustainable social existence that builds their dignity? The new labour movement, he said, is demanding an economic policy to achieve the following: for the white community, special treatment in British markets and particularly for demand for sugar.

But for the black and brown communities the call was for development assistance by way of loans at low rates of interest and large, free grants as reparations financing. Such funds, Lewis said, are to "make a radical attack on poverty – to

---

10. W.A. Lewis, *Labour*, 36, 37.

open up new areas and finance land settlement schemes, to improve housing conditions, to build new schools and finance the proper training of teachers, to build and equip hospitals and clinics, to drain swamps, and to supply drugs for a concerted attack on malaria, yaws, venereal diseases, children's diseases, and other ailments of the people".[11] Only a Caribbean economic development strategy, he concluded, based around the vision of the new labour movement, the grassroots Garveyites especially, could save the region from enduring poverty. But first, he said, the British government must pay back.

Reparations Development Approach

It would take "the next hundred years", said Lewis, for the West Indies to achieve any significant level of social transformation and economic development if the British government forced it to rely exclusively on local taxes, the expensive and unreliable imperial capital market, and welfare aid. British policy towards the West Indies would doom it to another century of mass poverty and human misery.

If, however, the British government could muster a sincere commitment to promoting people-centred progress in the region, transformation, he concluded, was possible. Development could be attained if a new policy called forth: (1) the adoption of "drastic measures" for economic change; (2) a reparations approach to social justice. Development, he said, could "only be done with British Government help" in the short to medium term. This was a clear statement of what was possible: no aid, but reparations.[12]

There had never been any credible reason to assume that the British government would adopt a development policy that called for an injection of significant capital into a post-slavery colony. Furthermore, the West Indians, having won the high ground in the pro-democracy, anti-colonial war, and effectively ending the legitimacy of British governance, were anticipating a severe backlash.

Lewis faced these realities head-on and asked the next question: "What claim have West Indians to demand such sacrifices from the British people?" His answer constituted the framework for a Caribbean economic development

---

11. Ibid., 37.

12. Ibid.; correspondence and memoranda between Lord Moyne and the War Cabinet, 30–31 January 1940, CO 318/443/6.

model based on reparatory justice. Before, during, and after the emancipation reform of the 1830s, he showed, the matter of a British debt to the enslaved and their descendants had been proposed, resisted and then ignored.[13] He connected his economic proposals to this historic narrative when he offered the following answers to his question: "It is the British who by their action in past centuries are responsible for the presence in these islands of the majority of their inhabitants, whose ancestors as slaves contributed millions to the wealth of Great Britain, a debt which the British have yet to repay. . . . Either Britain must help, or the people must remain very poor."[14]

Here, then, was the background to the West Indian ideological break with the British government and its instrument, the Moyne Commission. Lewis ruptured with British policy in order to support an economic development path, rather than the persistent emphasis on social welfare and the theme "Empire forever". His counter-vision of economic transformation required Britain to fund from its imperial reserves the capital-development projects the labour movement had planned and proposed.

Recognizing the future intention of the British to extract rather than inject capital, and not to be supportive of significant Caribbean economic development activity, Lewis was not optimistic. Britain, he knew, would not be inclined to support a capital-development grant as a precursor to nationhood. But his insistence on the need for a regional growth agenda, and that it was not inevitable "the people must remain very poor", met with British resistance, first from Lord Moyne and then from the minister for the colonies.[15]

For these reasons, Lewis was cautious in approach, but robust in tone and temperament. He noted, for example, by way of deflecting criticism from the Moyne camp and to appease the British government, that the "increased preferential treatment and grants and loans from the Imperial Treasury", elements of a reparatory justice payback, could "in the near future" assist the economic development of the region.

Such an initiative, Lewis thought, would trigger the beginning of the end of a time when the region would depend "permanently on the charity of Great Britain". Even small capital grants, he sought to clarify, could secure the region's

---

13. W.A. Lewis, *Labour*, 37.
14. Ibid.
15. Ibid.

independence in "the long run". Only such policies of a reparatory investment nature, he insisted, could begin to assist West Indian communities to "be able to stand permanently and prosperously on their own feet".[16] But this was clearly not what Britain wanted, despite its rhetoric. The diplomatic posture was nothing more than a strategy to avoid making any significant capital investment.

Lewis's development model, then, required a British reparatory capital injection in order to support sugar producers, promote access to US commodity markets, facilitate a comprehensive land settlement and redistribution programme, drive industrialization, and construct a fiscal framework to begin economic diversification. He was sure that future prosperity could not be achieved by further centring the sugar plantation sector. Not even increases in sugar prices were likely to deliver prosperity beyond the plantation great houses.

The future, then, suggested that development should be considered around non-sugar sectors and non-imperial markets. The United States, not Britain, he concluded, would be "the natural outlet for West Indian exports". The region should therefore begin its reorientation. New sources of revenue had to be found to "replace the existing staples". Britain had taken everything from the West Indies, Lewis understood, and was unwilling to give back beyond minimal social aid.

High on Lewis's agenda was a citrus industry, with food-related manufacturing, which he thought would "doubtless be profitable". He admitted that "it is difficult to feel much confidence in the future of agriculture" as it currently stood. But the development model he rolled out in 1939 proposed that the region's greatest "hope of permanent success" was to follow in the "footsteps of other agricultural countries into industrialisation". He stated, "There is scope for factories for refining sugar, making chocolate, utilising copra, making dairy products, etc. Such enterprises would need to be subsidised at the start while local labour was trained and the local market won, but after the initial period should be able to stand on their own legs. No other policy seems to offer such permanent prospects as the development of local industries."[17]

Lewis's clear thinking in the 1940s about economic development centred on laying foundations for industrialization initiatives. This was the first formally articulated reparatory justice strategy for anti-colonial transformation. He

16. Ibid., 38.
17. Ibid., 39.

affirmed and sought to present an economic framework for what the leadership of the labour movement had been saying in the prior decade.

The merger of anti-colonial political thinking and Lewis's critique and disruption of imperial extractive economics strengthened the vanguard of the democracy movement of the 1940s, which was rooted in popular mobilization against the empire. It was Lewis's intention to hasten the process by striking at the colonial business model that guided imperial operations. By promoting a Caribbean economic development strategy, designed to break endemic poverty and weaken economic dependency, he projected a much shorter time frame for West Indian political integration, nationhood and independence. In so doing, he positioned himself at the centre of the emerging nationalist movement and established his reputation as an activist and progressive scholar.

The empire struck back, as Lewis had anticipated, with specific recommendations found in the general narrative of the Moyne Report. Moyne pressed instead for "large expenditure on social service" and made tentative critical references to economic development.[18] The West Indian colonies, he said, cannot "hope to undertake from their own resources" the level of investment the moment requires. Hence his proposal: "We therefore recommend the establishment for this purpose of a West Indian Welfare Fund to be financed by an annual grant of £1 million from the Imperial Exchequer for a period of 20 years."[19] But, in respect of Lewis's call for a development programme to alleviate poverty and achieve nationhood, Moyne's response was precise, indifferent and negative.

Lewis was not surprised by Moyne's resistance to and attempt to discredit his ideas. He had gone far beyond the limit set by the British government, which still believed it could retain control of the region. His report stated, "It is essential, therefore, to seek means whereby the West Indian population of working age may otherwise be absorbed in useful activity. Some small increase in industrial employment may be afforded by the development of secondary industries; but these can at best only be of relatively unimportant proportions, and would be dependent for their prosperity on that of the main industry of the whole area, namely agriculture."[20] Furthermore, it added, "A new economic policy for the

---

18. *Moyne Report*, 427–28; Memos on Cabinet decisions, January 1940, CO 318/443/6; Colonial Development and Welfare, Report on the Operations of the Act of 31 October 1942, PP 1942–43, 9, 6422.P4.

19. *Moyne Report*, 427.

20. Ibid., 426.

West Indies must therefore be an agriculture policy, and development must be away from reliance on production for export."

Then came the core recommendation, which further rejected Lewis's idea of reparatory justice: "The need is not for the immediate grant of a large lump sum, but for a programme of development over a period of years, according to well-thought out policies and administered by an organisation in a position constantly to control and review the execution of such a policy."[21] Moyne's commissioners all accepted the British policy framework and they were determined not to step beyond their brief.

Moyne identified two moments in which he rejected Lewis's ideas for a West Indian industrial development option. First, he wrote, "The possibility of extending the local manufacture of coconut products is a subject much discussed in the West Indies and raises an important issue of official policy."[22] But he concluded, "Agriculture is the main basis of economic life of the West Indies; and, as will be evident from the foregoing survey of other activities, it must necessarily remain so. The possibilities of establishing new types of industry are being keenly discussed in several colonies, particularly in Jamaica; and various proposals have been submitted to us, raising issues of policy."[23] Lewis's West Indian development perspective, then, was actively considered by the commissioners and rejected.

The Moyne Report was supportive of Lewis on social policy issues, however. Moyne personally stood squarely against West Indian aspirations, while acknowledging and reaffirming Britain's intention to sustain colonialism.

Moyne was just the latest messenger of British economic-extraction policy. He stood at the crossroads of the crisis in which the call for financial reparation was maturing. The return of financial capital from the empire was necessary to facilitate the emerging West Indian nation. Moyne promoted the message that Britain owed no debt and had no responsibility to offer financial support to promote West Indian economic activity. British taxpayers, he intimated, had no liability to the region in respect of its economic development.[24]

The West Indies colonies, then, after being "sucked dry" of economic resources,

---

21. Ibid., 428.
22. Ibid., 15.
23. Ibid., 17.
24. See D.W. Stammer, "British Colonial Public Finance", *Social and Economic Studies* 16, no. 2 (June 1967): 194.

as Williams stated in 1962, were expected to be "financially self-sufficient". The endemic mass poverty and social degradation, therefore, against which the people had revolted, were considered by Britain a self-inflicted West Indian wound. British policy was set out thus: "the surest test of the soundness of measures for the development of an uncivilised people is that they should be self-supporting". An exception was tolerated in the case of the exceptionally poor.[25]

Although the West Indies were deemed "exceptionally poor" by the Moyne Commission, the approach was to make financial provision for social ameliora-tion through welfare aid, as set out by the 1929 and 1940 colonial development acts. Additional expenditures could be provided, but, to keep workers in check during moments of civil unrest, such special provisions were generally accom-panied by a "very strict degree of Treasury control over the Colony's finances".[26]

The 1929 and 1940 acts provided that any grant given to promote a minor development project had to conform strictly to stringent guidelines. It had to be shown, for example, that Britain would be the net beneficiary. D.W. Stammer noted: "A sum of £1 million per annum was to be made available for capital works, as much as possible of which was to be spent on British goods and materials (the contribution the Act might make to relieving unemployment in Britain was stressed in parliamentary debates). Preference in the allocation of funds of £9 million between 1929 and 1940 [in the empire] was given to projects which promised a fair rate of return."[27] Most of these funds were invested in Middle Eastern colonies. The West Indies were assigned to the margins.

The principal challenge Lewis faced was that everywhere there was the socio-economic and political dominance of the sugar plantations and their owners. Even in Trinidad, where the oil industry represented significant eco-nomic diversification, the number of people employed in the sector was rel-atively small and "did not greatly exceed those employed by any one of the large sugar companies".[28]

Lewis was concerned about the legacy of the sugar sector's link to the culture of white supremacy. This was as important to him as price and profit volatility

---

25. Ibid., 195.

26. Ibid.

27. Ibid.

28. Simey, *Welfare*, 5n3; Report of Herbert G. MacDonald, BWI Central Labour Org-anisation, 3 April 1945; 8 September 1945, CO 318/460/2; Gov. Sir H. Rance to Creech Jones, 4 May 1949, CO 537/4902; F.W. Dalley, "Notes of Some of the Personalities in the Trade Unions and Labour World of Trinidad", November 1947, CO 537/3814.

in the sector. Global price decline in sugar had been the West Indian norm for decades, in addition to the frequent ravages of nature caused by crop diseases, hurricanes and droughts. Lewis agreed, furthermore, with Simey, who stated in his 1946 book *Welfare and Planning in the West Indies* that "the economic foundation of life in the West Indies has been for many generations as uncertain as it has been weak, and this has had a profound influence on the moulding of the personality of the West Indian citizen".[29]

One regional result, and particularly for Jamaica, was the almost complete dependence on the British government for social welfare funding, as domestic economic activity was always suppressed. British control in respect of the economy had contributed to substantial US disinvestment between 1929 and 1939. But as American capital fled the region, colonial governments looked to the provisions of the 1929 act to fund social relief as well as to subsidize and stabilize sugar prices. In the mid-1930s, at least 20 per cent of Jamaica's domestic expenditure was funded by British grants in aid.[30]

Return to Race: Sambo and Quashee

It was only a matter of time in this context until a twentieth-century version of the nineteenth-century "lazy negro" stereotype, the Sambo-Quashee iconography of Carlyle-Trollope-Froude, surfaced. It was an intrinsic part of the ideological instrument used by Britain to push back against the West Indian agenda of economic development and reparations.[31]

Workers across the region understood that the Moyne Commission did not support a "reorientation of West Indian economic life". It was no shock to them when the commission supported the position that it would be "undesirable that West Indian Governments should either conduct or finance speculative industrial enterprises".[32] Labour leaders, therefore, expected Moyne to affirm that the primary economic purpose of his investigation was to consolidate the plantation system in order "to improve the markets for agricultural products". This was key to the British government's plan to consolidate political control over the West Indies.[33]

---

29. Simey, *Welfare*, 6.
30. Ibid.
31. Ibid., 130.
32. Ibid., 131.
33. Ibid., 132.

As the Second World War approached its end, mounting pressure on Britain in respect of colonial industrialization and economic development produced deeper cracks. The 1944 West Indian Conference, for example, hosted by Barbados, was the forum in which the Lewis paradigm was finally given centre stage. The conference resolved that a new industrial landscape was desired in the region and that only such a measure could reduce unemployment and generate additional wealth, thereby reducing poverty. The final declaration of the conference was, again, a rejection of the British vision for the region. It stated: "To this end it was recommended that governments should assist new industries by providing facilities for research, permitting the entry of machinery and material duty free, by granting other reliefs from taxation, by organising technical training, and by improving transport facilities."[34]

More significant was the agreement that "where a new industry would be of special value to the community, the government concerned might provide all or part of the capital". It was obvious, then, that the Puerto Rico policy of industrial development, which had benefited from Lewis's thinking about a post-plantation paradigm, was adopted in Barbados for the West Indian future. Even if "greatly diluted", given that the United States was considered the export market for possible manufactures, the message was clear that the region was breaking with the British Empire.[35]

Lewis found support in the influential 1945 finance report by F.C. Benham, consultant to the Jamaican government. An economic policy committee under Benham's chairmanship was established to do a systematic survey of the colony and to report on its prospects. Emphasis was to be placed on costs associated with government policy on providing mass employment. The committee supported the recommendations of the Barbados conference, but shifted attention away from public to private investment in developing new industries.[36]

The focus on private sector–driven industrialization in Jamaica added to conversations about the cost of production and the ethnic ownership of productive assets. Benham's recommendations were accepted by the local legislature and used as the basis of the decision to establish a cement factory with an 80/20 equity split between British and Jamaican investors.

---

34. Ibid., 131.
35. Ibid., 132.
36. Ibid.

While opposition elements in the House of Representatives saw local minority ownership as a perpetuation of the old colonial system, the domestic political environment had progressed to embrace industrialization for economic development. Furthermore, while Benham did not make explicit corporate recommendations to attract American industrial investments, readers assumed his commitment to such an approach. The Jamaican private sector accepted both the necessity and inevitability of this initiative.

Ironically, the Benham Report, aligned with local thinking, converged on an aspect of traditional imperial ideology, that the economic future of the region ultimately rested on the willingness of workers to commit to a culture of harder work and higher productivity. Significantly, it restated the climatic theory of labour when it noted that "most people in moist, hot, tropical climates . . . do not want to work very energetically for long hours; they seem to prefer to be satisfied with a lower standard of living and more pleasure".[37]

The assumption of low productivity and a weak work ethic in private sector–led industrial development was intended to illustrate that the new business landscape would be plagued by the "lazy negro" ideology of the old plantation sector. Sambo and Quashee were brought back, alive and well, into the post-development period in which the labour movement was officially entrenched.

The Benham Report, furthermore, was published the year following the Sir Frank Stockdale Report (1943–44), which had enlarged themes specific to Jamaicans' perceived attitudes to work in the urban and rural settings. Stockdale, too, had picked up on Moyne's ideas about the character and commitment of black workers. Everyone had concluded, colonialism notwithstanding, says Simey, that "the economic salvation of the West Indies depends in the final analysis on the awakening in the mind of the worker of a willingness to do more work".[38]

The notion that the mentality of workers was a threat to industrial development resonated, as a legacy of the plantation system and old colonial policy. Persistent racism enabled it to find a way into thinking about industrial diversification. Lewis's successful call for an industrialization agenda in the West Indies sent shivers down the old imperial spine. While he did not spell out the specific economic design of his proposal, his reputation as a macroeconomic specialist in colonial trade was enough to evoke political and academic responses.

---

37. Ibid., 136.
38. Ibid.

The effects of his ideas were far-reaching, resonating in spaces from grassroots West Indian organizations to British academia and the centre of imperial administration. The clarity of his narrative and at times the bluntness of his anti-colonial language reflected his eagerness to facilitate transformation that would lead in short time to West Indian development and the end of British rule.

The 1930s revolution had undermined the impact of the Moyne Commission Report and other lesser-known documents that suggested the need to consolidate the West Indian future around the white-supremacy system of the sugar plantation. This was the cry of the 1840s from the same quarter that had demanded no land for blacks, and the creation of a "slavery-like" post-slavery society.

The workers' response was to entrench and consolidate their 1930s revolution in more sophisticated political parties that would commit to the federation project. Nationalist negotiation, then, took place in the context of Britain's refusal to accept a new development paradigm in the region, based on the principle of a reparation debt to be repaid. The West Indians insisted, furthermore, that the post-plantation economy and society should be financially supported by the British imperial fund accumulated from two hundred years of free, enslaved and manumitted black labour.

The cascading demand for reparations positioned the labour parties to consolidate around the ending of imperial oppression as a precondition for economic justice. The British government, however, planned to rule the region for another century. The economic extraction principle, in addition to its racist abuse of military power, drove the popular call to condemn colonialism as illegal and unethical. The British rejection of Lewis's call for reparation economics triggered the movement towards independence.

In Jamaica in particular, the British ideological war against the workers' movement was most intense, militant and persistent. Simey recognized this in the early 1940s, but considered it a useless British backlash against blacks for their anti-colonial audacity. He noted: "The Jamaican is now a self-conscious citizen of the twentieth-century world. . . . The significant difference is that he is no longer willing to accept an inferior position for himself."[39] In respect of West Indians generally, he concluded: "The West Indians are awake, and there is no turning back from the stresses and doubts of contemporary social life." It was "an awakening that has borne fruit dramatically in recent years".[40]

---

39. Ibid., 30.
40. Ibid., 29.

W. Arthur Lewis, St Lucian anti-colonial development economist and Nobel laureate

C.L.R. James, Trinidadian socialist intellectual and pan-African activist

Robert Bradshaw, first premier of St Kitts and Nevis

Kwame Nkrumah, first Ghanaian president and pan-African intellectual

Norman Manley, Jamaican anti-colonial politician

Alexander Bustamante, first prime minister of Jamaica

Grantley Adams, Barbadian premier of the West Indies Federation

Eric Williams, Trinidadian anti-colonial scholar/historian and first prime minister of Trinidad and Tobago

Cheddi Jagan, Guyanese socialist anti-colonial politician

Harold Macmillan, British Conservative prime minister who presided over the rise and demise of the British West Indies Federation

Fidel Castro, leader of the Cuban Revolution

Dudley Thompson, Jamaican pan-Africanist politician and reparation activist

PART 3

Crushing Caribbean Aspirations

CHAPTER 9

Federation without Funding

Empire Strikes Back

The argument that self-government must be in step with financial stability is indeed relevant and can be used to a chosen audience. To some West Indians, however, such an argument is complete anathema; they believe, like the Irish, that His Majesty's Government is perpetually in debt to the West Indies for errors of omissions of the past three hundred years. The sum mentioned, in all seriousness, to liquefy this debt is astronomical and would undoubtedly provide financial stability for a greater or less number of years.

—Letter from C.Y. Carstairs to I.B. Watt, 5 September 1949, CO 318/487/1, no. 10

THE FEDERATION OF THE WEST INDIES project was short-lived – 1958–62. Much has been written and said about the causes of its rise and fall. Most arguments centre on the failure of what became in the end the British integration model, reflecting a colonial intention to merge the region into a cheaper governance package. A great deal has also been said and written about the corrosive political and personal conflict between regional leaders, particularly before and following Premier Bustamante's declaration of his desire that Jamaica should journey to independence alone, ahead of and finally without the rest of the region.[1]

The thesis presented here constitutes a departure from these popular paradigms. It begins by showing that Britain presented three distinct faces in its policy towards the federation. First, there was robust opposition, as federation was considered an aggressive West Indian anti-colonial strategy. Second, an evolved embrace of federation as a cost-reduction strategy, reflecting the

---

1. Samuel Hurwitz, "The Federation of the West Indies: A Study in Nationalisms", *Journal of British Studies* 6, no. 1 (1966): 139–68; Elisabeth Wallace, "The West Indies: Improbable Federation", *Canadian Journal of Economics and Political Science* 27, no. 4 (1961): 444–59.

reconsideration that unsupported political integration could foster a divide-and-rule culture, promoting the furtherance of rebellious anti-colonialism. Third, there was a final strategic, back-office diplomatic design formally to support but financially to subvert the federation by starving it of capital and fiscal development support.

This final face was hawkish and tactically intent on punishing the region for rising against the empire in the 1930s, an action that discredited British colonialism internationally and precipitated exit politics in African and Asian colonies. The West Indian revolt and demand for reparations in the form of capital-development support to establish "federated nationhood" ignited British vexation, leading to policy aggression that ultimately undermined the federation.[2]

To comprehend the implosion of the federation it is necessary to separate the two concepts of integration that converged in 1958 – the imperial and the nationalist. The former imagined that the integrated colonies would remain as such well into the twentieth century. Federation was, therefore, a fiscal strategy to cheapen colonial administration. The latter was a radical attempt to integrate the region as a precursor to disintegrating the empire and ending British domination of the region.

Arthur Lewis, reflecting on the collapse of the project, and setting out his explanatory recollections, presented several reasons, most of which are commonly cited in standard analyses. First on his list is that which provides the context and content for the argument presented here: that Britain ultimately chose to undermine the federation by means of financial strangulation. This deliberate action triggered intraregional contention leading to Jamaica's exit, followed by that of Trinidad and Tobago. Finally the project was ended by negative attitudes in Barbados and the eastern Caribbean islands.

Lewis noted, at the outset, that the federation could have been saved if there had been British commitment. He took this view even though it was known, according to an official policy paper, that "Her Majesty's Government's attitude to Federation . . . [is] to avoid any suggestion of a special obligation to support Federation in financial difficulty and any suspicion that Her Majesty's Government was trying to offload its responsibility for the West Indies". For

---

2. Charles H. Archibald, "The Failure of the West Indies Federation", *World Today* 18, no. 6 (1962): 233–42.

Lewis, financial-avoidance strategies explained why Britain slowed its negotiations with West Indian leaders to a crawl between 1950 and 1958. Lewis noted, nonetheless, that the federation could have been rescued if:

> the Colonial Office had set the second conference for 1950, when all the technical reports were in, instead of delaying it until 1953, and dragging out the date of Federation until 1958. The delay broke the connection between the desire for Federation and desire for self-government, since the West Indian politicians found in the fifties that each island could get self-government on its own, and federation then became a menace to local self-government.[3]

This, however, was not the result of bureaucratic foot-dragging by the British government. It was part of a deliberate diplomatic strategy by the government that ultimately saw how it could divide and rule the region more effectively within the context of weak, dependent, stand-alone island states, rather than an integrated, independent region with significant potential for democratic freedom and economic development.

This was also the opinion of Sir Kenneth Blackburne, who from his colonial base in Antigua in 1952 could not understand the slow pace of integration action in Britain. As governor of the Leeward Islands, he became increasingly disturbed at the delay in London in making the next move towards West Indian federation. It was necessary, he said, "to push ahead with the Federation" in order to avoid fractures among the political groups in the region, most of whom were "half-baked rabble-rousers" and very competitive among themselves.

The only way, Sir Kenneth concluded, to save the federation before it got started was if "Her Majesty's Government gives an imaginative lead". This quality of leadership was not to come. His warning was not heeded. Britain deliberately delayed action on the federation by five years when the region was deeply divided over its response to imperial strategy.[4]

It was an exercise, in the end, in effective diplomatic manipulation in plain sight. But behind the negotiations were shifty imperial tactics which even Sir Kenneth could not discern and found frustrating. This secretive approach ultimately won the day for British policy. But the background to the suffocation

---

3. See W. Arthur Lewis, "Epilogue", in Mordecai, *West Indies*, 455; British Government Policy Paper: CO 1031/1937, 18 April 1955; CO 1031/1937, no. 9, May 1955.

4. W.A. Lewis, *Labour*, 46. See Sir K. Blackburne to S.E.V. Luke, 15 August 1952, CO 1031/751, no. 512.

suggests that Britain had effectively planned and won the battle while the war to retain the empire was being waged.

"The Labour Movement", wrote Lewis in 1939, was "on the march". It has already behind it, he said, "a history of great achievements in a short space of time". It will make of the West Indies, he prophesied, "a country where the common man may lead a cultured life and prosperity".[5] This was his vision for the region, rooted in decades of democratic demands. The rise and defeat of the federation was central to his academic and advocacy work.

Lewis threw his intellectual energy fully behind the anti-colonial vision of ordinary men and women who wished to federate in order to rid themselves of British exploitation. What he might have underestimated was the power and persistence of British opposition. In response to his vision, the British government stepped up its rejection programme. The divisive policy of no financial support and minimal social aid, within a culture of diplomatic doublespeak, was again applied. "Federation yes, finance no" was the concept deployed to cripple the West Indian federation effort.

But British pushback against the ideas of the labour movement, and specifically the economic proposals from Lewis, hastened rather than halted democratic consciousness. By 1940, the drive to dismantle the empire was advanced on every front. Strategies to tear down militant, authoritarian colonialism came from every angle. There were loud statements of regional outrage against British governance. All roads within the labour movement led to the place called "West Indian nationhood", even though twists and turns along the way and the major reconnaissance rendezvous called "federation" defined and characterized the journey.

By 1945, the awareness of a radical change in the West Indies had finally seeped into British political consciousness. The "series of disturbances" in the 1930s, noted Simey in 1946, were in fact the harbinger of a "new order". Indeed, they had created a new West Indian dispensation. Simey added:

> In the first place, the fact that they extended throughout the Caribbean area was alarming in itself, for this had never happened before . . . this brought with it a new attitude to West Indian social problems. In the past a disturbance was thought of as a purely local affair, but the entire West Indies had received so unpleasant a shock in 1937 that a Commission of Inquiry was sent out by the

---

5. Lewis, *Labour*, 42.

Secretary of State to investigate the Trinidad riots, and a local commission was appointed for the same purpose in Barbados.[6]

The end of the Second World War represented the end of the colonial road. West Indians finally spoke in constitutional language about the beginning of nationhood. In the global arena it was recognized that West Indian democratic values were challenging British totalitarian rule. The West Indies became the Achilles heel of the British Empire.

The Moyne Report also made plain in 1945 Britain's unwillingness to offer financial support for a new economic and political order in the West Indies. When the report was circulated in the region, circumstances had radically changed. As a result, the British government, for the first time, began to seriously rethink its strategy of rejecting West Indian democracy. It started preparing to deflect the demands of the labour movement. The economic development agenda, for example, built on democratic reforms in the areas of collective bargaining and the insistence on a "minimum wage machinery", was finding its way to international legitimacy. So too were modern forms of industrial legislation, egalitarian taxation systems, programmes to assure that land and other productive resources were widely accessible, and, critically, the inevitability of more federation in the region.[7]

Britain saw industrialization and federation as the two heads of a West India hydra, placed there by the leadership of trade unions and the political parties they had spawned. They were the core aspects of Lewis's economic contribution to regional discourse on development. Federation, Lewis noted:

> is based on two sets of reasons; first, West Indian national aspirations, which are a powerful force in its favour; and secondly, the economy. The latter argument has been accepted by most official reports since 1897, and has long been obvious to the people themselves . . . the real stumbling block has been the opposition of small local potentates, fearful that their voices, all powerful in a small island, will be unheard in a Federation.[8]

In the interest of the region, he concluded, it is necessary to "ignore these small magnates and to proceed with the Federation of Trinidad, Barbados, the

---

6. Simey, *Welfare*, 25.
7. W.A. Lewis, *Labour*, 39.
8. Ibid., 45.

Windward and Leeward Islands and British Guiana in the immediate future, leaving Jamaica perhaps until a later date when better communications have been established".[9]

For these reasons, Lewis maintained, the Moyne Commission, speaking for the British government, would not be seriously supportive, committed as it was to the sustainability of colonialism. The Moyne Report had stated: "We recommend elsewhere the unification and reorganisation of certain of the social services; but without some central coordinating and directing authority any such measures would lose much of their value. Such coordination cannot, we consider, be provided by any feasible form of political Federation, as the necessary knowledge will not become available by any means of pooling inadequate resources."[10]

Moyne, then, in rejecting federation, sent the British message to the region. He confronted the vision of West Indian leaders and bluntly told them that their ideas and visions for federation were not only impractical, but irresponsible. On the other hand, he advised that the British Parliament should devote more time to discussing West Indian affairs. He suggested the establishment of a standing parliamentary committee that would function as an alternative layer of governance to pre-empt and diffuse the pressure for West Indian federation and nationhood. He stated: "We recommend that West Indian governments should be invited to accept the principle of local unified services and, if that is generally accepted, should address themselves to the task of giving practical effect to it at the earliest possible date. It should not be difficult to make a start by establishing a Unified Medical Service for the West Indies."[11] The battle lines, then, were drawn between Britain and the West Indian vision and aspiration of political federation. Moyne's negation of political integration was the first reaction to the dream of West Indian nationhood that was the obvious feature of the 1930s revolution.

The battleground of the 1940s, therefore, was an environment in which Britain, with its international imperial image bruised from visibly spilling workers' blood yet again, stood its ground against colonized West Indians and prepared to deny the region the right to self-determination.

---

9. Ibid.

10. *Moyne Report*, 429. See also C.Y. Carstairs, Report of the Standing Closer Association Committee, 21 June 1949, CO 318/487/2, no. 1.

11. *Moyne Report*, 429.

In 1943, British prime minister Winston Churchill, before the public had received the Moyne Report, stated in his grand speech before the international community on the Atlantic Charter, which called for the right of all people to choose the "form of government under which they will live", that his ideas of democracy and self-determination did not apply to the West Indian colonies. The principle of democracy, he said, "is quite a separate problem from the progressive evolution of self-governing institutions in the regions and peoples which owe allegiance to the British Crown".[12] Pressed on the contradictory nature of his comments, he explained arrogantly, "I have not become the King's First Minister in order to preside over the liquidation of the British Empire."[13]

Churchill's self-serving sermon was heard in every West Indian congregation. Lewis and other anti-colonial leaders understood in the most profound way that the agendas "for self-government, nationalism, and Federation were intimately linked"[14] and were threatened by the British government. The British Guiana and West Indies Labour Conference had taken the opportunity in 1938 to present the Moyne Commission with a full federation document, drafted by the irrepressible architect of the regional movement, Albert Marryshow of Grenada. By the time of Churchill's chastisement of the West Indian demand for democracy, the "spirit of nationhood at last seemed destined to triumph over longstanding insularity".[15]

There was undoubtedly a regional determination to rise against British resistance; "the new spirit of unity" pervaded all aspects and dimensions of regional politics. Added to the voice of Arthur Lewis were those of other academically acclaimed West Indians such as C.L.R. James, George Padmore and Eric Williams. If Lewis provided the economic analysis for the labour movement, Williams, James and Padmore injected an awareness of history and political theory that, when combined with those of other radical intellectuals in the tradition of J.J. Thomas, strengthened the movement with a sense of historically driven destiny.

Williams had stated in definitive terms that a federation of the West Indies was simply a matter of "common sense", given the non-sustainability of the dependency of the old colonial economy. Technocrats in the Colonial Office

---

12. Blanshard, *Democracy*, 354.
13. Ibid.
14. Wallace, *British Caribbean*, 93.
15. Ibid., 95.

of the British government meanwhile began looking seriously for a cheaper governance model to rule the colonies. West Indian nationalists at the same time were seeking the quickest path to independence. Imperialists began to reconsider whether "federating" the colonies, in part or as a whole, was the best answer to maintain the empire at a lower cost.

Federation, then, became a convergence point for opposing forces; a form of governance on which the oppressor and the oppressed could find consensus. The two, however, held different views on the endgame and the road map.[16] At the same time, then, West Indian and British swords were drawn over federation. For Britain, it was a cheaper governance strategy to simultaneously unite and divide the region. For the West Indies it was the beginning of an exit strategy that called for Britain to repay its debt to the region.

In Jamaica, long on the periphery of regional integration passions – of both the imperial and nationalist brand – Norman Manley's PNP threw its support behind the regional federation agenda. But the Jamaican legislative council in 1940 reaffirmed support for the imperial version. Britain had affirmed its preference for integrated social services rather than political sovereignty and regional economic development. The joint-services strategy articulated in the Moyne Report was a response to the fear of political federation as a precursor to independence.

The meeting of the Caribbean Labour Congress in September 1945 made real the foundation of a future that incorporated the Federation of the West Indies. It took place in Barbados and provided the regional leadership with the opportunity to respond to Prime Minister Churchill. Manley sent Richard Hart to represent the PNP, while Bustamante strategically sent no one to represent the Jamaica Labour Party. Hubert Critchlow (British Guiana), Grantley Adams (Barbados), Albert Marryshow (Grenada) and Albert Gomes (Trinidad and Tobago) deepened the leadership discourse and determined the direction.

It was significant that St Kitts also invited Hart to speak on its behalf. His intervention was forcefully anti-colonial. There was no doubt, when he called for a federation, that he wanted an immediate end to British rule. The British government responded, as predicted, that the West Indians, despite the rheto-

---

16. Ibid., 96. See also Sir S. Luke to P. Rogers, 2 February 1955, CO 1031, no. 67; Report of the Conference on Movement of Persons . . . in the Federation, 17 March 1955, CO 1031/1776, no. 140.

ric, were not ready for a federation, and urged the need for a more cautious approach, focusing on unitary planning around labour productivity, welfare, shipping logistics and communications services.

The not-so-subtle threat of the British government came from Creech Jones, colonial secretary. He informed labour leaders and politicians that their choice would mean a vote for financial independence, and that the British government would continue to assist only territories already dependent on grants in aid. A federal government in the West Indies, he warned, would be cutting financial aid from Britain, and as a result "should be financially independent". He walked this path during his career, leading West Indian leaders into believing in his support for development, while being unprepared to press his government to honour its financial obligations to the region.[17]

It was at the Montego Bay Conference, 11–19 September 1947, that West Indian leaders concluded the conversation on colonialism. It was there that they celebrated the trilogy of triumph – federation, independence and economic development. Manley, unable to attend, captured the mood of the meeting in a letter to delegates: "I put first, and . . . above all other things, the desire to see a West Indian nation standing shoulder to shoulder with all other nations of the world."[18]

Manley's sentiment symbolized the state of affairs in the region. The West Indian nation existed in the mind and heart of delegates. Colonialism, for them, was being read its last rites. Creech Jones, recognizing the inevitability of the empire's ending, stated that West Indians had long had a "dream" of federation. It was now as real as ever, he said, but urged that no leader should "prostitute the idea . . . for narrow political ends".[19]

The determination of the labour movement to federate the region as a first step to nationalist independence found formal expression in resolution 1 of the conference: "That this Conference, recognizing the desirability of a political Federation of the British Caribbean territories, accepts the principle of a Federation in which each constituent unit retains complete control over all matters except those specifically assigned to the federal government."[20] Democracy now

---

17. Wallace, *British Caribbean*, 98–99.
18. Ibid., 99.
19. Ibid.
20. *The Report of the British Caribbean Standing Closer Association Committee, 1948–1949* (Bridgetown: Advocate, 1950), 9.

beckoned, and leaders prepared to say "free at last", as plans were approved to institutionalize nationhood.

Racist Backlash: R.W. Thompson in Jamaica

The decade after the 1838 emancipation reform witnessed a literacy explosion of anti-black attitudes. Carlyle's discourse on the "Nigger Question", which promoted the first British national debate on the right of Africans to freedom, found expression a century later in R.W. Thompson's 1946 book, *Black Caribbean*. Like Carlyle, Thompson was a writer with a pretence to possession of the tools of the historian's craft. He travelled throughout Jamaica in 1944–45, collecting impressions of black communities as they prepared for federation and nationhood.[21]

Like Carlyle, and also Trollope and Froude, in the mid-decades of nineteenth-century Jamaica, Thompson sought to capture British response to black progressive politics, in particular the demand for democracy and political leadership. His narrative picked up where Carlyle's racial rhetoric had left off, presenting Jamaica as a symbol of post-slavery decay and decline. Jamaica, for Thompson, was Haiti for Carlyle, a failed experiment with the alluring idea of freedom, for which blacks were neither politically prepared nor culturally competent.

The idea of Jamaica's liberation from Empire terrified Thompson. It was equally terrifying for officials of the British government, and Churchill in particular. Thompson, as a literary figure, was licensed to express in non-fiction what official diplomacy could not comfortably communicate. Collectively, however, the imperial message, whether expressed in Thompson's book or squeezed between the lines of cryptic official correspondence, constituted an assault on the idea of West Indian federation and political freedom.

Before Thompson had arrived on the island he was exposed to "vague rumours of labour troubles and the evacuation of white families". Black agitators, he noted, were demanding something called "democracy", the "tragic expressions from the bowels of a bitterly abused subject people struggling for independence" or simply the "shallow shouting – the froth rimming the black melancholy of a dispirited race". He made reference to Churchill's already famous statement

---

21. Thompson, *Black Caribbean*.

about his not becoming the king's first minister in order to preside over the liquidation of the British Empire. He used it as a trope to define his role as a pro-imperial writer.[22]

Thompson described being greeted on arrival by a "little black monkey of a man cheerfully offering [him] pink gin", and giving an assurance that "everyone would be glad" to see him. The "black depression of arrival" notwithstanding, Thompson settled in for an adventure in the isle he grew to "love". The "easy negro laughter" he found infectious, and "pretty soon it cheered" him up. He celebrated the "negro faces breaking into broad friendly smiles" with their "sheer simple effervescence".[23]

In Kingston, he encountered the "saboteurs whose protestations" had become internationally known. He heard of "Bustamante, just released from internment to become an ally of an uneasy government, a labour leader, founder of his own 'trade union'". He described him as an "illiterate but powerful clown surrounded by his body guards of thugs, and overwhelming simple negro audiences with torrents of words, resembling the outburst of his Nazi-fascist models".[24]

Everywhere he journeyed in Jamaica, Thompson found evidence of the same anti-British political eruption that reminded him of the real threat that exists against "our Empire – the Motherland". He recognized the "slow stirring of Black Democracy, the body awakening, and finding its first voice through the cultured lips of Norman Washington Manley, and the raving, illiterate tongue of Bustamante". But democracy, he tells us, "if it can't and won't behave, must be controlled. A dangerous business, but a dangerous world."[25]

Freedom to participate in public governance, Thompson concluded, might be the aspiration of a few blacks from the emerging professional class, but as a colonial community they were simply not capable of its civic demands. His assault on the character of Bustamante was intended to ignite the legacy of the literary images of Sambo and Quashee, resurrected from the nineteenth century to decorate the twentieth. Jamaica was "no more fit to govern itself or for democracy, than is a month old baby to change its own napkins".[26]

---

22. Ibid., 60.
23. Ibid., 64.
24. Ibid., 66, 67.
25. Ibid., 70, 71, 82.
26. Ibid., 82.

Standing Closer for Federation

Resolution 6 of the 1947 Montego Bay Conference called for political machinery to advance the West Indian demand for federation. It recommended "the immediate constitution of a Standing Closer Association Committee composed of delegates appointed by the Legislatures of each unit in the British Caribbean area, not exceeding the numbers specified in the Schedule to this Resolution, and of a Chairman and Secretary appointed by the Secretary of State".[27]

Creech Jones skilfully and quickly moved to propose the appointment of a loyal chairman to control the dialogue between the West Indies and the British government.

Major General Sir Hubert Rance was chosen. He was favoured as an effective colonial governor who, like Lord Moyne in 1938, was to begin the business of protecting the British government by denying its responsibility for the economic development of the soon-to-be-federated West Indies. This was his project: to keep the West Indians away from the British treasury.

Rance had served as governor of colonial Burma for two years prior to his West Indian assignment. He was an army man with experience as an officer in both the First and Second World Wars. In Burma, his task was to administer the colony in the aftermath of the Japanese occupation. He retired from this service when, on 4 January 1948, Sao Shwe Thaik became president of Burma.

His duties in the West Indies were to carry on where Lord Moyne had left off; to promote reforms in sociopolitical governance at nominal financial cost to Britain – that is, to ensure that any West Indian development strategy would not be deemed a binding reparatory justice project. It would carry no significant cost to Britain, and West Indians would be led to expect no capital investments to fund the economic development aspects of their anti-Empire revolution.

Rance fully understood his mission, and, like Moyne, moved expeditiously to reject Lewis's argument that the British owed a debt to the West Indies, and, importantly, argued that Britain had no legal and moral responsibility to contribute to West Indian economic development and modernization.

The Standing Closer Committee comprised some of the principals of the federation project within the labour movement. The composition was as follows:

---

27. *Report of the British Caribbean*, 9.

Sir Hubert Rance	UK Chair
H.A. Cuke, OBE	Barbados Legislative Council (LC)
G.H. Adams	Barbados
C.V. Wright, OBE	British Guiana (LC)
T. Lee	British Guiana (LC)
W.H. Courtenay	British Honduras (LC)
F.R. Dragten, OBE	British Honduras
D.J. Judah	Jamaica (LC)
C. Hart	Jamaica
V.C. Bird	Antigua (LC)
M.H. Davis	St Kitts–Nevis (LC)
C.R. Meade	Montserrat
A. Gomes	Trinidad (LC)
L.C. Hannays	Trinidad (LC)
A. Winston	Dominica (LC)
J.B. Renwick	Grenada (LC)
G.H. Gordon	St Lucia (LC)
G. McIntosh	St Vincent (LC)

Rance was charged with leading this committee of prominent West Indians, most of whom were co-opted onto colonial legislative councils because governors had found them to be "responsible men". Grantley Adams was elected to his position, unlike his colleagues from other colonies, because Barbados had moved by constitutional reform to use a franchise for this purpose.

The committee constituted the first battleground where West Indian nationalism contested British control. Rance was ready to contest the West Indians on the financial front by suggesting that Britain would facilitate the region with nominal finance, but no significant capital support. In other words, the West Indians had fought against the empire and had won a battle, but were now on their own in terms of finance for economic development.

Deploying the regional rotation principle, the committee met for the first time in November of 1948 in Barbados and in March 1949 in Trinidad. The third and fourth meetings were convened in Barbados (June–July 1949) and Jamaica (October 1949) respectively. Meetings were held over a period of two weeks. The committee's findings and recommendation were published in Barbados in 1950 as *The Report of the British Caribbean Standing Closer Association*

Committee, 1948–1949. It became generally known as the Rance Report. It narrates the many conflicts between Chairman Rance and West Indian politicians on the critical matter of funding the federation.

From the outset, Rance was in a race to advance the policy of the British government: to slow, and, if possible, derail the process leading to federation. His first step was to establish that there was a direct relationship between the principles of political integration and financial viability. He stated: "It is now a truism to say that political independence is unreal unless it is based on financial stability which, in turn, must rest on a solid foundation of economic productivity – i.e. on an adequate income."[28]

The region, Rance noted, was accustomed to receiving "grant aid" from the British treasury through the provision of aid and welfare. The West Indian expectation of capital grants for development, however, went beyond the approved framework and was not likely to be fulfilled. He surmised that the West Indies had neither "economic stability" nor "financial solvency, both necessary for political federation and independence".[29]

West Indians, then, according to Rance, had no compelling argument for "adding a further political superstructure in the form of a Federation" to the already underfunded, fragile colonial governance system. There is "scarcely a territory", he added with an attitude of contempt, "even among the largest, whose finances do not give some cause for concern, and which might not, as a result of some by no means unprecedented misfortune or disaster, be brought to insolvency".[30]

While Rance made it clear that he was not opposed in principle to any form of political federation in the West Indies, and considered an imperial version of the idea a good one, his task was to impart to its advocates that the British government would not fund the West Indian version of the project. Also, his belief that independence was the last stop on the West Indian agenda hardened his tactical opposition to Federation.[31]

Rance's strategy was to advocate that the idea of federation and the robust demand for it as a strategy – to accelerate the anti-colonial agenda and end British rule – was largely an emotional and sensational desire. The bluntness

---

28. Ibid.
29. Ibid., 12.
30. Ibid.
31. Ibid.

of his anti-federation rhetoric was not always welcomed in the ruling British Labour Party, where there was no desire to see West Indian leaders presented as irrational, emotional and unrealistic.

Critically, there was also lukewarm support in the British Labour Party for Rance's idea that West Indian labour leaders had misled their public in terms of describing the benefits to be derived from federation. Rance noted:

> We do not claim that Federation will immediately and automatically solve the economic and fiscal problems of the region, or that it cannot fail. We do claim that it will put in the hands of men responsible to the region as a whole, powers and opportunities, particularly in respect to the pace of the region in world trade, which do not exist at present. . . . Federation as such will not solve our problems, but will provide the conditions in which they may be dealt with.[32]

Furthermore, he added, "Federation will not absolve the region from the necessity for physical and mental and moral effort – it may, if successful, help that effort to issue in greater productivity, more security and higher standards of living, than can the same effort exercised within the present political framework."[33] He pushed West Indian leaders back on their heels with the argument that they should look internally to their own financial resources. The federation, therefore, would have to examine its own inventory of assets, and look to raise loans to generate revenue through financial instruments "under its sole control".[34]

As an experienced colonial administrator, Rance effectively implemented the British resistance. He did not wish to be seen publicly as abandoning the smaller, less financially resourced islands in the Leewards and Windwards. But skilfully, using divide-and-rule techniques, he placed them in a special category, and in the process sowed seeds of dissension in the West Indian ranks. His public purpose was to show British concern for the less endowed colonies to camouflage the critical and substantive point that Britain was cutting off capital funds for the federation.

Rance's ultimate objective was to assure the short-term collapse of the ideology of independence, and with it the dream of the nationalist movement. He was aggressive in his assessment:

---

32. Ibid., 15.
33. Ibid.
34. Ibid., 20.

> We consider, however, that to continue the system of direct grants in aid from His Majesty's Government in the United Kingdom to the individual unit Governments concerned would seriously inhibit the development of financial responsibility and self-reliance in the region. Since in due course the territories must look to the Federation, and not to His Majesty's Government, for financial assistance when required, the Federal Government must learn to administer such assistance, and the sooner a beginning is made the better.[35]

The only window that would open to the West Indies, he noted, was if they applied to the British government for an annual grant – the equivalent of the grant aid each of the colonies had received for the five years prior to federation. The application for such aid would be made for a period of ten years. This way, the financially distressed colonies in the federation would have no access to capital grants from Britain, but would request such funding from the federal government. Federation leaders would "reduce to a minimum the necessity for applying to His Majesty's Government for financial aid", and "conduct their economic and financial affairs" with minimum British support.[36]

Then came Rance's final disclosure – the rejection of British reparatory responsibility for facilitating West Indian economic development. The Moyne Commission was used to dismiss any responsibility for an economic development strategy in which there was an industrialization policy and an economic reform agenda. Now the Rance Committee was being used to dismiss the West Indian official claim on Britain for funding for the federation.

Rance expressed his duty and loyalty to Empire with the following statement:

> At this point we feel bound to comment on a class of suggestion which has already been made in public discussion, and which may occur. It springs from the belief that any degree of political independence presupposes complete financial stability, and takes the form that in order to start off the Federation it would be necessary for His Majesty's Government to make a grant of a very large proportion – many millions of pounds have been mentioned – to a new Federal Government.[37]

There would be no reparatory justice approach to the end of Empire. "We do not exclude the possibility of some assistance by way of capital grant", Rance added, "for specific purposes e.g. the cost of setting up new Federal adminis-

---

35. Ibid., 22.
36. Ibid., 24.
37. Ibid., 25.

trative headquarters", but the "real independence of the region will only be won by its own effort, and founded upon resources thereby built upon".[38]

Resistance by Rance, then, played a similar part in West Indian politics to Moyne's role as the messenger of Empire: he sought to drive a nail into the coffin of West Indian demand for British reparations. Moyne had admitted that the positive effects of black emancipation on the West Indian economy were "mitigated by the payment of £20,000,000 from the British exchequer".[39] Rance, however, was not prepared to discuss development with West Indians. He bluntly dismissed proposals for large reparatory grants to the region and described them as "superficial attractions".

The West Indies, Rance added, needed long-term capital development – but Britain would not be the source. In dismissing the matter in respect of the federation, he wrote: "We do not however recommend any such scheme [a very large grant] for what appears to us the overriding reason that the availability of such a grant would not breed that spirit of self-reliance, and that determination to stand on our own feet economically and financially which are essential if we are to attain full independence."[40] Furthermore, he explained:

> It is we think a matter of human nature generally, and not of West Indian human nature only, that a grant for which the Federation was not accountable would not in fact be spent to the best advantage, and there would be a serious risk, if not a natural certainty, that when it was exhausted the region would find itself not with strengthened productive and economic resources but with heavily increased recurring commitments, and be further from, and not nearer to, real independence.[41]

The suggestion that West Indians, after a decade of revolt against destitution, were not to be trusted with reparatory funding was clearly meant to be confrontational. The funds in question would constitute just a minor portion of what had been extracted from the region. For the robber to argue that what had been taken should not be returned to the robbed because it would be put to improper use speaks to the nature of the white-supremacist thinking at the core of the British Empire's policy.

---

38. Ibid.
39. *Moyne Report*, 30.
40. *Report of the British Caribbean*, 25.
41. Ibid.

Proof of Punishment: No to Reparations

Now available for public access are the official documents of the British government in which the dealings with West Indian leaders on decolonization are set out. These data reveal the official response of Britain to funding the federation, nation-building and independence. Critically, they show the opposition to any form of reparations. Rance is revealed as the principal adviser to the British government on these matters while serving as chairman of the Standing Closer Association Committee. His role is revealed in crafting British policies to derail and discredit the federation project.

Secretary to the Standing Closer Committee C.Y. Carstairs, with Rance's permission, sent a series of back-channel documents to the British government in 1949. These communications clearly indicate that "genuine independence in the West Indies must remain a mirage" and its pursuit an occupation doomed to failure and frustration. The reason he gave was that "neither the small nor large territories have any real chance of moving very far from the margins of subsistence in public finance".[42] It did not matter, he added, that the West Indies can achieve as "a single political entity what its constituent units cannot achieve individually". What mattered was that their retention as colonies, even if federated, required their financial and political dependency. West Indian nationalists, therefore, as the champions of federation, should not be supported in the quest for economic development if the objective was political.[43]

Many such subversive statements sent to the British cabinet by colonial officials in respect of the federation were unknown to regional leaders. The content of this correspondence illustrates the anti–West Indian agenda of British officials, led by Rance and those to whom he reported. On 27 June 1949, for example, minutes prepared by H.T. Bourdillon were sent to W.L. Gorell Barnes at the Colonial Office capturing the discussion "on the financial arrangements for Federation".

These minutes were sent through Rance to C.G. Beasley, economic adviser to the British government on the West Indies.[44] The minutes began: "This is

---

42. S.R. Ashton and David Killingray, eds., *British Documents on the End of Empire*, ser. B, vol. 6, *The West Indies* (London: Institute of Commonwealth Studies, 1999), 9.

43. Ibid., 10. See C.Y. Carstairs, Report on the Standing Closer Association Committee, 21 June 1949, CO 318/487/2, no. 1.

44. Ashton and Killingray, *British Documents*, 12; H.T. Bourdillon to Gorell Barnes, 27

the file dealing with the financial arrangements for the West Indian Federation if it comes off. . . . There seems to be a number of trends of opinion relative to this matter in the West Indies, not all of them pulling in the same direction. In fact it would hardly be going too far to say that there are some fundamental contradictions in the West Indian attitude."[45] They were divided, Bourdillon said, on the issue of financing their "hypothetical federal authority" and some of them believed that His Majesty's Government is "foisting federation on the West Indies in order to escape from financial responsibility".[46]

The contents of enclosure no. 4, and the telegram within enclosure no. 6, show the advice given to the British government if the "Federation is allowed to become a financial reality". It should be made clear from the outset, noted an influential voice, that "financial self-sufficiency" should be the expectation. The federation should be provided with no significant capital at the beginning and its creation and sustainability should be seen in these terms.

Enclosure no. 6 spoke to the provision of a small "block grant for five years based on the average aggregate of grant in aid in the recent past". This sum would be "evidence of generosity on the part of His Majesty's Government", and should be handed over with the clear understanding that "the Federal authority would do its utmost not to come back for more".[47]

These statements referenced the regional belief, officials noted, that as with the Irish, "His Majesty's Government is perpetually in debt to the West Indies for errors or omissions of the past three hundred years". The sum of money mentioned as colonial debt to be redressed as reparations startled the British, but the principle was not officially rejected. The report stated: "in all seriousness to liquefy this debt is astronomical and would undoubtedly provide financial stability for a greater or lesser number of years". Lewis had defined the debt as an accumulation of liability for two hundred years of free labour. He offered no sum in terms of monetary value.[48]

Reference to the "large sum" expected by West Indian leaders, and the acknowledgement that it would go a long way to "provide financial stability" for the region, connected to the admission that a debt was indeed owed. Without

June 1949, CO 318/486/3.

45. Ashton and Killingray, *British Documents*, 12.

46. Ibid.

47. Ibid., 13; H.T. Bourdillon to Gorell Barnes, 27 June 1949, CO 318/486/3.

48. Carstairs to Watt, 5 September 1949, CO 318/487, no. 10.

reparations, the government official reiterated, West Indian "politicians and prominent persons may well advance the theory that the enthusiasm shown by Her Majesty's Government for Federation is due mainly to the desire to rid herself of the financial liability" for the weaker regional economies.[49]

Anxiety in the British government over the debt owed the West Indies dominated discussions throughout the 1950s. Fear of "the large sum" expected kept policy discussions confined to a small sum. In Britain, there was considerable concern in particular about the posture of Bustamante, who officials said was building his anti-federation sentiment on the refusal of the British government to fund the federation. Enclosure no. 6 contained a statement attributed to him. It stated that in his dealings with the British he "will overestimate the cost of the federal structure and will bid for a fantastic grant from the British Government before he is prepared to give his support. He will know that a refusal, or even silence on the part of the British Government regarding his bid, will present him with excellent material against Manley's People's National Party."[50]

The British financial offer to West Indian leaders of a small grant for ten years, the equivalent of the "grant in aid" provisions for the previous five years, was not expected to be supported. It was assured to irritate Bustamante and fuel Jamaica's opposition. The grant in aid for the region (excluding Honduras) for 1952–53 was a mere £600,000. An official informed that the sum proposed "will be successful only if it leads to further economic development, and that it is incumbent on His Majesty's Government to provide the basic conditions for success by providing initially, funds for development". The "supplementary financial assistance for economic development", the official concluded, would undoubtedly increase significantly the sum expected from the government.[51]

Reflecting on the inability to satisfy West Indian politicians with development funding, colonial official Mr Burke expressed frustration with having to think in terms of how "to bribe the West Indies" into accepting small sums. Politics aside, he said, the "most important point" is "that by and large the West Indies, what with underemployment and rapidly increasing populations, are going economically downhill".[52]

---

49. Ibid.
50. Ibid.
51. "Financial Aspects of West Indian Federation", Bourdillon to Lyttelton, January 1952, CO 1031/760, no. 9.
52. Ibid.

Another official, Mr Luke, broke ranks with Burke and argued the case for reparations. He called for a serious policy discussion and backed the West Indian argument: "While we may deride the claim that Britain owes a debt to the West Indies for the fortunes taken out of them in the plantation days, the fact remains that until quite recently nothing was done to put money back into these islands in order to expand their economy, and that the effects of this neglect are now being felt."[53] He acknowledged that Britain created the colonial mess that West Indian politicians were dealing with. The "walking-away" policy, he argued, should, therefore, be re-examined.

Writing in support of a significant reparation package to assist the region, he stated: "Overpopulation in relation to economic resources becomes daily a more serious problem, and matters have been made worse by the phenomenal rises in costs . . . over the past few years. These facts impressed themselves on both of us during our tour of the West Indies a year ago, and we both felt grave doubts whether CD&W [Colonial Development and Welfare] assistance on the present scale is sufficient to stop the rot."[54] He concluded: "We are only scratching the surface . . . the economic problem . . . will advance without considerably greater capital outlay both in terms of loan and grant that falls within our present plan, towards solving them."[55]

The West Indies, then, noted Luke, were within their rights to press for reparations and "require increased assistance irrespective of the Federation". "I have felt", he added, that federation "must be supported by His Majesty's Government with a new measure of capital assistance if hopes are not to be frustrated and if the new political unit is ever to be more than a façade".[56]

The case for a substantial reparations grant was made by Luke and a minority group within the British government in 1952. Their argument was based on the principle that three hundred years of capital extraction and no injection had left the region to decay and decline. The group suggested that the British government had "never attempted to coordinate their economic activities" in the region and a grant based on "a coordinated plan for economic development worked out in the region itself" would be the answer. Such a strategy, noted the British official, "is primarily economic, in that without such assistance we

---

53. Ibid.
54. Ibid.
55. Ibid.
56. Ibid.

may be confident that the economic situation of many of the . . . territories will go from bad to worse".[57]

These officials began the task of considering what an effective reparatory-development capital grant for federation would look like. One made reference to the process as "crystal-gazing", searching for a calculation that they "might ultimately have to offer if they were to make a realistic yet not extravagant response to the much larger reports which the West Indians themselves would no doubt produce".[58] As a group they expected that West Indian leaders would make a proposal for a large development grant in order to begin serious talks about reparations.

The dialogue among British officials, in the end, moved from reference to a "large sum" to a rejection of any sum. Fear drove the retreat – that the request would be for an "astronomical financial" package. Some officials remained prepared to compromise as a negotiation strategy, but the consensus was to advise the minister to dismiss any reparations claim from the West Indians.[59]

The tactical, diplomatic suggestion was that the minister should entertain West Indian leaders on the reparation matter, encourage their line of thinking, and then at the right strategic moment issue a refusal. The minister was advised by his diplomats to carry out the plan as follows:

> After subtle remarks about the financial straits of the United Kingdom and the impossibility of promising anything, to say that they could not even consider such requests except on the basis of a coordinated and practical plan for economic development, designed to achieve the viability of the whole region. It would then be for the West Indians to go away and work out such a plan . . . and by the time it had been produced we might in any case be moving towards the era when the Treasury will be willing to consider further CD&W assistance to the colonial empire as a whole.[60]

The minority element within the government, led by Luke, that supported reparations was thus silenced.

The deceptive strategy to dismiss the West Indian claim for reparatory development revealed the lengths to which the British government went to

---

57. Ibid.
58. Ibid.
59. Ibid.
60. Ibid.

derail the popular aspirations for a prosperous federation. The tactic was to slow them down, without causing offence, and then redirect West Indian efforts with a view to shutting them down within the context of a plan for the wider empire. This confirmed what was known: that the British government, despite rhetorical statements of support, was not predisposed financially to helping the West Indians with either the federation or economic development. Indeed, Britain's intent was more to humiliate than to encourage West Indian leaders. This was the payback for the 1930s anti-colonial revolution.[61]

Most British officials were committed to proceeding along these strategic "lines from a tactical point of view". Enclosure no. 12 in the documents, for example, reveals the sense of victory they felt in successfully refusing capital funding. They indicated how the matter could be laid "to rest until . . . comments of the West Indian Governments" were received. They noted, further, that it was necessary to inform "both our Ministers and the Treasury" that they should prepare, as set out in enclosure no. 9, for a large West Indian reparations bill to His Majesty's Government. The estimation, they noted, for "the final bill . . . though it may not be presented for a year or two is likely to be a good deal bigger than £20 million over five years".[62]

There was, therefore, a systematic attempt by the British government to block and deny the just West Indian claim to development with reparation finance. The capital starving of the federal project was carefully and ruthlessly pursued and implemented. Officials who supported the idea of a significant West Indian capital grant to promote economic growth and political integration were brushed aside by hardliners who schemed and plotted against development. They degraded West Indian politicians in formal meetings and other gatherings. Their correspondence illustrates clearly that the character assault on key politicians was intended to diminish their standing in the West Indies and beyond, rendering them less capable of serving the development needs of their region.

By the time of the 13 April 1953 conference in London, the British government had already prepared an internal scheme to neutralize the West Indians in terms of a meaningful financial plan for the federation. The official report of the conference, and communique no. 14, which summarized the proceedings,

---

61. Ibid.
62. Ibid.

make no specific reference to the expected reparation funding for the West Indies. This was a surprising turn of events.[63]

The British government nonetheless drew up plans for the suppression of reparations demands around federation. The alternative plan was also developed in the event that tactical rhetoric was required. Provision was made in the following way:

> Subject to the approval of Parliament, Her Majesty's Government would make available to the Federation in the first ten years, grants intended to cover the budget deficits of those units which in spite of their best efforts could not pay their way. The annual amount to be paid in each of the first five years would be negotiated nearer the time of Federation but would not be less than the average of the ordinary deficits of grant-aided colonies during the three years [not five] previous to Federation.[64]

In addition, it was agreed to make a social welfare contribution of £500,000 "towards the capital cost of establishing the Federal Headquarters".[65]

The persistent subversion of the thinking and proposals of West Indian leaders continued. Sir Hugh Foot, commenting in 1956, noted, "I know very well that West Indian leaders often take all the aid they receive far too much for granted." He added, "I realise of course that financial assistance is never given without strings and if assistance is given there should be something given in return." In a letter to the secretary of state, he added, "What we have said is that the fact that the British taxpayer is forced to make a very substantial contribution to the West Indies remains an argument as to why Her Majesty's Government should continue to have an opportunity of supervising the expenditure of the money."[66]

This sentiment preceded and informed the plans for the 1956 London Conference, at which it was agreed to constitutionally establish the federation. It was stated: "Put shortly, . . . Her Majesty's Government cannot increase its present financial commitments . . . as stated in the Secretary of State's circular despatch no. 411 of April 26, 1955, there may be later on some small further

---

63. *Report on the West Indian Federation Conference*, communique no. 14, April 1953, CO 1031/751, no. 308.
64. Ibid.
65. Ibid.
66. Sir Hugh Foot to Alan Lennox-Boyd, 16 January 1956, CO 1031/103, no. 65.

allocation out of the existing reserve to West Indian territories among others."[67]

As the time approached for the conference, the British government intensified the conversation in respect of choking funding obligations to the West Indies. The language became more stringent and the tone increasingly disrespectful, less generous and more dismissive. When, for example, regrets were expressed over increasing from £500,00 to £1 million the contribution to establish federal administrative facilities, the fiscal commissioner made it clear that the revised sum "was the absolute maximum that could be given, and . . . that he hoped that this would be regarded as a generous donation".[68]

The negative West Indian response to the offer was read as undiplomatic, not recognizing the financial constraints of Her Majesty's Government. West Indians replied it was hoped that "Her Majesty's Government would understand that their own difficulties in the West Indies were even greater". Furthermore, they revealed, it was their intention to put forward a proposal in short time for a loan of £2 million at a low interest rate "to provide the working capital for the Federation". The donation, they concluded, was "not as generous" as the fiscal commission declared.[69]

The federation, then, came into being in an environment filled with the hostile attitude of the British government. As a major project it was identified with independence and reparations and the pressing of demands for significant capital-development support. In the British cabinet and the Colonial Office, opposing positions were crafted and refined, intended to deny the regional reparatory right to resources.

Britain understood that federation, democracy and independence meant the end of its empire in the West Indies. As a result, it took an aggressive posture against all calls for capital support to promote economic development. Once again, Britain had succeeded, despite intense West Indian pressure, in distancing itself from the ideas Lewis had outlined in 1939. Its strategy was to deny a debt was owed to the region.

---

67. "UK Financial Assistance", CO brief no. 22, 1 February 1956, CO 1031/1737, no. 39.
68. Ibid., 126; see also "Sources of Federal Revenue", 13 February 1956, annexes 2 and 3, CO 1031/1754, no. 4 (53)3.
69. Ibid.

CHAPTER 10

Punish West Indians, Promote East Indians
The Colombo Plan

In 1957, the Standing Committee on Federation submitted a Resolution to the Secretary of State for the Colonies pointing out that the union would begin "with an inherited situation of poverty and unbalanced and inadequate economic development". Hence, it asked the British Government to give the new Federation prompt and substantial aid of at least £100 million, plus an equal sum for the second five years of its life. West Indian ideas about the financial assistance which could be expected from the metropolitan power were influenced by their needs, their belief that Britain had a moral obligation to them, and envy of the United States' massive contribution to Puerto Rico.
    —Elisabeth Wallace, *The British Caribbean: From the Decline of Colonialism to the End of Federation*

THE SUM DEMANDED FOR ECONOMIC DEVELOPMENT in 1957 was £200 million. West Indian leaders requested that Britain pay this amount into a capital fund to make the federation financially viable. The reparations sum was expected to be invested over a period of ten years. Britain refused the request.

Bustamante thought more should have been demanded. He later "lamented the failure to extract from the United Kingdom a firm promise of 'millions of pounds'".[1]

Two hundred million pounds was considered a modest, indeed conservative, estimate of what a West Indies development fund should look like, given the vast debt owed to the region. Britain's rejection was swift and blunt. The West Indies, federated or not, one government official stated, should begin accepting

---

1. Wallace, *British Caribbean*, 113; "The Plan for a British Caribbean Federation: Report of the Judicial Commissioner", Cmd. 9620, London, 1955, 1–20.

responsibility for its own financial sustainability by standing on its own feet. It promised instead to increase the grant in aid to the region from £500,000 to £1 million. Then it rejected a soft-loan request from Premier Manley of Jamaica for £2 million. Finally, it agreed to establish a loans council to coordinate debt requests from the region instead of development grants.[2]

The details of the British counter-offer are set out in the official report of the 1956 federation conference. West Indian leaders considered it unacceptable. It was presented as follows:

> The UK delegation then outlined the requirement of the federation with regard to the initial expenditure as they saw it. The Fiscal Commissioner had worked on the assumption that Her Majesty's Government would make a grant of £500,000 towards the cost of the Federal Capital, leaving £1,750,000 to be found; this sum could be met by annual contributions of £60,000 and, when the time came to raise a loan, the interest charges could similarly amount to £60,000 per annum. The situation had now been altered by Her Majesty's Government's consent to increase the amount of the capital grant to a total not exceeding £1 million. It was not the wish of Her Majesty's Government to impose any restrictions on the expenditure of the capital grant in relation to the expenditure from local funds; they would be quite happy to see their contribution used first.[3]

The intense debate that followed attracted this response from Lord Lloyd to a question posed by Mr Gomes of Trinidad and Tobago: "In addition to the grant of £1 million towards the cost of the Federal Capital, Her Majesty's Government would, of course, continue to make available Colonial Development and Welfare Funds, grants-in-aid to unit governments as at present. . . . Only a limited amount of capital was available for overseas investment by the United Kingdom, and demands for capital were presented to the United Kingdom from all over the world."[4] This response represented the final brush-off. The West Indians were told to join the global aid queue and wait in line.

The impolite dismissal set the tone for the birth of the federation. It was a West Indian project refashioned and then betrayed by Britain. Its financial

2. Wallace, *British Caribbean*, 114; *British Caribbean Federal Capital Commission Report*, Col. no. 328 (London, 1956), 15–20. See David Lowenthal, "The West Indies Chooses a Capital", *Geographical Review* 48 (1958): 336–64.

3. Report of the Seventh Plenary Session of the London British Caribbean Federation Conference, 15 February 1956, CO 1031/1754, no. 9.

4. Ibid.

viability was dependent on British policy and attitudes. It was, therefore, a vulnerable enterprise that could not survive Britain's intention to punish the region for its rejection of Empire, a process that had set the tone for other colonies to follow. Williams stated four years later that the British mood had evolved from anger to indifference and disrespect.[5]

It is necessary to trace the background to what had happened up to 1956/58, leading to the rise of the federation and then to its demise in 1962.

In 1913, Marcus Garvey published an essay entitled "The British West Indies in the Mirror of Civilization: History Making by Colonial Negroes". In it, he made the following reference to the idea of a West Indian federation: "There have been several moments to federate the British West Indian islands [imperial attempts to merge colonial governance], but owing to parochial feelings, nothing definite has been received. Ere long this change is sure to come [from below] because the people of these islands are all one. They live under the same conditions, are of the one race and mind, and have the same feelings and sentiments regarding the things of the world."[6] Garvey referenced the British imperial efforts to federate the colonial administration of West Indian colonies – primarily the Leewards and Windwards with Barbados, Jamaica with Cayman, Turks and Caicos and Belize – in order to facilitate cost reductions.

Garvey's call, however, was for a federation of the West Indies as one nation with a common yet diverse Caribbean heritage and creole culture. Federation from below, as Garvey envisioned it, was the end project of national liberation. It would be the most ambitious political undertaking coming out of the post-slavery West Indies.

The British government, therefore, received "federation from below" as an enemy agenda and secretly planned for it to be discredited and discarded. Recognizing its popularity in the region, however, Britain responded cautiously, but knew from the outset that it would be starved of financial resources. Federation, then, did not fail in 1962. It was defeated by the British with the help of internal allies.

---

5. See Dudley Seers, "Federation of the British West Indies: The Economic and Financial Aspects", *Social and Economic Studies* 6 (1957): 119–214; Dudley Seers, "Federation in the British West Indies: An Exercise in Colonial Administration", *Economist*, 11 April 1960, 17–19; "The Plan for a British Caribbean Federation: Report of the Fiscal Commissioner", Cmd. 9618, London, 1955.

6. See *Africa Times and Orient Review*, October 1913, cited in Hill, *Marcus Garvey*, 53.

The persistent notion of internal failure has since then focused on the fatal eruption of an insular consciousness in West Indian politics, centred on the rise of professional politicians who took centre stage in the labour movement during the 1950s. There has also been some focus on the technical incompetence of these politicians and their public servants in terms of managing the mechanics of integration.

West Indian political leadership was constituted mostly of men with enormous public support and invested with considerable reputations in their respective countries. But the region was governed by Britain, which for three centuries practised the politics of insularity, fostering animosity between neighbours. In addition, the region was a theatre for Britain to pursue its militarized scorched-earth policy. Further, it was an economic zone managed by Britain with exclusive trade and investment practices. The legacies of these realities made integration politics contentious and corrosive.

These were the headwinds blowing against the supporters of federation. The dialectics of decolonization, furthermore, suggested that a colonial backlash was inevitable. When it came, it took the form of choking off the funding stream needed for federation. What happened during the late 1950s and early 1960s was classic British imperial manipulation in action: celebrate the birth, since there was nothing you could do about it, then starve the infant.

At the 1956 London Conference, the British government confirmed its willingness to support the federation, with the caveat that it should immediately "stand on its own feet economically and financially". This was the first move in the British strategy of strangling the unwelcome stranger. The conference produced a critical piece of administrative architecture, the Standing Committee on Federation, made up mostly of West Indian leaders and chaired by a well-known colonial staff member with lead responsibility for colonial welfare.[7]

West Indian members of the committee wasted no time in making the case for reparatory justice. Their proposal was specific, and written in the rhetoric of legitimate expectation. The committee heard the West Indian case that the federation would inevitably begin its life "with an inherited situation of poverty and unbalanced and inadequate economic development".[8]

---

7. Wallace, *British Caribbean*, 113.
8. Ibid.

The request was made that "the British Government give the new Federation prompt and substantial aid of at least 100 million, plus an equal sum for the second five years of its life".[9] In total, West Indian leaders were asking for a development grant of £200 million.

The cash injection was considered a reparations payment, based on the belief "that Britain had a moral obligation". The federation concept was cast within a reparations model, and expectations were high. This was the context in which Bustamante thought, on reflection, a stronger public demand for development support should have been made, since the British owed the West Indies "millions of pounds". Furthermore, he stated, these funds should have been insisted upon as reparations claims when, in the 1940s, the ending of colonialism was being discussed.[10]

Exiting the empire "on the cheap", and amicably, with Britishness as a respected brand in the region, was Britain's long-term objective. The government worked to disavow West Indian demands. It offered instead a patronizing package of small grants, aid, loans and social welfare support.[11]

Wallace noted that while West Indian "demands may have been unrealistic, their needs were undeniable", a position some British officials considered true. Britain proceeded, nonetheless, to implement the suffocation of the federation.[12] The final offer was £1 million in cash up front, and the doubling of "its capital grant . . . from £500,000 offered in 1953 to £1 million".[13]

The West Indian moral position was no match for British financial power. The critical aspect of the British victory was shifting the conversation from an expectation of reparations to a discussion about loans and reaffirmation of welfare provision within the "grant in aid" colonial methodology. Importantly, support for small commercial or public sector projects would be subject to a quid pro quo principle. The Loans Council steered the demand for capital-development funding from reparations to a culture of debt. In every instance, the British government had the final say.

The deepest nail Britain drove into the coffin of federation was to ensure that the federal centre was weak financially and incapable of successfully lob-

---

9. Ibid.
10. Ibid.; J.F. Marham to H.A. Hankey, 15 June 1959, CO 1031/2039, no. 96.
11. Wallace, *British Caribbean*, 113.
12. Ibid., 114.
13. Ibid.

bying for substantial development capital. Britain intended this to facilitate intimate bilateral relations with individual territories, keeping them dependent while frustrating core administration. Federation policy, in this system, was minimized, leaving territories vulnerable to manipulation from London. The obvious outcome of this strategy was to render the federation unstable and lacking power to enforce its relevance.

Britain's success in dominating the discussion about structure, finance and governance placed the survival and operations of the federation inexorably in the hands of colonial officials. West Indian financial dependency was enforced while officers of Empire referenced their commitment to the region's development.

The British rejection of any reparatory obligation to promote economic development and integration in the region also served to define imperial policy. Colonial officials insisted that the federation should "obtain revenue from profits on the issue of currency" and from mandatory taxes levied in the areas of custom duties and excise taxes. Such federal revenue, they said, should be shared up front with unit governments.[14]

When, on 2 August 1956, the British Parliament passed legislation to enable the formation of the "British Caribbean Federation", it did so knowing that it had structured the governance model that assigned to the region responsibility for its neocolonial economic development and financial sustainability.

The queen was fully endowed with executive powers vested in her by the act. Her ability to exercise royal authority over the federation was administered through a governor general, intended to disempower Caribbean leadership. Britain had crafted a colonial federation at an anti-colonial time. It then proceeded to dispense with what it had created.

Federation governance and financial arrangements were finalized by Britain and sent to the West Indies with a message that no development funding was forthcoming to empower the labour movement. Manley called for "strength and patience and wisdom", but when his £2 million loan request was rejected, he too realized that the federation would soon be harpooned by Britain.[15]

The West Indian federation model, then, was re-engineered in London by colonial officials, remade in their imperial image, and sent back to the West Indies for implementation with an identity that contradicted Caribbean

---

14. Ibid.
15. Ibid., 122.

consciousness. It was understood domestically that the "foreign" version of federation would result in weak economic performance.

At the outset it was required to absorb operational costs of BWI$4,785,000, with BWI$2,175,000 coming from Kingston and BWI$2,413,000 from Port of Spain.[16] In this way the Jamaican and Trinidadian economies were expected to carry federation costs at a level West Indian leaders had not expected. Despite the impact of bauxite and oil production in Jamaica and Trinidad respectively, which did raise national income, mass poverty was the norm. Upon these weak economies Britain imposed the responsibility of funding the federation.

In 1956, the "average per capita annual income in Jamaica was BWI$510, as compared with $612 in Trinidad, and $283 in other British islands". In Jamaica, between 1952 and 1958, national income "more than doubled" and "exports increased by some 250 per cent". In Trinidad, the establishment of the Industrial Development Corporation in 1958, after Williams's 1956 electoral victory, facilitated a five-year development plan with a projected expenditure of BWI$250 million.[17]

Impressive growth rates were projected for Trinidad relative to Jamaica, but the glaring result was the revenue gap between these two islands and the rest of the much poorer region. This economic gap began to grow at a visible and alarming rate.[18] The wealth and income disparity, in the absence of British capital funding, created the context for colonial officials to manipulate concerns over inadequate funding and to stir up discontent in order to entrench division.

In Jamaica, for example, in the theatrics between Manley and Bustamante, the former was celebrated for his intellectual, regionalist rhetoric, while the latter was feared as the champion of workers' power. Both, however, agreed that Jamaican popular opinion was for federation as the fastest track to national independence. This, strategically, in the end, allowed Britain to take final aim at federation. It manipulated and managed a "Jamaica exit" option, with the policy shift that neocolonial dependency was better secured with multiple independent units rather than a sustainable federation.

On 3 January 1958, three million West Indians were federated under the governorship of a Conservative Party hardliner, Lord Hailes, whose reputation in the West Indies as an aggressive imperialist identified him as unsuited for

---

16. Ibid.
17. Ibid., 129.
18. Ibid.

the task. His choice by Conservative prime minister Harold Macmillan was intended to send a clear message to West Indian political leaders. There was no forgiveness in the heart of British politics for their violent revolt against the empire two decades earlier. No payout was the imperial payback message. Lord Hailes was sent to the region with this directive.

Managing Manley, Bustamante, Williams, Adams, Bradshaw and others was an impossible task. Lord Hailes's default plan was to muddy the waters in order to cause disagreement in respect of federation. In addition, he would buy time for his government to further its thinking about the region in order to stay credible for the rest of the century.

Lord Hailes cast West Indies leaders in the image of Oliver Twist – eternally ungrateful and wanting more! This perception of the federation festered among the British government and bred resentment. Hailes, like Moyne and Rance before him, sought to distance the British treasury from the dream of the West Indies of economic development.

The federal government received from the Colonial Development Corporation, not surprisingly, a paltry £9 million between 1959 and 1964. Most of his was distributed as follows:[19]

Dominica	£1,000,000
St Lucia	£900,000
Grenada	£540,000
St Vincent	£540,000
Barbados	£500,000
Jamaica	£250,000
Caymans, Turks and Caicos	£150,000
Trinidad and Tobago	£100,000
Federal government	£3,240,000

Hailes's thinking that led to this distribution was obvious: the richer countries would receive less and the poorer more, inflaming passions in the region because Jamaica and Trinidad would carry the bulk of costs incurred by the smaller islands. His divide-and-rule strategy of stoking factionalism was obvious to regional leaders, who could not but respond predictably. Hailes was in a hurry, as Rance had been.

---

19. Ibid., 153.

Most West Indian leaders understood the British strategy, but few were prepared to publicly oppose it. Some believed that standing close with the British government, on an individual basis, would yield greater results for them. This was the fragmented governance environment Britain had created using the Colonial Development and Welfare Fund.

Robert Bradshaw, the charismatic federal minister of finance from St Kitts, understood the issues better than most, and emerged as a vocal critic of the neocolonial version of federation. As a body without legs, he said, it could only "crawl along financially". He was adamant that without British reparatory funding, and with no other reliable sources of development capital, the federation could not achieve economic advance. The entire federal budget for 1959 was BWI$11,301,832, while Trinidad's budget, as approved by its domestic legislature, was BWI$140,000,000.[20]

But West Indian leaders persisted in the face of Britain's machinations and rejection of responsibility for its debt to the region. They were also aware that with or without a reparatory decolonization model, they had to "produce more, export more, work harder, invest more, and cooperate more fully". This was the only sustainable way to create "the nation as a viable political entity in this competitive world".[21]

In February 1960, the Jamaican representative at the meeting of the Regional Council of Ministers severely criticized the British government for drastically reducing colonial development and welfare funding for development projects. Premier Williams, feeling insulted by the sum allocated to Trinidad and Tobago, requested that the paltry amount be transferred to the University College of the West Indies in order to facilitate the creation of the St Augustine campus.

Williams also took the opportunity to expose the causes and consequences of Britain's deliberate underfunding of the federation. The financially weak centre, he concluded, could not push through the regional development agenda nor lay the foundation for the transition to independence for all. Angered that Britain had backed away from supporting the federation with the expected finances, he proceeded to lay out a road map for the singular independence of Trinidad and Tobago. Being "spiritually free" of British colonialization, Williams said, was the top priority of his government.

---

20. Ibid., 154. See Alan Lennox-Boyd to Sir Hugh Foot, 23 June 1956, CO 1031/1741, no. 319.
21. Wallace, *British Caribbean*, 154.

But this was precisely what the British were hoping to achieve in phase one – the fracturing of regional commitment to the federation. The British response was undoubtedly manipulative, conceding a little more ground, and then to impose their own judgement on the Caribbean discourse. Ian MacLeod, secretary of state for the colonies, informed the federal leaders in 1960 that "while independence implies an ability to stand on one's own feet financially as well as politically, Her Majesty's Government recognizes that the West Indies may not be able to assume at once the whole weight of the financial burdens which would normally fall to an independent member".[22] At the same time, he added, his government was "most concerned that the Federation was struggling to create an effective financial sovereignty".[23]

The British government moved the following year to establish a "Development Loan and Guarantee Fund" with a capital injection of BWI$8,200,000, half of which came from the US government. The objective was to promote projects in the region classified as developmental by the Colonial Development Corporation.[24] In March 1961, Prime Minister Macmillan, concerned that West Indian leaders had run out of patience in the expectation that there would be a respectful conversation around appropriate British funding, visited the West Indies to hold talks with the federal government.

Macmillan reiterated the doublespeak policy that his government would support the federation as a stabilizing and development institution, subject to the availability of funds. While leaders were happy to hear from him in the aftermath of his strong prior anti-apartheid speech on South Africa, they could not but agree that his presence represented the final brush-off, intended to finish the federation and restore West Indian political fragmentation as the ideal within the empire.

The cracks in the cheaply constructed "imperial" federation were everywhere appearing. In all parts of the region, underfunding was held to be the main cause of political tensions. In some social circles it was mischievously uttered that regional tensions originated in the lecture rooms of Oxford, referencing that Manley, Adams and Williams were graduates of the ancient British

---

22. Ibid., 170. See *Report of the British Caribbean Federal Capital Commission*, Sir F. Mudie, Col. no. 328, 1956; September 1956, CO 1031/1791, no. 177.

23. Wallace, *British Caribbean*, 170.

24. Ibid., 178.

university. Publicly, it was understood that British underfunding pressures were responsible for the crumbling.

It was Bustamante who, as victim and then as advocate of British policy, struck the first official domestic blow to the federation. While his language appeared inflammatory in terms of West Indian integration, the truth was that the federation, as it was recrafted at the 1956 conference by British hands, stood in the way of Jamaica's progressive anxiety about its national independence and the end of Empire.

Williams shared, even if privately, similar sentiments, but as the master of local politics he had achieved what Bustamante lacked: full, unquestioned control over his society. First, he had to overcome the influence of Manley. The decision to take Jamaica out of the federation was Bustamante's strategy to take Jamaica away from Manley. But in order to succeed he found it necessary to demonize the federation. He described it as an institution designed to impoverish rather than enrich Jamaica, and to reduce the nationalist image of Jamaica to a place run by the policies of the leaders of its smaller neighbours.[25]

Increasingly, Adams, as premier of the federal government, was forced to comment on the mounting evidence in Jamaica of dissent and anti-regionalism. After months of silence, he stated: "I have no comment to make, but if I said anything it would be an atomic bomb." This was as clear an admission of defeat and finality as could be expected from the former Barbados premier.[26]

Meanwhile, fear in the federation that Britain would use backroom channels to support Bustamante and turn the financial screws even tighter, especially in the Leeward and Windward Islands, had considerably increased. Independence for Jamaica and for Trinidad and Tobago would be the final cutting of the federal umbilical cord, which also meant the end of funding from the Colonial Development Corporation, on which they heavily relied. But Britain's dread of West Indian independence, in the hands of "socialist" labour leaders, was greater than its fear of a federation.

Williams, the historian, never lost sight of the signs of British tactics in respect to subverting the federation. He returned frequently to the recommendations of the 1897 Royal Commission report, in which it was admitted that the British, having brought black people from Africa for the sole purpose of

---

25. Ibid., 181; see Sir S. Luke to P. Kennedy, 20 September 1956, CO 1031/1743, no. 3.
26. Wallace, *British Caribbean*, 184.

enslavement for their enrichment, had a financial responsibility to them and the region. The federation, he concluded, was yet another twentieth-century opportunity that enabled Britain to shed this responsibility.[27]

Meanwhile, Adams continued in vain to call for meaningful capital support from Britain, above and beyond that provided within the social welfare paradigm. Press reports in the region intensified the perspective that the West Indian concept of federation had been restructured by Britain into a "Beggar's Opera".[28] The mother country, it was cynically stated, had decided to keep the West Indians in a federal union at a level to which they had always been accustomed.

The level of aid the federation received was not celebrated nor respected in the region, leaving imperial officials to comment on an alleged West Indian culture of ingratitude. Responses to expressions of this impression in the West Indies were invariably swift. The chief minister of St Vincent, for example, noted that proper and timely funding of the federation by Britain would have enabled the West Indies to achieve its development objectives.[29]

When the Leewards and Windwards pressed their claim for financial support, British officials directed the conversation to the constitution of the federation. The result was "a bitter attack . . . on Britain, whom they held responsible for all West Indian ills, from draining the islands of their wealth in past centuries to neglecting them in the twentieth. They insisted that Britain owed them a debt, and that the most appropriate way to honour it was with significant funding of their participation in the Federation. Without quality funding, they concluded, 'independence was meaningless'."[30] The leadership of the eastern Caribbean islands, following Arthur Lewis, was more inclined to be focused on the reparations agenda. Their tendency was to speak, not as one, but from multiple angles, even when it was with the same message. St Lucia, Montserrat and St Kitts, for example, expressed outrage at Britain's pushback on their proposals for development funding.

Finally, the eastern Caribbean came together and drafted a reparations plan for federation independence. They demanded "an interim payment of

---

27. Ibid., 186–87. See also CO brief no. 6 for the UK delegation at the London British Caribbean Federation Conference, 30 January 1956, CO 1031/1785, no. 2.
28. Wallace, *British Caribbean*, 188.
29. Ibid.
30. Ibid.

BWI$28 million and a guarantee of large additional grants to the Federation in the decade following independence to offset hardships caused by the moratorium on freedom of movement". Once again, the islands were fobbed off with clichés by London.[31]

This time, however, chief ministers in the Leewards and Windwards were vocal in their resentment of Britain's disrespect, and accused the government of breaching a prior agreement to provide significant project funding. The dialogue ended, according to Wallace, with participants "at each other's throats".[32] The ill will that overtook relationships within the federal government, then, originated in the British refusal to respect West Indian legitimate expectation. Anger towards Britain was internalized in West Indian politics and later determined the demise of the federation.

The deep rift that opened in the relationship between Manley and Williams, to the extent that they were not acknowledging each other, was rooted in Britain's refusal to provide adequate finance. The quarrel over customs union revenue – levies, taxes and other relatively small sums of money – festered as inflexible British positions pitted them against each other. Bustamante's hostility to the federation was part of a narrative that the underfunded federation was a "useless luxury" Jamaica could not afford. The contribution Jamaica was expected to pay to the federal budget was at least 43 per cent of the colony's total expenditure.[33]

The internal Jamaican divide, then, was deepened in large measure by the absence of adequate British funding. Manley made the impressive point that Jamaica had federal and regional obligations to be met with or without federation, such as support for the University College. Bustamante asked the local electorate, in an attempt to denigrate the federation, "Have you ever heard of federating poverty?" The poor would pay for the rich who would enjoy the spoils, he insisted, and Jamaica was subsidizing both Britain and the smaller islands, particularly in the eastern Caribbean.[34]

The decision by the British government in early 1962 to agree to Jamaica's

---

31. Ibid. See "Mr Manley's Seven Propositions", CO brief no. 15 for the UK delegation, 1 February 1956, CO 1031/1696, no. 369.

32. Wallace, *British Caribbean*, 189.

33. Ibid., 192.

34. Ibid., 193, 194, 196. See "UK Financial Assistance", CO brief no. 22, 1 February 1956, CO 1031/1737, no. 39.

secession from the federation, even though there were no articles of secession in the federal constitution, and to facilitate the process in London, was understood in West Indian circles as Britain's ultimate strategy to scuttle hopes of West Indian solidarity.[35]

West Indian political fragmentation was a British objective. Bustamante described the federation as Jamaica's "experimental trial marriage", which was peacefully terminated in a democratic fashion. Donald Sangster described it as a pause along the way to independence. Both concluded that to continue with the federation would be to impoverish the island. Bustamante by this time was also regretful that he had not publicized his view that reparations from Britain should have been paid as a precondition to federation.[36]

The bill to dissolve the federation followed a meeting in London in the first week of February 1962. The British Parliament debated it on 31 May and the House of Commons passed it on 2 April. Williams accused the British government of deception in not informing his government of these developments. When Adams went to London to meet government officials on 13 March, having heard of the British prime minister's intention to facilitate Jamaica's exit, he was kept waiting for a week, during which the wheels were greased to accelerate the end of federation. The same passion with which West Indian leaders were moving to end the empire was applied by the British government to end the federation.

While in London, the premier of the federation read reports of the British parliamentary debates and decisions in the daily press. He called it "shabby treatment" and "highly immoral", but it was much more than that. It was the final blow administered to rising West Indian political dignity by the hand of the dead empire.[37]

At the last sitting of the federation, Wallace noted, the British government was condemned for its subversion. Also deplored was that "successive Secretaries of State for the Colonies had made no effort to preserve the Federation".[38] It took five days for Adams to see Secretary Maudling, noted Wallace, and then the meeting lasted only fifteen minutes. At the stroke of midnight on 31 May

---

35. Wallace, *British Caribbean*, 207.
36. Ibid.
37. Ibid., 211. See Summary Record of the Third Plenary Session of the London British Caribbean Federation Conference, annexes 2 and 3, 13 February 1956, CO 1031/1754, no. 4.
38. Wallace, *British Caribbean*, 212.

1962, the West Indian dream died, buried by the British Parliament that never intended to see it succeed.[39]

Britain's was identified as the hand that held the dagger. Every reparations request placed before it was denied. Its cavalier setting aside of the idea of a debt to be repaid found a temporary resting place in Jamaica's federal exit, and in the personal humiliation of Adams. The federal government certainly felt betrayed by the secession politics of Jamaica and Trinidad and Tobago, but held to the conviction that it was ultimately Britain that had blood on its hands. A.N.R. Robinson of Trinidad and Tobago, for example, then a federal supporter, added that Britain, "having assisted in the formation of a weak and ineffective Federation, played an equally prominent role in its floundering".[40]

The demand for a reparations approach to decolonization had permeated West Indian thought about the federation from inception to ending. Equally, it featured centrally in the British government's strategy to extricate itself from any sense of responsibility for West Indian development. Britain held on to the self-serving notion that the West Indies, federated or not, should be financially forced to stand on their own feet.

This posture was understood in the region as strategic and discursive rather than a serious economic policy position. It shamefully illustrated how the economic exploitation of the region did not leave behind any legal or moral reflection on the consequences. Some British colonial technocrats, however, understood that the underdevelopment of the region was severe and required a significant capital injection.

The defeat of federation by Britain, in a tactical, warlike fashion, was never intended to be an end-of-the-line mission. Rather, it was part of a general post-1930s approach to suppress regional anti-imperialist culture and to bend the West Indian mind into subservience. By fostering in the region a compliant neocolonial mentality, built around an aid and debt approach to development, rather than economic partnership and development, West Indian nationhood was intended by Britain to be a dependent construct.

Britain ultimately intended to benefit from its own narrative and guidance of these events. It anticipated that the West Indian masses would emerge critical of labour leaders and consider neocolonialism a good choice, and furthermore,

---

39. Ibid.
40. Ibid., 214–15; Robinson, *Mechanics*, 46.

that the colonial heritage and its imperial support system would offer a better future than the nationalist alternatives. In other words, they would validate the legitimacy of British colonialism and perceive the nationalist strategy as not founded in carefully thought-out choices.

By juxtaposing old Empire with emerging nationalism, Britain sought to carry the marginalized "back to the future". The only way this could be achieved was discrediting the latter. The defeat of the federation was a key component in this long-term strategy. Keeping the "natives" in check and under control had been, from the beginning of colonial settlement, the principal imperial imperative. The objective was to craft the federation into an acceptable and ultimately rejectable shape, facilitate its dismantlement, bury it and prepare the region for a "dependent" independence – the new, post-imperial ideal.

The Colombo Plan: No West Indies, Yes East Indies

Popular rebellion in the West Indies was matched, and in some instances exceeded, by similar developments in the "East Indies". The empire was experiencing everywhere a groundswell of internal resentment, driven by nationalist surges that were stimulated by Garvey in the "West" and Gandhi in the "East". In 1919, for example, peasants and the landless poor in India rose up in the Amritsar community and demanded the end of British rule and independence. Mohandas "Mahatma" Gandhi, like Marcus Garvey, had raised popular consciousness above and beyond what the empire could absorb.[41]

The leader of the British troops wasted no time, as he did at Morant Bay, Jamaica, in 1865, in giving instructions to troops to fire on protesters. Over four hundred people were murdered by the military and at least one thousand wounded. General Dyer, commander in chief, was recalled, much like Governor Eyre in Jamaica, but not convicted of murder. Protest and rebellions continued across India during the 1920s. As in the West Indies, they reached a rebellious climax in the late 1930s, leading into the Second World War.[42]

---

41. See David Pierce, "Deolonisation and the Collapse of the British Empire", *Inquiries Journal/Student Pulse*, 1, no. 10 (2009), http://www.inquiriesjournal.com/articles/5 /decolonization-and-the-collapse-of-the-british-empire; Edwin Reubens, "Economic Aid to Asia", *Far Eastern Survey*, 10 January 1951, 6–12.

42. P.J. Cain and A.G. Hopkins, *British Imperialism, 1688–2000*, 2nd ed. (Harlow, UK: Pearson Education, 2002), 560–62; "Netaji and Gandhi: Two Titans of the Independence

Critical to the intensity of the Indian anti-colonial movement was the leadership of Subhas Chandra Bose and Jawaharlal Nehru, both to the radical left of Gandhi. They succeeded at the Madras Congress in 1927 in passing a resolution calling for the full, constitutional independence of their country. The Congress Party, backing the bravery of Bose, unanimously voted him president in 1938. He was subsequently arrested and imprisoned by the British government until the Second World War ended in 1945.[43]

In that year another popular rebellion took place in Calcutta, 21–24 November. This time the colonial police shot over two hundred protesters, killing thirty-three. Workers' rebellions continued across the country despite constitutional reform in 1942 in which dominion status was granted as political appeasement to anti-colonialists and for loyalty to the empire in the war effort.[44]

In much the same way that Churchill was satisfied that the Moyne Commission report in 1945 had pacified the West Indies, he thought it possible that the enormously publicized Sir Stafford Cripps Mission in 1942 would cool Indian political temperatures. The Cripps Mission, however, was a dismal failure. Rebellions and mutinies became the order of the day.

In response, the British government deployed Field Marshal Sir Archibald Wavell to win the hearts and minds of the Indians in his role as governor general and viceroy. As the political situation degenerated, Wavell issued the now-famous statement in 1946 that India had become "ungovernable", implying that its political independence was inevitable and should be immediate.

The British Empire in the West Indies at this time was surviving on fumes, while in the East Indies it was burning to the ground. India pressed for its independence and won it in 1947, followed by Ceylon and Burma in 1948 and Malaya in 1957. In 1948 West Indian leaders had agreed to the federation of the region en route to independence. But in 1950 the East Indies had generally detached from the empire and were preparing for transformative economic development and democracy.

Struggle", *India Abroad*, 24 January 1997; Ramesh Majumdar, *Three Phases of India's Struggle for Freedom* (Bombay: Bhavan, 1967), 57–60.

43. See Ranjan Borra, "Subhas Bose, the Indian National Army, and The War of India's Liberation", *Journal of Historical Review* 20, no. 1 (2001). See also Susmit Kumar, *Modernization and Islam and the Creation of a Multipolar World Order* (n.p.: Susmit Kumar, 2008), 16–20.

44. See Susmit Kumar, "Hitler, not Gandhi, Should Be Given Credit for the Independence of India in 1947", in Kumar, *Modernization*.

The Japanese invaded British Burma in 1942, illustrating British imperial weakness in the region. In March 1946, Prime Minister Attlee informed the House of Commons that the empire in the East Indies was rapidly crumbling. *Time* magazine of June 1947 featured Gandhi on its cover, symbolizing the American perception of the end of the British Empire in the East Indies. The West Indies, meanwhile, were prepared for the retribution Britain could not impose upon the liberated East Indians. While Britain humbled itself before them, it expressed intense hostility in response to the demands of the decolonizing West Indians.

But this was not where the divergent attitudes ended. Arthur Lewis had outlined an economic development plan for the West Indies that required Britain, and its allies the United States and Canada, to agree to a framework to guide structural transformation and economic modernization. Lewis intended also to promote policies to facilitate the mobilization of grant capital and other forms of financial support. The East Indians wasted no time in placing their requests for development support before Britain within the context of its leadership of the Commonwealth. The difference in response to the East Indies was extraordinary.

The East Indians, as did the West Indians, prepared for a postcolonial "comprehensive attack upon the problems of poverty and under-development". Taking advantage of their independent status and anti-colonial solidarity, Asians pushed forward with a vision of development intended to detach each country from Britain. Fully aware of their enormous potential for both capitalist and socialist transformation within the post-war global ideological divide, they transcended the binary choice with a strategy to give primary focus to capacity-building for economic production.[45]

Britain, initially driven by anger, eventually embraced the East Indian agenda. Embittered by the collapse of the empire in the East, government officials looked to the future and saw economic opportunities. They saw markets for British manufacturers and further options to cheaply extract Asian resources. Thinking of its own long-term economic expansion, Britain imagined the four hundred million colonial Asians as consumers of its exports. These circumstances coalesced to forge a reactive postcolonial diplomacy that provided the East Indies with the vital economic development framework denied the West Indies.[46]

---

45. Charles S. Blackton, "The Colombo Plan", *Far Eastern Survey* 20, no. 3 (1951): 28.
46. Ibid.

Britain and East Indian leaders agreed to use the meeting of foreign ministers of the Commonwealth, 9 January 1950, in Colombo, Ceylon, as the venue to present the vision. Ernest Bevin, British secretary of state for foreign and commonwealth affairs in the Labour Party government, agreed to support the development strategy wholeheartedly. It was also decided that Australia, and to a lesser extent Canada, would back the project, to be presented by Jawaharlal Nehru and Don Senanayake, representing India and Ceylon respectively.

The strategy was framed to provide Australia, representing a Euro-Asia bridge, with special lead responsibility on par with Ceylon. It was presented as a "Commonwealth initiative" but welcoming of the support of all Southeast Asia, Japan and the United States. In effect, Britain acting in support of the East Indies, had found and embraced a design to pull the Western world into alignment with Asian postcolonial economic development plans.[47]

The proposal became known as the Colombo Plan. It was bold, courageous and unprecedented. As a project, it called for "assistance from developed to developing countries [that] comprised both transfer of physical capital and technology as well as a strong component of skills development. Hence, while infrastructure by way of airports, roads, railways, dams, hospitals, plant fertilizer, cement factories, universities and steel mills were constructed in member countries . . . a large number of people were simultaneously trained to manage such infrastructure and the growing economies."[48] The idea of the plan originated in the thinking of K.M. Panikkar, a distinguished Indian diplomat, who saw an opportunity to encourage the departing British to remain relevant in South and Southeast Asia for mutual material benefit.[49]

The Commonwealth hurriedly established a consultative committee to workshop the concept. The first meeting took place in Sydney, Australia, 15 May 1950, under the guidance of Britain, but was chaired by the Australian external affairs minister, Percy Spender. The committee hammered out a three-year Commonwealth programme for East Indian economic development that entailed technical and capital support. Non-Commonwealth countries with an interest in the project were invited to participate.[50]

---

47. Ibid. See also G.M. Bryant, "The Colombo Plan: A Decade of Cooperation", *Australian Quarterly* 33, no. 2 (1961): 7–17.
48. See "The Colombo Plan", http:/www.colombo-plan.org/.
49. Ibid.
50. Blackton, "Colombo Plan", 28.

The United States endorsed the programme and issued a public statement of support. Britain hosted subsequent meetings of the committee later in the year which were chaired by the economic affairs minister, Hugh Gaitskill, signalling the beginning of a new era in East Indies postcolonialism. The six-year development plans of Ceylon, Pakistan, Malaya, Singapore, North Borneo, India and Sarawak were discussed and supported unanimously by the committee. The British government published the white paper on 28 November 1950. It was formally declared "The Colombo Plan for Cooperative Economic Development in South and South-East Asia" and was officially launched on 1 July 1951.[51]

Like the West Indies, "The Colombo Plan area", noted G.M. Bryant, an early critic, "is beset by illiteracy, poverty and low industrial and agricultural production which, allied to such killers as malaria, reduce human productive capacity and expectancy of life". Members of the plan were urged to pool their financial resources and enter bilateral development cooperation with Britain and the United States that served as its post-war patron with the Marshall Plan.[52]

The funding and technical support provided by Britain made West Indian leaders dizzy when they contemplated the dollar values. The enormous sums reinforced their belief that Britain's intention to punish the region was racist in origin and shamelessly self-serving. Britain had received since 1945 the sum of $6 billion in Marshall aid loans and grants from the United States and skilfully diverted some of these funds into supporting the Colombo Plan.

Britain, furthermore, resolved to use these resources to "provide a substitute for the declining idea of imperial tariff preference as a means of strengthening the British world system" and to promote the Commonwealth as "the most successful experiment in international organisation". In addition, investing Marshall Plan resources in the Colombo Plan did "help the United Kingdom to retain its position of primus inter pares in the Commonwealth".[53]

What Britain saw as a tangible result was an East Indian future in which it "would benefit further from improved sources of raw materials and enlarged markets for its industrial products". Estimates of £1.8 billion were considered reasonable to deliver the plan within six years.[54]

Britain, then, had shifted its gaze from the West Indies to the East Indies,

---

51. Ibid.
52. Bryant, "Colombo Plan", 7.
53. Blackton, "Colombo Plan", 30.
54. Ibid.

and was entering a new period and strategic place in terms of postcolonial engagement. The transition from an aid approach to an investment orientation contributed to the meteoric economic rise of the East Indies and further ruin in the West Indies. Charles Blackton noted: "Total British funds allocated to Far Eastern colonies under the Colonial Development and Welfare and other programmes will reach £47 million by March 1951. In addition, since July 1947 Marshall Plan funds have been utilized by Britain in some of her Far Eastern possessions; for example, $498,000 has gone for road-building in Malaya, North Borneo, and Sarawak. Burma, though no longer a Commonwealth member, received in 1950 a loan of £6 million", backed largely by the United Kingdom.⁵⁵ Only South Africa, which had declared itself an apartheid regime in 1948, was not invited to be a part of the massive British-led Commonwealth effort to rescue the East Indies from postcolonial disaster. The West Indies, meanwhile, abandoned by Britain in anger, were left to navigate the unsupported North Atlantic postcolonial globalization.

---

55. Ibid., 27.

Michael Manley, Jamaican prime
minister and democratic socialist

Maurice Bishop, leader of the Grenada
socialist revolution

Walter Rodney, Guyanese anti-
colonial academic/political activist

Lloyd Best, Trinidadian development
economist

Kari Levitt, Canadian-Caribbean
development economist

George Beckford, Jamaican
development economist

Norman Girvan, Jamaican
development economist

Clive Thomas, Guyanese development
economist

CHAPTER 11

Independence
Britain Exits on the Cheap

The fact is that financial assistance to several of the territories is at present required on a scale which is incompatible with the reality of political independence. If the Caribbean Federation is to become a full member of the Commonwealth there will have to be a combination of economic growth and assumption of the burden of assistance by the wealthier territories, in order to enable the Federal Government to pay its own way without being dependent for its very existence as such and as it may receive from outside.

—Alan Lennox-Boyd to Sir Hugh Foot, 23 June 1956, CO 1031/1741, no. 3/9

AS WEST INDIAN LEADERS MOVED ON from the demise of the federation to discuss independence, they took with them the prior claim for reparatory funding. There was persistent pressure on Britain to pay reparations in the form of economic development support, an expectation deeply embedded in the decolonization process. The theme took centre stage in every significant discussion. Successive British governments listened to such West Indian demands, and prepared to reject them with social welfare counter-discourses.

Independence emerged from the ashes of the federation. There was little time between the demise of one and the advent of the other. Heated debates ensued on Britain's debt to the region. Having publicly denied and denounced the debt, while privately acknowledging its legitimacy, British government officials expected the renewed advocacy.

British political historian Gordon Lewis suggested that West Indian leaders were "incredible optimists". While they understood that independence meant the creation of citizens with a full sense of national responsibility, he argued that they were not prepared to relinquish the reparation debt they believed was due to them as a right. He noted also that their ancestral loyalty in particular remained a central part of their thinking. This meant that the two centuries of free enslaved labour that Britain had extracted from the region to fund its own development could not be exorcised from their political imagination. The independence agenda kept the expectation of reparatory justice alive and active.[1]

Pressing the reparation claim was not seen as clinging to Empire for a financial handout. Neither was it, as Lewis noted, "the game of blaming the ex-colonial power for everything, however historically justifiable it may be". It was about demanding justice and standing taller at a time when to do so was considered a human right. Not to insist on reparatory economic demands would be to accept and ignore the crimes of slavery and colonialism and by so doing promote a culture of political apathy.[2]

Nation-building took the shape of a political and constitutional project that had resulted from the crimes of chattel slavery, indenture and brutal colonization. It reflected a commitment to economic development and detachment from the shackles of imperial legacies. It was simultaneously the struggle against external exploitation and internal class oppression. Reparations to support nation-building meant a "golden handshake" by which imperialists and nationalists settled a debt and agreed to move on. It was a special financial embrace, an injection of investment for independence, within the broad political policy of reparatory justice.

Independence, in effect, was a call on newly constituted citizens to take direct responsibility for accepting and alleviating the historical ills that persisted. The nation inherited the colonial mess, the socio-economic consequences of imperial wealth extraction, and sought to turn their legacies into a modern society. This would be the most burdensome and formidable aspect of nation-building. It was also expected that the passion which informed decolonization would typify nation-building.

Bustamante and British Contempt

In the first week of July 1962, British colonial secretary Reginald Maudling met with a Jamaican delegation in London led by Premier Bustamante. The purpose of the meeting was to discuss in broad reparatory terms "a financial settlement with Jamaica".

---

1. G. Lewis, *Growth*, 414–15.
2. Ibid.

Britain's finance advisers were keen to conclude a discussion that centred on providing Jamaica with a small grant based on a sum that was consistent with the aid received during the years of the federation. Bustamante's objective, however, was to maximize a capital contribution from Britain as part of Jamaica's independence. Britain's aim was to turn the screws on Jamaica more tightly and walk away from the discussion.[3]

The content of the Jamaica-Britain reparation negotiations was to set what was to be the norm in British dealings with the West Indies in their transition to independence. The British strategy, its officials noted, was to use a "needs" analysis in settling the basis for an objective jettisoning of Jamaica that could stand up to public scrutiny in the event of a diplomatic dispute. Jamaica, these officials noted, might have the largest number of slums, the greatest number of unemployed, the most illiterate people per capita, but it could also claim a high per capita income, twice that of the Leewards and Windwards, one and a half times that of Barbados, and seven times that of East Africa.[4]

Using this approach, British officials did not consider it a difficult negotiation to push aside Jamaica's insistence on reparatory grant funding for independence. What was required to accomplish this task was the application of technical calculations to extricate the British government from significant financial obligations. D. Kirkness, rising to the occasion, noted with typical Colonial Office aggression: "They have little claim on us, and our object should be to give them the least we can." It would be possible, he noted, to get away with a good deal with Jamaica on a "take it or leave it" basis. If they "want independence, let them have it on our financial terms".[5]

Kirkness was far from kind in his assessment of Jamaica's claim for capital assistance. He further added: "In view of the recent ministerial decision that new or increased overseas commitments could be accepted only if they were of exceptional importance to UK interests . . . no case could be made for the future of Jamaica falling within that category." Chancellor of the exchequer Selwyn Lloyd had announced in July the previous year that "the overseas aid budget of £180 million was the maximum the UK economy could sustain". The decision to keep Jamaica in the petty-cash end of financial

---

3. Notes of a meeting between Mr Maudling and a delegation led by Sir A. Bustamante, 2 July 1962, CO 1031/3489, no. 44.
4. Ibid.
5. Ibid.

support was consistent with the finance and foreign governance policy of the government.[6]

Before Bustamante entered the discussion, the stage was set for Britain's rejection or minimization of his requests. British officials had already determined that he was not intellectually capable of discerning their preparations and would be an easy prey for entrapment. They were confident in their expectation of the meeting and its outcome. One official stated: "The Jamaica delegation submitted a request for grants of over £2 million and loans of £10 million for the period up to the beginning of a new ten-year development plan in 1963, with assistance thereafter bringing the total to £14.5 million." Another added that from the perspective of the budget department of the colonial office, Bustamante's request was "preposterous".[7]

Angered by the rejection of his minimum request for independence financing, and unwilling to withdraw the proposal, Bustamante insisted on the need to negotiate further. When invited by the secretary of state to do so, he made the following statement:

> Jamaica's needs fell into two broad categories: First, there was the problem of immediate requirements. On assuming office, the new Government had found that it had inherited a liability of £6.1 million for the period up to March 31, 1962, with the result that no reserve funds were available for emergency purposes. There was also a deficit of about £4.5 million for the current year which could be met only by external loans.[8]

The Jamaica government, then, on attaining independence, had inherited a financial mess, and was considered fiscally compromised, if not bankrupt. The existing colonial government had dealt the new nation its first financial blow, from which it would not recover. It was forced to dig itself further into the hole by international borrowing.

Jamaica, therefore, at independence had inherited from imperial Britain the need for a fiscal bailout plan from Britain. It was an irony of history as unimaginable as it was immoral. As a colony since 1655, and the site of Britain's greatest wealth extraction, Jamaica had good reasons to feel further disrespected. Bustamante believed that Britain owed Jamaica a huge debt, and he was in

---

6. Ibid.; see also "Jamaica and the Common Market", 29 June 1962, CO 852/2064, no. 5.
7. "Jamaica and the Common Market", 29 June 1962, CO 852/2064, no. 5.
8. Ibid.

London to collect a part of it. His argument for taking his country out of the federation was that Britain had turned its back on its financial obligation to the region. He continued his plea: "The new government had also inherited a heavy commitment for the purchase of railway stock and the Industrial Development Corporation had borrowed from the banks over £1 million for the construction of factory buildings. Secondly, there was the need to secure low-interest-bearing loans for the proposed 10-year development plan which represented the minimum rate of growth possible which was satisfactory given the political economic circumstances in Jamaica."[9]

Furthermore, he considered it necessary to add that all available internal resources had been earmarked for the national plan and no more could be raised domestically by the issue of treasury bills. The private sector, he added, particularly the bauxite and hotel sectors, could not be called upon for additional funds. Jamaica, therefore, on the eve of ending colonialism, was in a severe fiscal bind and would enter independence with its back against the wall.

The British team did not accept Bustamante's case and rejected his narrative. The island, Bustamante concluded, stood alone "among a sea of discontent" in the West Indies. He emphasized that "the overall increase in . . . wealth in recent years had hardly touched the small man; 18% of the working forces still remained unemployed". In support of his leader, Edward Seaga chimed in and stated forcefully that "there was no correlation between incomes and the level of unemployment". Furthermore, "industrial development had resulted in only 8,000 jobs being found whereas 18,000 were required".[10]

Seaga's intent was to discuss the nature of the mess Britain left behind. He noted that the country had "secondary school places for only 7½% of children of school age and the house-building programme was meeting only one tenth of what was needed". Jamaica's development, Seaga emphasized, was strangled, despite the best local effort, without British capital support.[11]

The secretary of state responded that he was "very surprised" at the extent of the financial assistance sought by Jamaica, which was "completely out of line

---

9. Notes of a meeting between Mr Maudling and a delegation led by Sir A. Bustamante, 2 July 1962, CO 1031/3489, no. 44; see also Fraser to Brooke, 6 July 1962, CO 1031/3489, no. 41A.

10. Notes of a meeting between Mr Maudling and a delegation led by Sir A. Bustamante, 2 July 1962, CO 1031/3489, no. 44.

11. Ibid.

with what was expected; with what Her Majesty's Government might be able to afford, and with what other newly independent countries had sought". He dismissed Bustamante's requests as "unreasonable". Also considered unacceptable was his "assumption that external assistance would be available at three times the level at which it had been previously".[12]

The British response, then, was immediately packaged in language that defined as "preposterous" Jamaica's request, beginning with the belief that Britain owed it a debt. The negotiation that ensued between Chancellor Lloyd, the Colonial Office and the Jamaica delegation reinforced the British position that any reparatory request from the West Indies was outrageous. Government officials, nonetheless, were keen not to shame the Jamaica delegation, but to let it down gently with a trivial contribution.

The exchequer had identified the ceiling of £100 million for financial engagements within the crumbling empire. The small sum of £5.25 million was earmarked for the entire West Indies, excluding Guiana; Jamaica was expected to receive "at least £1½ million as appropriate". Officials agreed to inform Bustamante that no special financial provision would be made for Jamaica's first national strategic plan, and that he would receive what was set aside for "the Aid Programme forecasts".[13] The final financial package agreed consisted of

1. A grant of £600,000
2. A grant of £300,000 for the University of the West Indies (and its teaching hospital)
3. Grants of £100,000 to support national expenditure on regional services
4. A loan of £250,000 to support the 1962–63 development plan.

There was no capital injection that could be considered as reparatory in the context of colonialism. The £14.5 million Bustamante requested in grants and loans was knocked down to £1.2 million in total.[14]

The meeting led to an escalation of aggression against the West Indies by the British government. This was reflected in the tone and texture of the final discussion. Britain was moving full steam ahead to block the global discussion by the independence movement surrounding expectations of reparatory justice

12. Ibid.
13. Fraser to Brooke, 6 July 1962, CO 1031/3489, no. 41A.
14. Ibid.

funding. Defeating the West Indies' claim was top priority. High commissioners on the ground in the region provided the necessary intelligence that enabled the formulation of policy and its successful implementation.

High Commissioner Sir A. Morley on Bustamante's Jamaica

The British government's position on Jamaica, on the eve of its independence, was that the country was prosperous and not eligible for development financing to support nation-building. It made frequent references to the colony having a higher income per capita than the "small islands" and all of East Africa. This argument, critiqued by Seaga's intervention at the London meeting, was intended to steer Jamaica's leadership away from the reparations discourse. This was achieved, a government official indicated in July 1962, by giving Jamaica "the least we can".[15]

The second line of defence to Bustamante's reparations claim was to show that Jamaica's economic problems were of the making of its own politicians and not rooted in colonialism. British officials identified the island's main economic development challenge as residing not in mass poverty and the human-resource disaster Lord Moyne had seen in 1938, but in its "unfavourable wage/cost problem", the creation of an irresponsible labour union/politician alliance. The good news, the British government reported, was that Bustamante was not proposing nor practising "economic nationalism" or "Jamaicanization" and was "an effective supporter of the West".[16]

British high commissioner to Jamaica Sir A. Morley was asked to provide his government with an objective assessment of Bustamante's character and leadership and the country's potential for economic development. His report, submitted through Duncan Sandys, dated 23 October 1962, is uniquely instructive on how Britain prepared to subvert Jamaica and its leadership on the eve of national independence. After setting out a detailed historical analysis of the island's evolution as a colony, with special reference to its race, class and cultural features, he turned to the matter of Bustamante's character and ability as a political leader.

---

15. Notes of a meeting between Mr Maudling and a delegation led by Sir A. Bustamante, 2 July 1962, CO 1031/3489, no. 44.

16. Ibid.; "Future Prospects for Jamaica and for Trinidad and Tobago", note for Cabinet Committee, 20 December 1962, CAB 134/2153, LAC.62 (14).

The principal purpose of Morley's report was to discredit Bustamante so as to establish the argument that political failure on the island was an entirely domestic affair and should not be remedied with finances from the British tax-payer. Local leadership was foregrounded, rather than the 307 years of British wealth extraction. It would be "rash", furthermore, Morley said, to assume that the Jamaicans "fully understood" Westminster democracy, as borne out by the fact that "Sir Alexander could even toy with the thought of making himself Governor General".[17]

The harshness of Morley's opinion of Bustamante also reflected the British tendency to be disrespectful of leaders whose ideas about colonial exploitation they did not wish to hear or engage. Morley stated, in respect of Bustamante:

> In his seventy-nine years at least, he is scarcely capable of discursive thought or even of coherent oratory . . . his paternalistic appeal is essentially to the "quashies" (as the small farmers are known) . . . Although . . . [he] is somewhat of an opportunist and a demagogue – the final destruction of Federation was essentially his doing – his political position in most matters is to the right of Mr Manley and is even more uncompromisingly anti-communist.[18]

He argued further that Jamaica must bring "wage increases under some form of control", reduce the "high birth rate" and "export a proportion – some say as much as half – of her population" otherwise "all plans for development" will fail.

The unlikelihood of Bustamante achieving economic development targets, noted Morley, was due to his "age and limited intellectual capacity". Success would depend, he said, on Bustamante showing "himself capable of the statesmanship to throw off his past as a trade union boss and give Jamaica the leadership it needs". Without this, he concluded, "all might yet come to nought through plain inefficiency, too slow a tempo of work, and the lethargy which is the curse of the West Indian islands".[19]

However, Morley could not ignore the colonial legacy. He admitted, "For a substantial part of the British connection, we tended to neglect the West Indies." But if the Jamaican government "will act rationally, even if mistakenly, and free from the blind emotion of economic nationalism, the relationship with

---

17. "Future Prospects for Jamaica and for Trinidad and Tobago", note for Cabinet Committee, 20 December 1962, CAB 134/2153, LAC.62 (14).
18. Ibid.
19. Ibid.

Britain can be fairly bright". Also, if it could steer clear of "Jamaicanization", and allow British firms to operate with Jamaicans having a share of equity, the country would recover from the "current economic stagnation".[20]

Eric Williams's Rejected "Golden Handshake"

In November 1962, Williams addressed a gathering at the London School of Economics on British imperial exploitation of the West Indies. Few could claim a better knowledge of the subject than Williams, whose 1944 seminal historical text *Capitalism and Slavery* was globally celebrated.[21]

Before the speech, Williams was on record as saying the British government had politically betrayed the federation by financially subverting it. This position was commonly articulated in Trinidad and Tobago. He looked behind the popular rhetoric that Bustamante's withdrawal of Jamaica was the prime reason for its collapse. He understood first-hand that the British underfunding strategy had been effective. As a veteran researcher of British colonial policy, and the methods used to secure outcomes, he was not deceived.

For nearly thirty years, Williams had been a critic of British colonialism in the Caribbean. He had an extensive record of advocacy against the economic exploitation of the region, both as a public speaker and prodigious writer. He spoke and wrote about the subhuman conditions in which more than half of the black and Indian workers in the region were trapped. The white-supremacist economic system that did not sustain decent life for the social majority was his main target. "Sucking the orange dry" best captured his view of British rule.

Following Bustamante, it was Williams's turn to make a claim for British financial support within the framework of reparatory justice. In March 1962, he began the campaign for "significant economic assistance" from Britain. Colin Palmer's study of his strategy provides an excellent insight.

Trinidad and Tobago, Williams insisted, required reparations in order to sponsor nation-building. Without this support, he said, the region would choose the communist decolonization path championed by Castro in Cuba and Jagan in British Guiana. Democracy and economic development, he insisted, were the twin paths Trinidad and Tobago had chosen. The sustainability of the

---

20. Ibid.
21. Palmer, *Eric Williams*, 149.

emerging nation, he said, required the reparatory financial package known as "the Golden Handshake".[22]

Amicable future relations required this transaction as evidence of political integrity and ideological commitment to a shared vision of the future. Williams expected, therefore, a respectful "golden handshake" from Britain, and not the brush-off given to Bustamante. Williams was hopeful that Britain would provide him with a significant sum of capital in addition to traditional "financial aid for social improvement".[23]

Reparations for Independence

Williams referred to the financial reparations he requested as support for the "Equipment for Independence". He utilized concepts found in the Marshall Plan that highlighted the role of external capital injection on a large scale in financing economic development. Arthur Lewis had recommended such a plan in 1939. Williams's "Equipment for Independence" plan, then, was an attempt to frame a West Indian reparations strategy. A "golden handshake", he argued, was to equip his country with technical and infrastructural capacity as compensation for centuries of extractive colonial exploitation.

In the document submitted to the British government, Williams presented the case for "substantial British support on the occasion of . . . independence". It was designed as a moral discourse calling for justice against the background of historical wrongs and debilitating current legacies. The language was respectful, though tense and steely. This was no "beggar's opera". He made reference to "a parting gift" which he said was the right of a "departing colony". The expectation of a "gift", he said, was not "unreasonable".[24]

Capital was necessary, Williams noted, to "adequately equip" the economic vehicle for the journey to nationhood within the "Commonwealth caravan". He said, "It is of little value to question why we do not now possess all that we now require to play our part [in] ensuring the continuous progress." He concluded, "This is no time for recrimination over past neglect."[25]

---

22. Ibid., 139.
23. Ibid.
24. Ibid.
25. Ibid., 140.

Williams informed the British government that his country was not adopting a mendicant posture and had made very significant economic strides under his leadership. His government, he said, in the six years since 1956, had done more for the country than Britain had done in fifty years. The expected contribution to national development, therefore, was an excellent endowment.

This was not a Bustamante-style negotiation. Britain recognized the difference at the outset and in rejecting the claim, prepared for wrath from Trinidad and Tobago. Williams wrote:

> If the achievements of Trinidad and Tobago in the sphere of economic and social development during the past five years are to provide an argument for rejecting the new nation's request for reasonable assistance then, at the least for the benefit of those territories still on the road to independence, it should be made abundantly clear that self-help is a disqualification and that the United Kingdom would prefer to help those who do not help themselves.[26]

The "Equipment for Independence" plan called for funding to support national security and defence, social reform, economic institutional strengthening and capacity-building, and an extensive investment in social capital. Education, skills training, transport, public health and technological modernization occupied the plan's core. It was a comprehensive catalogue of development-support items that Williams placed before the British government.

As was the case with Jamaica, the local British high commissioner was called upon to provide the first line of attack by discrediting the request. There was a great emphasis, noted Sir N.E. Costar, high commissioner in Port of Spain, "on new industrial development", but it was "high-cost" and would not make "much impact on the growing unemployment". Dismissing Williams's claim, he advised his government that the premier and his ministers "need to concentrate on using better the resources already available and on tackling the country's problems – mainly labour unrest, unemployment and the strangling growth of population".[27]

The tactic of deflecting responsibility for the oppressive legacies of Empire, the colonial mess, was now the standard tool in the British political kit. Costar

---

26. Ibid.

27. "Future Prospects". See also "Jamaica and the European Free Trade Association", Cabinet External Economic Relations Committee on a proposal that Jamaica should join EFTA 14 June 1963, CAB 134/1777, EER (63) 78.

outlined in a report the many problems confronting the young country and placed these fully at the feet of Williams, soon to be "father of the nation". Using the concepts of wastage, inefficiency and incompetence, the British government, he said, could effectively blame Williams for their proliferation.

This was the same strategy used by High Commissioner Morley against Bustamante. He informed the secretary for the colonies:

> The Development Plan for the period 1958–1962 included new roads and bridges, hospitals, airport runways, schools and houses. . . . In the process employment was created, though much of it only temporary employment. In 1961 (and suspiciously close to elections time) the Government found some BWI$6 million for a "Crash Programme" of work to provide employment. But the funds were badly administered, and the programme amounted to nothing more than a "dole" for a few thousand workers for a few weeks. This same inefficiency of administration was evident throughout the whole Development Programme.[28]

It angered Williams that the British government, which had never conceived or implemented a development plan for Trinidad and Tobago, was intensely critical. But Costar did not end there. He listed the specific technical, professional and educational limitations of Trinidad and Tobago and implied that, as a consequence, Williams's development ambitions were doomed to failure.

"Inefficient administration", Costar added, was accompanied by "an acute shortage of competent staff in government, at both the administrative and technical levels". Projects were planned, he said, but left incomplete:

> A new technical college is built with Colonial Development and Welfare funds but stands empty, having neither teaching staff nor equipment . . . millions are spent on a splendid new road to open up a beach, while overcrowded hospitals and slums fester. The government is full of ideas and ideals but lacks the talent, the know-how and the drive to implement them. In part, this lacuna stems from the Prime Minister himself.[29]

The "blame the leader" tactic was a standard element in the art of colonial management. It was ingrained into British national consciousness not to take official responsibility at any time for the hardships experienced by the colonized.

Costar saw his task in these terms: to belittle Williams's political ambition

---

28. "Future Prospects".
29. Ibid.

and to rescue Britain from an official conversation on reparations. His official reports are replete with the suggestion that Williams's alleged wastage and incompetence should discredit his claim for any significant development finance from the British treasury. He noted: "The Government's second priority in these five years was the attraction of new industries by means of incentive legislation and the creation of an Industrial Development Corporation. It sought to achieve additional employment and a diversification of its industrial activity. But neither of these objectives was achieved."[30] Williams was now "short of cash", Costar stated, and his new government had turned to all sources in "the quest for capital for future developments". The nationalist government was seeking contributions from major companies in the territory, Costar stated, and so far had received firm promises of BWI$26 million. Furthermore, it announced on 21 November that the US government had agreed to give it BWI$51 million in grant finance over five years. But its "immediate preoccupation", Costar concluded, was with the United Kingdom, as a market for exports and critically for the "raising of finance for continued development".[31]

Costar's cynicism and criticisms gave Williams no space with which to negotiate with the British government. He stated that Williams's tour of Europe, and his financial bid before it, had been widely publicized to his electoral base, who will now "undoubtedly expect him to return weighted down with European money bags". He added that he feared, however, "that the Prime Minister himself may have to learn the unpleasant truth that there are no vast sums waiting to flow . . . into the public sector developments".[32]

The Big Let-Down

While Williams was making his bid for the golden handshake, the British government was planning a bronze goodbye. The specifics of his request were:

£750,000 in grants for national security
£3,000,000 in loans for working-class housing and slum clearance
£2,000,000 in loans (no more than 2 per cent in twenty years) for infrastructure
£3,100,000 in loans and grants for Tobago's economic development

---

30. Ibid.
31. Ibid.
32. Ibid.

£100,000 for a University of the West Indies campus

£2,500,000 in loans for a modern national telephone system

Altogether, with additional smaller requests, Williams's demand was for nearly £12 million – £2.2 million in grants and £9.3 million in loans. He expected that Britain would "bear a reasonable portion of the cost of such operations as a contribution to the economic development of the islands".[33]

In addition to these capital requests, Williams informed the British government that his new five-year development plan, designated as the independence transformation strategy, carried a price tag of £10 million annually. He considered the request for British capital support modest, noting that his government would be taking responsibility for four-fifths of the sum and Britain a mere one-fifth. According to Palmer: "Colonial officials must have experienced apoplectic fits in reading these detailed and often sharply worded documents. Although they had grown accustomed to Williams' caustic comments about imperial behavior and neglect, these documents were requesting the kind of financial assistance that they were unwilling to imagine, much less contemplate."[34] Williams was not prepared to genuflect to the British government on the matter of its imperial obligation. He was a scholar of the outflow of wealth from the West Indies, and considered an inflow at the end of Empire an ethical matter.

It did surprise Williams, nonetheless, that Britain was cold in responding to his expectation. He was informed by Hugh Fraser, a colonial office insider, that he was way out of line, from Britain's perspective, and rather than £12 million, a £2 million proposal was a more likely figure for serious discussion. That conversation took place on 10 July 1962. Two days later, news reached Williams that the British government had rejected his request and had also turned down his prior one-off request for a short-term loan of £589,000 to meet an urgent national challenge.[35]

The British government was sending Williams a clear message in phases, driving a wedge between the anti-colonial scholar/activist/prime minister and his nation, and reaffirming the imperial policy of retreating scot-free from its

---

33. Palmer, *Eric Williams*, 142. See also CO brief no. 23, 11 January 1962, CO 1031/4269, no. 42; on the collapse of the federation, see Sir H. Poynton to Maudling, 19 March 1962, CO 1031/3509, no. 12B; on the possible federation of the Little Eight, see memorandum by Mr Maudling for Cabinet Colonial Policy Committee, 6 April 1962, CAB 134/1561, CPC (62) 14.

34. Palmer, *Eric Williams*, 142.

35. Ibid., 143, 144.

harmful colonial legacy. Williams went on the offensive, communicating his outrage to Britain for seeking to bury his young nation as it had the federation. He told his party supporters that they must start with national independence, understanding "Britain is not going to help" and had no interest in the West Indies whatsoever. He concluded that "in the United Kingdom everybody was absolutely fed up with the West Indies".[36]

Britain had adopted a penny-pinching position in dealing with the West Indies, which had been the primary external source of its early wealth and economic development. Trinidad and Tobago was officially placed at the bottom of the benefit bucket, on the basis that it had the highest per capita income in the West Indies. Colonial officials knew that the oil economy had created a super-rich elite who lived above and far beyond the masses of very poor people. The same argument was used to jettison Jamaica's request.

The oil income, Williams stated, like that of bauxite in Jamaica, had grossly distorted income per capita calculations. He knew that Britain would use this methodology against him. The British position on capital support was made even clearer to him on the eve of independence, when Costar advised: "our object, therefore, will be to give the least we can", and "if Trinidad wants independence, especially in a hurry, our aim should be to let it be on our own financial terms".[37] The identical advice was given to the British government by its high commissioner in Kingston, Sir A. Morley.

When the dust settled, Williams was made an offer which he had no choice but to refuse. Its timing was intended to back him in a corner and to make him absorb the lesson in how the British Empire could strike back. Two ungenerous gifts were presented – both of £500,000. One was for support to acquire four Viscount aircraft for British West Indian Airways (already on charter) and the other unspent funds allocated by the Colonial Development Corporation. There was also a development loan of £1 million.[38]

Meanwhile an internal quarrel had developed in the British government between officials in the colonial office and those in the treasury department in respect of the harsh treatment meted out to Williams. The former wanted to

---

36. Ibid., 144.

37. Ibid.; see also N.E. Costar to Sir Garner, 31 August 1962, CO 1031/3494, no. 37; "Note on the Finances of the Federation of the Little Eight", 24 October 1962, CO 1031/3376, no. 258.

38. Palmer, *Eric Williams*, 145.

go beyond the bare-bones approach insisted upon by the treasury, which they admitted was "little better than a calculated snub" – worse than that given to Bustamante. Nevertheless, within this context Williams understood that his "Equipment for Independence" plan, and other specific reparations requests, were a dead matter.[39]

Knowing he had been treated with deliberate disrespect, Williams, in outrage, wrote a letter to Macmillan informing him of his "inability to give serious consideration to his offer". In turn, the British government informed Williams that his letter to the prime minister was a grossly disrespectful missive, beyond the pale of appropriate political correspondence.[40]

Williams's rage could not be contained nor regulated by any British official. The treatment he received was consistent with what he had known about British colonization. First there was Adams, then Bustamante, and now himself. His expectation of a change of policy was informed by what he considered a new beginning. Trinidad's departure was also the ending of the empire in the richest West Indian colony, strategically significant because of its oil resources.

Williams was a master politician with the finest British education. But the British knew of no other way to deal with him other than with spite and a fair measure of malice. Despite recognizing his considerable intellectual capacity and domestic public adulation, British officials juxtaposed him with Bustamante, whom they considered beneath them. Williams, more than any other leader in the region, had all the necessary knowledge to understand that Britain simply wanted the cheapest possible exit from its West Indian imperial obligation.

The disrespect shown to West Indian leaders by the British government had much to do with the lingering bitterness in Britain over the popular uprising against the empire in the 1930s. It was believed that its leaders were guilty of driving the deepest nail into the imperial coffin. Britain's first colonies were turned into a battlefield, leading in short time – less than thirty years – to the collapse of Empire in Africa and Asia.

By seeking to save face before a watching and democratizing world, Britain was forced to participate in the demise of its imperial glory. The West Indies, where the mighty empire began, had signalled to the world that a small axe could fell the mightiest tree. The British government was determined, with cloak-and-dagger diplomacy, to punish them for their audacity.

---

39. Ibid., 148.
40. Ibid.

P.J. Patterson, Jamaican prime
minister, pan-Africanist and
reparation advocate

Jean-Bertrand Aristide, Haitian
president and reparation activist

Ralph Gonsalves, prime minister
of St Vincent and the Grenadines,
reparation and social justice activist

Mia Mottley, prime minister of
Barbados, reparation advocate and
anti-colonial strategist

Portia Simpson-Miller, Jamaican prime minister, feminist and reparation supporter

Gaston Browne, prime minister of Antigua and Barbuda, anti-colonialist and reparation advocate

Lord Anthony Gifford, British law lord and legendary reparation advocate

David Comissiong, Barbadian pan-Africanist and reparation leader

CHAPTER 12

West Indian Nation-Building, or Cleaning up the Colonial Mess

An administering power is not entitled to extract for centuries all that can be got out of a colony and when that has been done to relieve itself of its obligations by the conferment of a formal but meaningless – meaningless because it cannot possibly be supported – political independence. Justice requires that reparations be made to the country that has suffered the ravages of colonialism before that country is expected to face up to the problems and difficulties that will inevitably beset it upon independence.

—Sir Ellis Clarke, address to the United Nations Committee on Colonialism, 1964

SIR ELLIS CLARKE, TRINIDAD AND TOBAGO'S representative to the UN's Committee on Colonialism, was emphatic in the 1960s that Britain should not be allowed to walk away from the West Indies without paying reparations. Speaking at the United Nations that year, he pressed the case. Britain mobilized its power in the international forum to oppose the West Indian argument. It was a historically determining display of global authority by one of the world's largest imperial powers.

Sir Ellis situated his call for reparations in the context of Britain's intimidation of West Indian leaders who had championed the cause for three decades before Jamaica and Trinidad and Tobago finally opted for national independence in 1962. He spoke in solidarity with the leadership of emerging West Indian nations in much the same way that Arthur Lewis had done in 1938.[1]

Gordon Lewis summarized Sir Ellis's 1964 seminal statement as the West Indians' first attempt to place the matter of reparations on the global agenda. It was a powerful presentation that ran into a wall of European opposition.

---

1. See G. Lewis, *Growth*, 410.

The West Indian case, however, had arrived at the apex of global diplomacy.

The most effective way to describe the British strategy, Lewis added, was that it tried "to fob off West Indians with independence on the cheap". It succeeded "in an evasive fashion" in achieving this outcome by insisting that "West Indian domestic difficulties" were home-grown, and not of an imperial nature. This discursive notion was used originally as a tactic but evolved into "an excuse for British inaction to meet the moral issue involved".[2] Furthermore, he summarized West Indian resentment and outrage:

> West Indians, generally, felt this kind of attitude to be shabby treatment. They were, after all, they felt, entitled to something better as, historically, the first of all British colonies to be settled. They quoted the observations of the greatest of all Royal Commissioners ever sent out to the region, as the West Indies could claim, that Britain had placed the labouring population of the West Indies where it was and could not divest itself of the responsibility for its future.[3]

It was not possible to deny, Lewis insisted, that Britain's "divestiture of responsibility was in hard truth the . . . motive throughout". The government intended all along to punish the West Indians for their rebelliousness. That much was clear, he surmised. But what West Indian leaders found most disturbing, he noted, was the way in which the ill treatment was executed, with a disgraceful disregard for "British manners" and the "code of the English gentleman class".

The disrespect shown the West Indians, for example, by colonial secretary Reginald Maudling, said Lewis, was in showing "his face set angrily" as he chastised them like an "ill-tempered schoolmaster". This was the "crowning humiliation". It was the final, obvious proof that Britain intended to punish the region for its insistence that a debt was owed and should be paid.[4]

Gordon Lewis, then, confirmed the general proposition advanced in this analysis of British policy towards the West Indies. This intention was obvious to all who participated in the negotiations. His reference to "anger" in the face of Secretary Maudling and the abandonment of "manners" in dealing with West Indian leaders reflected the rage against them within the British government.

With the defeat of the federation in 1962, the West Indian community crumbled into conflicting and acrimonious independent nations. The process

---

2. Ibid.
3. Ibid.
4. Ibid., 411.

of separateness was celebrated with the same triumphant carnivalism that had accompanied the federal achievement. By the end of the decade, Jamaica, Trinidad and Tobago, Barbados and Guyana had raised national flags, setting in train a trajectory for the remaining colonies. Britain had won.

The dust raised by this parade had blurred the political atmosphere, but some leaders saw clearly that Britain was quietly slipping away from the spirited colonial scene in celebration of its own strategic achievement. It too had danced to the sound of decolonization, but paid just a few pounds for the privilege.

Colonial officials recognized that West Indian revolt had shortened the projected life of the empire. Against this background they recommended to their government that the pound sterling should not finance post-rebellion West Indian development.

The two decades that followed the 1944 winning of adult suffrage in Jamaica represented the period during which which Britain won the war to de-finance decolonization. First, it fiscally suffocated the workers'-movement version of federation and, second, it effectively turned the colonies against each other in a competitive, divisive political catastrophe. The finessing of the federation defeat was followed by the even more successful strategy of denying capital obligations to the region. With the bamboozling of Bustamante, the punishing of Williams, and the diminishing of Adams, Britain effectively pushed aside the empty, outstretched West Indian hands.

With the federation defunded and defunct, and with underinvestment in the transition to national states, Britain had achieved its objective of impressing upon West Indians that they were on their own. Using the language of imperial authority, the region was told that it was to stand on its own feet. It was the first time in three hundred years it was told to do so. Significantly, it was done with anger and aplomb.

The critical success of Britain, however, in exiting its West Indies obligation was to convince its leaders that the underdevelopment caused by centuries of wealth extraction was now theirs to address as nation-builders. The attempt to persuade Jamaican leaders, for example, that the country's extreme and persistent poverty was rooted in overpopulation and high wage costs made significant inroads in national consciousness.

The penetration of the imperial narrative enabled Bustamante to accept that endemic poverty and extreme inequality in the new nation were an inevitable part of the order of things. The social degradation of the poor within the economic systems of the rich was effectively normalized in the assumptions of national planners. The critique of mass poverty was tentative and its alleviation considered as the exclusive responsibility of the state.

The discourse surrounding British debt was driven underground and soon vanished from official communications and parliamentary discussions. This state of affairs became the norm across the region, though Williams, whose distinguished academic mind was dedicated to revealing how British imperialism had sucked dry the West Indian "orange", continued to deny Britain victory by declaring Trinidad and Tobago a republic.

Meanwhile, Arthur Lewis had prepared to adopt the United States as his new home. He minimized professional contact with Britain, which had disrespectfully dismissed his vision and strategy for West Indian development.

His thinking evolved considerably between the 1930s and 1970s. He moved some distance away from his original position in respect of development policy recommendations. Lewis did not, however, abandon the core belief that Britain owed the region a debt for two hundred years of unpaid labour. The evolution of his early ideas, and the embrace of market-driven economic development concepts at the core of his pragmatic advice to West Indian governments, was not an intellectual retreat. Rather, he chose to focus on what each moment could bear, seeking always to confront realities with solutions that seemed financially practical and politically viable.

For Williams, the veil that had partly hidden the British intent to punish and push aside West Indian leaders finally came down, in two phases. First, on return from a tour of Britain and Europe, he unsuccessfully made the case for development funding; second, he received intelligence that the "measly million" offered him by the British had been upstaged by a "golden handshake" of £50 million offered to Kenya and Malta.[5]

It was at this moment that Williams finally digested the British anti-development design as it was set out by Sir N. Costar, high commissioner to Port of Spain. "Surely we could afford to spend some money in the West Indies", Williams informed Costar, "and not put it only into places where we had a strategic interest like Kenya and Malta". Williams, Costar concluded, "is clearly

---

5. See Costar to Sykes, 29 July 1964, FO. 371/173580, no. 57; see also 27 November 1964, no. 99.

irked at our £50 million independence settlement for these two countries".[6]

Why did the West Indies not receive an "independence settlement" of millions of pounds in development grants, as did Kenya and Malta? The first part of the answer is clear: that Britain had moved on from the West Indies in terms of its strategic interests. Indeed, Costar had informed his imperial bosses that "our best interests might be served by further withdrawal as occasion permits". Furthermore, he said, current West Indian nationalists like Williams, who believed that Britain owed the region and should "help it on its way with a large endowment", were an impediment to the West Indian cause.[7]

On 15 March 1965, the British government issued a memo on the state of the West Indies and their relationship to the empire. West Indian leaders, it noted, continued to believe that Britain owed them a significant sum of reparatory finance, an approach which on every occasion was rejected. Furthermore, they were having challenges realizing that they "no longer have the strategic and commercial importance for Britain they had in the eighteenth century".[8] The region was of great commercial and strategic value during the height of the era of sugar and slavery. West Indian leaders, the British government quibbled, needed to wake up and realize that the eighteenth and twentieth centuries were quite a long distance apart.

While fine-tuning perspectives in the 1960s on reduced commitment to the West Indies, British officials were clear that the region's marginalization was the inevitable outcome. When, for example, Colonial Officer Greenwood informed the cabinet that West Indians needed to embrace their twentieth-century strategic irrelevance, he also commented that they were far more important from the American vantage point, "located as they are in an internationally sensitive area". The Americans, then, for geopolitical purposes, he said, should be urged to take more interest in their future welfare. The time had come to send the region on its merry way.

Costar was in broad agreement with Greenwood. Commenting in 1964 on the growing conflict between Williams and Bustamante, leaders of the two independent states, he advised the Colonial Office that the West Indies were threatening to become high-cost as a consequence of their constant demand

---

6. Costar to Sykes.

7. Ibid.

8. Greenwood to Cabinet Defence and Overseas Policy Committee, 10 March 1965, CAB. 148/26, OPD (65) 51.

for development support: "To sum up, I would at present advise against any avoidable involvement in the domesticities of the West Indies. Indeed, our best interests might be served by further withdrawal as occasions permit. But when some of today's leading West Indian personalities move off the stage, more positive British encouragement of Caribbean cooperation might be generally welcome. This will be the time to help."[9] He wrote, furthermore, with obvious glee, that Williams was "irked" by the "independence settlement" offered to Kenya and Malta.

It was obvious from his correspondence that Costar held a considerable measure of disregard for Williams both as a scholar and anti-colonial statesman. He wrote in respect of Williams's scholarship:

> In his mind, colonialism is the cause of most of the trouble in the Caribbean; indeed, of most of the troubles in the world. The theme of his book, "Capitalism and Slavery", recently reissued, was that Britain gave up slavery, not on humanitarian grounds, but just because it no longer paid. Likewise, he says that today we give up our colonies because they too no longer pay, and that the ex-colonial power still maintains a position of economic advantage.[10]

Furthermore, he noted: "It is true that in recent years Dr Williams has frequently condemned Britain for a lack (in his eyes) of a Caribbean policy. But this really means, to him, the lack of a policy to bring the Caribbean under his sway, and to help it on its way with a large endowment." He concluded that the end of Williams would be "the time to help" the region with a supportive policy.[11]

The £50 million reparations settlement offered to Kenya and Malta informed the beginning of Williams's cold war with Britain. The data assembled by British diplomats were released as follows: "Over the past years Britain has disbursed in aid to the Caribbean area, including British Guiana, and Trinidad and Jamaica before independence, a sum of about £88 million. British aid to British Honduras and the territories of the eastern Caribbean in colonial development and welfare money and grant in aid is now running at about the rate of £4½ million in a year."[12] But it was not Williams alone who placed these aggregates in their proper, minuscule per capita context, but the Americans.

---

9. Costar to Sykes, 27 November 1964, FO 371/173580, no. 99.
10. Ibid.
11. Ibid.
12. Ibid.

They came to Williams's defence and expressed concern over Britain's under-funding of the West Indies. Since the Bay of Pigs military disaster they were keen to expose Europe for the impoverished state of the Caribbean – which was on their doorstep.

The Americans' policy target was Britain's refusal to support West Indian independence with a reparatory settlement similar to, or greater than, what was offered other colonies. They did not accept as satisfactory the British idea of granting development support according to Britain's own strategic objectives. To this end Washington critiqued London's unsupportive trade and investment policy in the West Indies. The State Department, in contrast, formulated an approach to development that led to negotiations with independent countries in the Caribbean. Canada similarly opted to invest in the region, providing a significant source of capital for private sector projects.

The United States and Canada, therefore, prepared to fill the development void created by Britain in the West Indies. Canada increased its annual development grants to the region between 1962 and 1968 from $2 million to $10 million. The United States offered to match this sum, leaving the United Kingdom politically embarrassed. The UK ambassador to Washington commented on this circumstance: "The aid we are giving [the Caribbean] does not begin to compare with what the Dutch, French and Americans have done for their territories. Moreover, if it ever got out [as it would] that we had turned down the American initiative, our name would be mud in the British Caribbean."[13] He understood the extent to which Britain's treatment of its West Indian colonies, on the verge of their independence, was not ethically sound within the Euro-American context.

Washington embassy officials reported comparative covert intelligence on the circumstances. It was stated in a formal communiqué: "Internal inquiries in the Colonial Office revealed that in 1963 the French had given $95 million (in aid and loans) to Martinique, Guadeloupe and French Guiana." The evidence of Britain's meagre development support in the West Indies became a flashpoint in global diplomacy.[14]

In specific respect to the Windward Islands, Colonial Officer Kirkness minuted the following for the British cabinet:

---

13. Ibid.
14. Ibid.

> After a visit to the Windward Islands, there is a need for a higher level of develop-
> ment assistance if we accept, as we have done tacitly for years, that these islands
> must have a level of services a good deal above what we would think necessary
> in Africa or Asia. The condition of the schools and hospitals . . . is in most cases
> deplorable, because such aid as we have been able to provide has had to go to
> more important economic priorities.[15]

He indicated that the American initiative to invest in the West Indies not only
compromised the British, but validated the claim that his country, compared
with the French, was mean-spirited.

The Americans offered to increase the value of grants and loans far above
the British threshold, but invited the British to match it in the interest of
the region. British officials, still pushing back against West Indian requests
for funding for development, advised their government that if it should take
up the American offer, "It should be in the form of loans and not grants." In
their opinion, the American suggestion of matching funds was "unfair". They
recommended that Britain, as a "good political gesture", and no more, should
"make some part" of the increase "available in the form of soft loans", if only
to appease Dr Williams, who had been "clamouring" for them.[16]

The decision of the British government to accept the American and Canadian investment intervention was driven by fear of the West Indian backlash.
The truth, said M.Z. Terry of the Colonial Office, was: "The UK Government
will continue, as in the recent past, to be unable to do anything substantial
to help. We can keep them ticking over at their present low level by means of
our grant in aid 'dole'. . . . [S]ince there is virtually no local capital available
to promote development, the only hope is to attract external capital aid from
non-UK sources."[17] Her suggestion was followed by additional statements in
support of the North Americans coming to the rescue of the West Indies. She
added:

> Nor do I think that we need be unduly disturbed that the Americans have asked
> for an indication of our own likely aid to the area before committing themselves.
> These territories were, after all, a strictly British responsibility, (and no one who
> has seen them can be too complacent about our trusteeship). These are not,

---

15. Ibid.
16. Ibid.
17. Ibid.; M.Z. Terry, minute on the new American proposals, 8 February 1965, OD 20/234.

however, an American responsibility, and it is a generous and imaginative gesture they are making in suggesting that they might help to share our burden.[18]

The eastern Caribbean islands badly needed development support, she stressed, and Britain "can no longer afford to give" them what they asked for. Critically, she added, it could only be "helpful to long-term British interest to attract American aid into the area", since without "substantial development", the United Kingdom "will be forced to go on paying out grants in aid till the end of time".[19]

Britain decided, in a benign fashion, to promote North American participation in filling the financial needs of the West Indies, while taking an arm's-length approach. Building on the judgement that the region was of greater "strategic and commercial importance" to the United States than to the United Kingdom, it was expected that the British government would step back and allow the United States to step forward.[20]

The British decision to encourage a federation of the eastern Caribbean (the Little Eight) required the convening of a conference in London in 1965. The invitation to show an expression of interest went out to the leadership in the subregion. The responses to the invitation were not what the British government expected. It had announced previously that it was not taking up the responsibility of funding the proposed new federation. Greenwood informed the cabinet:

> At one stage, the Governments concerned declined to come to a conference at all until the British Government had stated how much aid it was prepared to make available to a Federation during the first 10 years of its existence. They tried in fact to get the British Government to guarantee the finance for the full cost of the proposals of the Economic Survey . . . estimated at about £59 million over a 10-year period. This the British Government declined to do.[21]

The proposed federation came unstuck precisely on the same broad issue – Britain's refusal to compromise with West Indian leaders in respect of development finance.

---

18. Terry, minute.
19. Ibid.
20. Ibid.; Greenwood to Cabinet Defence and Overseas Policy Committee, 15 March 1965, CAB 148/20, OPD (65) 51.
21. Greenwood to Cabinet Defence.

The British counterproposal in each instance was the dismissive treatment that killed interest, deflated energy and redirected the discourse in the opposite direction. The counterproposal from Her Majesty's Government, on this occasion, Greenwood reported, outlined the well-known refusal guidelines. It stated:

> Government gave them the assurance in February 1964 that if Federation can be brought about on satisfactory terms, British aid will continue and that over the first five years of Federation, the amount will be not less than these territories are together receiving from Britain at present. They have again said that they do not regard this assurance as satisfactory; but they are prepared to come to a conference without imposing any preconditions about aid though they will not finally agree about Federation until the question of their external aid is decided.[22]

Again, the position of the British government was to brush aside the proposal by offering minimum financial support.

Britain's shifting of development responsibility in the West Indies to the Canadians and Americans was based on the advice of its diplomatic and colonial officials. Greenwood ended his cabinet briefing with the following statement:

> The fact that the area requires so much external economic assistance lends urgently to the need for encouraging other external donors – notably the Americans and Canadians – to be active in this field. Canada aid to the area has recently been stepped up . . . my officials are now working with officials of the ODM [Overseas Defence Ministry] on a plan which, it is hoped, will succeed in inducing the Americans to renew their aid programme to these territories.[23]

It was understood, both in the eastern Caribbean and in London, that the standard paltry aid package, without economic development funding, would keep West Indian countries aid dependants to the end of time (table 12.1).

What was required to manage the bad press Britain was receiving in the West Indies, officials reported, was a high-profile public relations programme built around the small donations that would "win the confidence" of political leaders and provide "discreet promotion of the British interest in the region". This was Britain's most cynical diplomatic approach. It was rolled out in the

---

22. Ibid.
23. Ibid.

Table 12.1. The Eastern Caribbean 1963–1966

Country	Estimated Population 1965	Approx. Recurrent Revenue 1964 (£)	British Grant in Aid Approx. 1964 (£)	Colonial Development & Welfare Funds Available 1963–66 (£)
Barbados	260,000	6,000,000	nil	592,000
Montserrat	13,000	240,000	170,000	271,000
St Kitts	66,000	1,000,000	200,000	678,000
Antigua	61,000	2,100,000	nil	666,000
Dominica	70,000	800,000	220,000	738,000
St Lucia	102,000	1,500,000	nil	682,000
St Vincent	96,000	900,000	230,000	674,000
Grenada	106,000	1,400,000	300,000	587,000

Source: Greenwood to Cabinet Defence and Overseas Policy Committee, 15 March 1965, CAB 148/20, OPD (65) 51.

most vulnerable, crisis-riddled communities – the eastern Caribbean colonies.[24]

The public relations programme began in January 1966, with the establishment of a "British Development Division" in the West Indies, headquartered in Barbados. W.L. Bell was its director. He had served as head of Colonial Administrative Services in Uganda (1946–53) and at the time of his appointment was secretary to the governor of Westfield College, University of London.

Bell was expected, as head of division, to win hearts and minds in the eastern Caribbean while preserving British interests in the region. He noted that the Caribbean audience "is one of the easiest, not the most difficult to reach. English is spoken, each territory is so small that minor events make news; and the grapevine is splendidly efficient. Canada produces a mini project, the US a handful of scholarships, and the publicity is deafening." He was confident, then, that it ought to be no major challenge "to keep Britain in the eye of the beholder".[25]

---

24. Ibid.; D. Sharpe and H. Hawkins, minutes, British Development Division in the Caribbean, 25–28 June 1965, OD 28/80.
25. Sharpe and Hawkins, minutes.

The strategy, Bell declared, was to use the printed and electronic media to maximum effect in order to create a public perception of British goodwill. To this end he suggested the release of "a short press release" on every UK aid project "as soon as it is approved". Media savvy, he said, was the key. He noted, "Not all newspapers and radio will bite – but most will."[26]

The truth was, Bell added, "simple and speedy publicity beamed to a territory about that territory will meet with response; the big picture should be painted after the audience has been secured – for it can't itself secure it".

Furthermore, Bell added, in derogatory language: "This is calypso country; and the most popular and hence most successful calypsos are bluntly phrased, attractively packaged, slap up to date, intensely local, savoured by illiterate and sophisticated alike . . . this really is a golden opportunity."[27]

The eastern Caribbean islands were his chief target. H.C.G. Hawkins, the government official who framed Bell's remit, could not have been more cynical about the project. He said, "If Federation of the little 5, 6, 7, or 8 does not come to fruition, then they should be held together by a common services regime." Similar doubt was cast on the integration process and its advocates by an official of the UK embassy in Washington, who wrote in December 1964: "They are so given to quarrelling among themselves, particularly over anything to do with money, that the chances of their operating joint disbursement aid with any success are extremely remote. There would also be a loss of UK control over the administration of our aid which might be unacceptable to Parliament." Therefore, the official noted, any aid to the eastern Caribbean might include the United Nations in a monitory role.[28]

Prior to this decision, the relevant sections of the British government had recommended that the best way forward in "our Colonial history . . . must be to liquidate Colonialism" and, importantly, to do so without significant financial cost. The overriding strategy, it was noted, was to emerge "without any stigma of colonialism".[29]

The idea of holding the international conference in London in May 1965 was to give effect to the disposal strategy. The conference document was entitled "Future of the Remaining British Colonial Territories". Williams rejected the

---

26. Ibid.; see also W.L. Bell to K.G. Fry, 20 October 1966 OD 28/9, no. 35.
27. Bell to Fry.
28. Ibid.
29. Ibid.; see also Sir H. Poynton to Gore Booth, 28 September 1965, FO 371/179142, no. 5.

proposal on the basis that he wanted nothing to do with Britain seeking to find yet another back door to rid itself of its West Indian obligations. This was not about a governance problem in the West Indies, he argued, and should not be discussed as a political matter. Britain's emphasis in the region, he concluded, "should be on economic aid."[30]

Britain's concern, however, was more with appeasing the international community. The world was turning its face against colonialism and Britain did not wish to be tarnished as a global offender. In this regard, Sir H. Poynton made the critical observation that Britain had moved on: "So far as purely British interests are concerned, this might not really matter. We have no great commercial or defence interest in these islands any longer; and the ties that we have with them are largely cultural, moral and sentimental."[31] The United States and Canada were now invited to assume official leadership of financial responsibility in the subregion.

Britain placed on the US's plate the project of addressing the colonial hardship – the hardcore poverty south of Miami. Poynton further added: "Our principal ally, the United States, is, however, very sensitive about anything that happens in these territories and would not welcome a situation developing in which Britain withdrew and left seven little Haitis and Cubas on their doorstep."[32]

Britain had tactically manoeuvred the "little 5, 6, 7, or 8" out of its foreign policy package of concern. By the end of 1965, its principal issue was no longer economic support for these islands, but how to handle them in a way that did not cause it any shame in the "international community". This was a top priority, Poynton said, as "Britain would find it embarrassing to be responsible for the Caribbean mess". This meant the offer of "full internal self-government for the islands with Britain remaining responsible for "defence and external affairs".[33]

In the next two decades the remaining colonies became independent:

Antigua and Barbuda	1981
Bahamas	1973
Barbados	1966
Dominica	1978
Grenada	1974

---

30. Poynton to Gore Booth.
31. Ibid.
32. Ibid.
33. Ibid.

Guyana	1966
Jamaica	1962
St Kitts and Nevis	1983
St Lucia	1979
St Vincent	1979
Trinidad and Tobago	1962

None received a reparatory justice programme, but all demanded one. The founders of each state carried into the nation-building process a profound sense of betrayal by Britain. Their legitimate expectations were dashed.

In the mid-1960s, Britain walked away from its legacy of broken public institutions, poorly functioning operational systems and political corruption rooted in imperial racial arrogance and class inequalities. In each colony, black and brown children were still set to work by white plantation owners, while their parents were considered too expensive to employ. The social and mental violence associated with white-supremacist rule was intended to break the spirit of black and brown citizens. Again, the people rose up in the 1970s and led movements with righteous indignation demanding democracy and justice.

The cost of cleaning up the colonial mess left behind in the Caribbean was computed by British officials as beyond the capacity of the national treasury. It was better for the government to bury the debt. Refusal to accept it made it an easy matter to deflect, using diplomatic codes, the requests for financial support and economic justice.

Each West Indian nation, then, began its independence journey with the massive British legacy of social decay. Systemic economic exploitation and environmental ruin weighed down each ship of state as it set sail. It became the norm for international observers and writers to narrate the beauty of the Caribbean against the background of the enduring poverty of its urban environment or rural interior.

With Britain rejecting ownership of its legacy, taking full responsibility for the West Indian catastrophe became the mandate of nation-builders. But it was evident that they would soon be overwhelmed by the colonial burden. In a short time, political leaders and innovative entrepreneurs came to terms with the resilience of poverty and the antisocial culture it bred.

Social aid for the new nations rather than economic development remained the mantra of the British. While nation-builders clamoured for capital to promote economic and social development, the British state remained resolute in providing just enough to prevent further economic mayhem. Within a decade of the last independence celebration, in St Kitts in 1983, West Indian economist Trevor Farrell noted:

> The Caribbean is clearly in crisis. If we step back and look at the trajectory of events over the last decade and study where current trends seem to be leading, the situation can only be described as grim, and the prognosis, poor. Jamaica and Guyana for example are now well on the way towards fulfilling Naipaul's prediction that the future of the Caribbean is Haiti. Over the last decade, these economies have not just shown little growth. They have contracted.[34]

Farrell did not promote the blame game. He went deeper into the "inner plantation world" of the region, insisting that full responsibility should be taken for the colonial legacy:

> To my mind three things are clear. One is that we have failed. The second is that it is our decisions at governmental level that are primarily to blame. The third is that our failure is in the final analysis our responsibility. None of this is to deny that imperialism or rapacious corporations, or untoward international events or power-hungry trade unionists exist. They do; but enemies, rivals, obstacles and capricious fate are facts of life that one has to live with, overcome or get around. To blame everything imaginable for our failures and exonerate ourselves after decades and more of "independence is silly".[35] [37]

To discern the difference between defeat and failure in the academic discourse has not been an easy task, and few researchers have been willing to sift through the ashes for the evidence.

A truth to be confronted is that the size and resilience of underdevelopment have been downplayed by nationalist politicians, trade unions, domestic entrepreneurs and other nation-building stakeholders. It was the mandate of the postcolonial collegiate to research the full dimensions of the colonial mess and reveal its oppressiveness. The multidisciplinary research literature has focused on the economics and sociology of the resilient plantation and called attention to its capacity to confront nation-builders with its heritage and hegemony.

---

34. Trevor Farrell, "The Caribbean State and Its Role in Economic Management", in *Caribbean Economic Development: The First Generation*, ed. Stanley Lalta and Marie Freckleton (Kingston: Ian Randle, 1993), 200.

35. Ibid., 201.

The "plantation school" took prominence in new explanatory frameworks, while socialism as a metaphor for social justice turned development discourse upside down. By the end of the 1990s, most "independent" nations to which Britain had refused reparatory financial support had fallen into the debt orbit of the International Monetary Fund and World Bank. There, once again, in their political independence, they became reliant on the "welfare aid approach" of Britain. In this regard, Empire was reinvented by colonialists without colonies.

The debt Britain owed the West Indies, first framed by Arthur Lewis in 1939, has now attracted the attention of the global community. The legitimate expectation of those against whom crimes against humanity were committed are better known today than at the moments of emancipation, federation defeat and national independence.

Everywhere today in the West Indies the word "reparations" rolls from native tongues, the sound of justice that refuses to be silenced. There is no carpet in Britain big enough for black and brown debt to be brushed under. The post-independence generations have struggled hard to build foundations for the elusive sustained economic growth.

Where Farrell's assessment of "exit from colonialism" via independence adds significant value is in the conclusion that the regional effort failed rather than being defeated. While admitting this, almost in an irritated way, he recognizes that the imperial extraction model still has potency. More important for him, however, is that West Indians have failed to uproot colonialism, a necessary condition for sustainable nation-building.

The logic of his argument extends to the notion that independence and decolonization are one and the same process, without reference to time frames. How long should it reasonably take for a colony to become meaningfully independent? Farrell's conclusion that political independence served to sustain systems of economic colonialism, because of the superficial nature of national symbolisms, is significant within the "failure-defeat" binary.

What is evident, using Farrell's markers and criteria, is that the economic reality in the West Indies at the outset of the century conforms to the description of underdevelopment. His analysis also calls for the burden of the "colonial mess" to be reassessed. The intention of the regional effort has been to remove debilitating forces while pushing ahead with socio-economic transformation. Meanwhile, Britain intended to block, subvert and derail these efforts in order to install and sustain compliant neocolonialism.

The defeat-failure binary discourse then, hinges upon the relative values assigned in weighing these processes. Farrell stated in 1983:

> The blunt truth, however, is that all this is largely epiphenomenal. The reality is that the English-speaking Caribbean remains essentially colonized. What has changed is the form of the colonization, the mechanisms through which it operates, and the colonizing agents. This is not to say that no change has taken place. Change has in fact taken place, and more will follow. The dynamic of events in the Caribbean . . . thrusts toward ultimate and real decolonization. But that time has not yet arrived.[36]

And furthermore, he added, twenty years after the high point of independence, "the metropolitan strangle-hold has once again simply shifted its grip".[37]

This evolutionary process, then, has two dialectical features. The West Indians fighting for genuine political freedom, constitutional liberation and popular democracy against the force of the British Empire; and the persistence of British power that "simply shifted its grip" – hence the emphasis on the endurance of British control rather than ownership.

Where Farrell's discourse climaxed was in a place not far removed from where most West Indian social scientists of his generation had landed. There was a pedagogical crusade in the Caribbean academy calling for economic reform and authentic independence, breaking away completely from the colonial framework that held the regional economies in place as distant assets to be effectively managed, if not completely owned. Grouped together, the advocates of transformational change were tagged variously as the West Indian "dependency school" and "the plantation economy school", which opposed the legitimacy of the narrative of "independence" within neocolonial structures and relationships.

The politics of nationalizing imperial assets did originate from the economic-injustice discourse of the 1970s and 1980s, but the acquisition of these resources did not mean the ending of Empire. From the 1990s into the twenty-first century, the British extraction model transitioned as new sectors such as global finance, wealth and asset management, and tourism took centre stage in the West Indian economy. With new sources of wealth creation and extraction,

---

36. Farrell, "Decolonization", 5.
37. Ibid., 7.

the British postcolonial control was strengthened. In this way, economically marginal citizens remained the main victims of incomplete nationhood.

In summary, then, Britain was offended by the 1930s workers' anti-imperial revolution, and considered audacious the 1940s "end of Empire" economic development and democracy movements. The empire struck back and succeeded in retarding, derailing and defeating many of the critical political projects and strategies advanced in the region. The effects of Britain's success in halting socio-economic transformation, rejecting its debt to the region and frustrating the visions of leaders and strategic thinkers created significant doubt in the region about its long-term ability to defy British imperial power.

At each stage of the decolonization and democracy process, from emancipation to national independence, the racist British approach, disguised as diplomacy, is captured in their official records. The inflexible policy of ignoring the West Indian call for reparatory justice in the nineteenth century, and development financing in the 1930s, denied the region the opportunity to partner with Britain in cleaning up the colonial mess. The federation was subverted by the lack of funding, and the refusal to give the region a "golden handshake" as reparations at independence in the 1960s was blunt.

Persistent poverty, the primary expression of underdevelopment, remains the principal legacy of Britain's exploitation of the region. Britain initiated and popularized the racist argument that West Indians lack the qualities needed to promote their own development, and that they must "get over" the historical damage and present-day injury of colonialism. In this way it further embedded the impulse towards institutional racism at the heart of its empire.

West Indians were expected to reverse, in the independence era, the effects of three hundred years of socio-economic exploitation and to transcend by their own efforts the debilitating legacies of five centuries of slavery and colonialism. Britain legally invented and perfected chattel slavery, resulting in a holocaust of Africans in the West Indies. The continuing suffering arising from these crimes against humanity remains evident in most aspects of West Indian life today.

From Africa as a source of enslaved labour, Britain turned to Asia, in particular India, and developed the replacement system of indenture in order to sustain wealth-extraction colonialism in the Caribbean. From the time of these crimes to today's denial of responsibility for financial reparations, Britain has buried its head in the sand.

Verene Shepherd, Jamaican historian and reparation activist

Olivia Grange, Jamaican grassroots politician and reparation leader

Tony Blair, British Labour prime minister who rejected apology for slavery and reparation negotiations

David Cameron, British Conservative prime minister who rejected apology for slavery and reparation negotiations

Epilogue

THE CARIBBEAN CALL FOR REPARATIONS WILL resonate with increasing intensity in the political and diplomatic corridors of British-Caribbean relations until it is answered and matters brought to a settlement by means of formal resolution. The evidentiary basis of the case has long been established. It points overwhelmingly to the conclusion that Britain and other colonizing and slave-owning European nations have a case to answer in respect of the multiple crimes against humanity they committed in the region.

In 2013, I published a monograph entitled *Britain's Black Debt: Reparations for Caribbean Slavery and Native Genocide*. The front cover shows a photo of Queen Elizabeth II and her cousin the seventh Earl of Harewood on his sugar plantation (the Belle) in Barbados in 1966, while the island was in independence celebration mode.

The sugar plantation was bought by the first Earl of Harewood in 1780 with 232 enslaved Africans, and remained in the family into the mid-twentieth century. In 1922, the Harewoods, former leading slave barons of the island, married into the royal family, hence the 1966 meeting of cousins, queen and duke, in the plantation mansion overlooking the cane fields that took labour and life from thousands of enslaved and manumitted blacks.

The photo, furthermore, speaks to the several themes of this work, which traces the reparations discourse from its roots in native genocide and slavery in the seventeenth century to the postcolonialism of the early twenty-first century. In many respects, then, this work is a sequel to *Britain's Black Debt*. It responds to the argument that the nineteenth century, which witnessed the abolition of chattel slavery, brought to an end the crimes of enslavement. Also, that the legislation of the 1830s was "a long time ago", disconnected from the deprivation and suffering being experienced today by the descendants of the enslaved.

This tactical exercise in debt avoidance by Britain is countered here with the evidence of the continuity of colonialism, in which the savagery of British governance flourished under the legal guise of freedom. The evidence shows that the 1830s emancipation reform of the criminal system of chattel slavery was just the beginning of Britain's long-term strategy to sustain the violent, racist system of colonialism.

The British state might have been pressured to dismantle the slave-based system, but it worked hard to keep the essence and core relations of slavery in order to facilitate the economic extractive model that gave colonialism its value.

The importation of thousands of indentured workers from India was intended to prolong wealth creation and appropriation in the same way as slavery. Resistance and rebellion also characterized the conduct of the indentured, who also desired freedom and self-determination. They too felt the sting of slavery-like plantation harshness.

A long century of British colonial brutality followed emancipation, until the workers' anti-colonial revolt in the 1930s toppled the imperial architecture. It was a bloody interlude. The colonial state, empowered by imperial directives, tortured and executed the rebellious masses in ways directly reminiscent of the slavery period. The crimes committed against the poor were endemic. Extreme police torment accompanied military massacres across the region, designed to deny the popular will for social justice, economic participation and democracy.

The discrediting of the colonial state by grassroots populism in the 1930s consolidated the democratic impulse in the region's political culture. These developments were rooted in the intention of workers and their professional and intellectual allies to end once and for all the oppression of the imperial order. This was also the moment that signalled the beginning of Britain's determination to extend colonialism, its ideologies, structures and relations by subverting Caribbean commitment to economic development and political sovereignty.

Poverty is the primary product of British rule. The enslaved, the indentured and their descendants were its systemic victims. The collective mass impoverishment is the underdevelopment of the region. Twentieth-century colonialism was the last harbinger of twenty-first-century persistent poverty. The perception of the West Indies as a place from which to extract profits produced an industrial relations culture that remains.

British reactions to indigenous freedom and struggles for democracy were not only repressive; they were vicious and bloody whenever and wherever boldness erupted from the social base. Political oppression and social degradation were the tools used to maintain maximum wealth extraction. The cumulative effects of this colonial policy served to determine and sustain the economic backwardness and underdevelopment of the region.

Deep resentment grew within regional communities that knew all too well that the extraction by the British of free and cheap labour over a period of three hundred years had gone a long way towards financing and furthering their own economic growth and industrial development.

By 1940, when the workers' anti-colonial revolt entered the negotiation phase, it became obvious that there was resentment towards the region among British governments. This much has been captured in the official records of the period. These records show the hardening of British negative attitudes to West Indian development initiatives. The impulse to oppose and destroy Caribbean visions and policies evolved into a politics of humiliation. It also illustrates an intent to punish the region for its revolt. Official correspondence expresses glee at the ability of officials to deny the region financial support while offering significant assistance to colonies elsewhere.

The politics of decolonization in the West Indies, then, was characterized by an aggressive determination by the British government to ignore responsibility for mass poverty and financial support for the development agenda. The British framed their counter-narrative with the argument that the nations breaking under the weight of the colonial burden were fully responsible for their own underdevelopment. According to officials, decline and decay were the fault of incompetent nationalist leaders rather than centuries of extreme colonial wealth extraction.

Denied access to reparatory justice in terms of capital funding for development, nationalist leaders embarked on nation-building on the assumption that they would take responsibility for cleaning up the colonial aftermath as a precursor to economic and social development. Unable adequately to fund the basic needs of nationhood, such as primary and secondary education for all, basic public health care, housing for the poor, running water for communities, and roads, nation states eventually accepted, though reluctantly, that British opposition and indifference were crippling.

The empire did strike back. The massive slum-clearance project that was a top priority in nation-building became the scene of multiple problems, including crime and security. The combined legacies of mass illiteracy and endemic poverty provided the context for the intergenerational economic marginalization that defined the postcolonial state.

Allied to this circumstance was the persistent white-supremacy culture that allowed for racial economic differences to be explained in terms of culture and skin colour. The poor were poor because they were black and the rich were rich because they were white. Blacks were assigned to the labouring role because they were black, and whites were assigned to ownership and management because they were white. The race mixture of these two groups slotted in between. This was the race pyramid of slavery and colonization. It remained rooted in the economic and social structures of the new nation states.

The economic underdevelopment of the nationalist project was the outcome of British policy. In the 2014 and 2016 UN Human Development Reports, the region is defined as having one of the world's most extreme wealth and income disparities, despite being the longest integrated and engaged part of Atlantic modernity.

The regional and international reparation movement has, however, exposed the colonial damage done to the region. Britain is invited to return to the scene of the crimes and to participate in a reparations-for-development programme. The call is for the "colonial wealth extractor" to join with the region at a reparations-for-development summit, during which a mutually agreed partnership for prosperity would be conceived and implemented.

The global Black Lives Matter movement has endorsed this reparations claim and approach. There is no escaping the demands of this moment. Public political consciousness has caught up with the crimes of colonialism and their legacies. These are captured in every aspect of every day in the region. The mass suffering remains evident everywhere. Only a reparations response can resolve this crisis. For two hundred years, the Caribbean has been calling for this conversation. Britain, the nation of "No", must become a community of "Yes, we will".

Selected Bibliography

Books

Ashton, S.R., and David Killingray, eds. *British Documents on the End of Empire*. Ser. B, vol. 6, *The West Indies*. London: Institute of Commonwealth Studies, 1999.

Augier, F.R., S.C. Gordon, D.G. Hall and M. Reckord. *The Making of the West Indies*. London: Longman, 1960.

August, Eugene, ed. *The Nigger Question: The Negro Question*. New York: Crofts, 1971.

Ayearst, Morley. *The British West Indies: The Search for Self-Government*. London: Allen and Unwin, 1960.

Beachey, R.W. *The British West Indies Sugar Industry in the Late 19th Century*. 1957. Reprint, Westport, CT: Greenwood, 1978.

Beckford, George, ed. *Caribbean Economy*. Kingston: Institute of Social and Economic Research, University of the West Indies, 1975.

———. *Persistent Poverty: Underdevelopment in Plantation Economies of the Third World*. Oxford: Oxford University Press, 1972.

Beckles, Hilary McD. *Britain's Black Debt: Reparations for Caribbean Slavery and Native Genocide*. Kingston: University of the West Indies Press, 2013.

———. *Centering Woman: Gender Discourses in Caribbean Slave Societies*. Kingston: Ian Randle, 1999.

———. *Chattel House Blues: Making of a Democratic Society in Barbados – From Clement Payne to Owen Arthur*. Kingston: Ian Randle, 2004.

———. *The First Black Slave Society: Britain's "Barbarity Time" in Barbados, 1636–1876*. Kingston: University of the West Indies Press, 2016.

———. *Great House Rules: Landless Emancipation and Workers' Protest in Barbados, 1838–1938*. Kingston: Ian Randle, 2004.

———. *Natural Rebels: A Social History of Enslaved Black Women in Barbados*. London: Zed Books, 1989.

Blackburn, Robin. *The Overthrow of Colonial Slavery, 1776–1848*. London: Verso, 1999.

Blanshard, Paul. *Democracy and Empire in the Caribbean*. New York: Macmillan, 1947.

Bleby, Henry. *The Reign of Terror: A Narrative of Facts Concerning ex-Governor Eyre, George William Gordon, and the Jamaica Atrocities*. London: William Nichols, 1862.

Bolland, O. Nigel. *On the March: Labour Rebellions in the British Caribbean, 1934–1939.* Kingston: Ian Randle, 1995.

——. *The Politics of Labour in the British Caribbean.* Kingston: Ian Randle, 2001.

Brown, Christopher. *Moral Capital: Foundations of British Abolitionism.* Chapel Hill: University of North Carolina Press, 2006.

Bryan, Patrick. *The Jamaican People, 1880–1902, Race, Class, and Social Control.* London: Macmillan, 1991.

Butler, K.M. *The Economics of Emancipation: Jamaica and Barbados, 1823–1843.* Chapel Hill: University of North Carolina Press, 1995.

Cain, P.J., and A.G. Hopkins. *British Imperialism, 1688–2000.* 2nd edition. Harlow, UK: Pearson Education, 2002.

Carlyle, Thomas. *Occasional Discourse on the Nigger Question.* London: Thomas Bosworth, 1853.

Carrington, George. *Our West Indian Colonies.* London: Anti-Bounty League, 1898.

Carter, Henderson. *Labour Pains: Resistance and Protest in Barbados, 1838–1904.* Kingston: Ian Randle, 2012.

Checkland, S.G. *The Gladstones: A Family Biography, 1764–1851.* Cambridge: Cambridge University Press, 1971.

Chester, Rev. Greville John. *Chester's Barbados: The Barbados Chapters from Transatlantic Sketches (1869), Barbadian Heritage Reprint Series.* Bridgetown: National Cultural Foundation, 1990.

Clubbe, John, ed. *Froude's Life of Carlyle.* Abridged ed. Columbus: Ohio State University Press, 1979.

Cole, Hubert. *Christophe: King of Haiti.* New York: Viking, 1967.

Craig, Susan. ed. *Contemporary Caribbean.* Vol. 1. Port of Spain: Susan Craig, 1981.

Craton, Michael. *Testing the Chains: Resistance to Slavery in the British West Indies.* Ithaca: Cornell University Press, 1982.

Cross, Malcolm, and Gad Heuman, eds. *Labour in the Caribbean: From Emancipation to Independence.* London: Macmillan, 1988.

Davis, R. *The Rise of the Atlantic Economies.* London: Weidenfield and Nicholson, 1973.

Demas, William. *Essays on Caribbean Integration and Development.* Kingston: Institute of Social and Economic Research, University of the West Indies, 1976.

Draper, Nicholas. *The Price of Emancipation: Slave Ownership, Compensation and British Society at the End of Slavery.* Cambridge: Cambridge University Press, 2010.

Dunn, W.H. *James Anthony Froude.* 2 vols. Oxford: Clarendon, 1963.

Eisner, Gisela. *Jamaica, 1830–1930: A Study of Economic Growth.* Manchester: Manchester University Press, 1961.

Escobar, Arturo. *Encountering Development: The Making and Unmaking of the Third World.* Princeton, NJ: Princeton University Press, 1995.

Farrell, Stephen, Melanie Unwin and James Walvin, eds. *The British Slave Trade: Abolition, Parliament and People*. Edinburgh: Edinburgh University Press, 2007.

Finlason, W.F. *The History of the Jamaica Case*. London, 1869.

Foner, Eric. *Nothing but Freedom: Emancipation and Its Legacy*. Baton Rouge: Louisiana State University Press, 1983.

Fraser, Cary. *Ambivalent Anti-Colonialism: The United States and the Genesis of West Indian Independence, 1940–1964*. Westport, CT: Greenwood, 1994.

Froude, James Anthony. *The English in the West Indies: or, The Bow of Ulysses*. 1888. Reprint, New York: Scribner's, 1897.

——. *Two Lectures on South Africa*. London: Longmans, 1880.

Geggus, David. *Slavery, War and Revolution: The British Occupation of Saint-Domingue 1793–1798*. London: Oxford University Press, 1982.

Girvan, Norman. *Foreign Capital and Economic Underdevelopment in Jamaica*. Kingston: Institute of Social and Economic Research, University of the West Indies, 1971.

Green, William. *British Slave Emancipation: The Sugar Colonies and the Great Experiment, 1830–1865*. Oxford: Clarendon, 1976.

Hall, Catherine. *Civilizing Subjects: Metropole and Colony in the English Imagination, 1830–1867*. Chicago: University of Chicago Press, 2002.

Hall, Douglas. *Five of the Leewards, 1834–1870: The Major Problems of the Post-Emancipation Period in Antigua, Barbuda, Montserrat, Nevis and St Kitts*. Aylesbury, UK: Caribbean University Press, 1971.

——. *Free Jamaica: 1838–1865: An Economic History*. New Haven, CT: Yale University Press, 1959.

Haring, C.H. *The Spanish Empire in America*. New York: Oxford University Press, 1947.

Hart, Richard. *Labour Rebellions of the 1930s in the British Caribbean Region Colonies*. London: Caribbean Labour Solidarity and the Socialist History Society, 2002.

Henry, Paget. *Peripheral Capitalism and Underdevelopment in Antigua*. New Brunswick, NJ: Transaction Books, 1985.

Heuman, Gad. *Between Black and White: Race, Politics, and the Free Coloureds in Jamaica, 1792–1865*. Oxford: Oxford University Press, 1981.

——. '*The Killing Time*': *The Morant Bay Rebellion in Jamaica*. London: Macmillan, 1994.

Heuman, Gad, and David Trotman, eds. *Contesting Freedom: Control and Resistance in the Post-Emancipation Caribbean*. Oxford: Macmillan, 2005.

Higman, B.W., ed. *Trade, Government, and Society in Caribbean History*. Kingston: Heinemann Caribbean, 1983.

Hill, Robert A., ed. *The Marcus Garvey and Universal Negro Improvement Association Papers*. Vol. 2: *August 1919 to August 1920*. Berkeley: University of California Press, 1983.

Holt, Thomas. *The Problem of Freedom: Race, Labour, and Politics in Jamaica and Britain, 1832–1938*. Kingston: Ian Randle, 1992.

Hoyos, F.A. *Grantley Adams and the Social Revolution*. London: Macmillan, 1974.

Hume, Hamilton. *The Life of Edward John Eyre*. London, 1867.

James, C.L.R. *The Black Jacobins: Toussaint L'Ouverture and the San Domingo Revolution*. New York: Random House, 1963.

James, Winston. *Holding Aloft the Banner of Ethiopia: Caribbean Radicalism in Early Twentieth-Century America*. London: Verso, 1998.

Kale, Madhavi. *Fragments of Empire: Capital, Slavery, and Indentured Labor Migration in the British Caribbean*. Philadelphia: University of Pennsylvania Press, 1998.

Kidd, Benjamin. *The Control of the Tropics*. London, Macmillan, 1898.

King, David. *A Sketch of the Late Mr G.W. Gordon, Jamaica*. London: Oliphant, 1866.

Knight, Franklin. *The Caribbean: Genesis of a Fragmented Nationalism* NY, Oxford University Press, 1978.

Kumar, Susmit. *Modernization and Islam and the Creation of a Multipolar World Order*. N.p.: Susmit Kumar, 2008.

Lalta, Stanley, and Marie Freckleton. eds. *Caribbean Economic Development: The First Generation*. Kingston: Ian Randle, 1993.

Lambert, David. *White Creole Culture: Politics and Identity during the Age of Abolition*. Cambridge: Cambridge University Press, 2005.

Lawrence, K.O. *Immigration into the West Indies in the 19th Century*. Bridgetown: Caribbean University Press, 1971.

Lee, Debbie. *British Slavery and African Exploration: The Written Legacy*. Philadelphia: University of Pennsylvania Press, 2002.

Lewis, Gordon. *The Growth of the Modern West Indies*. London: MacGibbon and Kee, 1968.

———. *Main Currents in Caribbean Thought: The Historical Evolution of Caribbean Society in Its Ideological Aspects, 1492–1900*. Kingston: Heinemann Caribbean, 1983.

Lewis, Rupert. *Marcus Garvey: Anti-Colonial Champion*. London: Karia, 1987.

Lewis, Rupert, and Patrick Bryan. eds. *Garvey: His Work and Impact*. Trenton, NJ: Africa World Press, 1991.

Lewis, W. Arthur. *Labour in the West Indies: The Birth of a Workers' Movement*. London: Victor Gollancz; the Fabian Society, 1939.

Livingstone, W.P. *Black Jamaica: A Study in Evolution*. London, 1899.

Macmillan, W.M. *Warning from the West Indies*. Harmondsworth, UK: Penguin, 1936.

Majumdar, Ramesh. *Three Phases of India's Struggle for Freedom*. Bombay: Bhavan, 1967.

Marshall, Woodville, ed. *The Colthurst Journal: Journal of a Special Magistrate in the Islands of Barbados and St Vincent, July 1835–September 1838*. Millwood, NY: KTO.

———, ed. *Emancipation III: Aspects of the Post-Slavery Experience of Barbados*. Bridgetown: National Cultural Foundation, 1988.

McDonald, Roderick. ed. *West Indies Accounts: Essays on the History of the British*

Caribbean and the Atlantic. Kingston: University of the West Indies Press, 1996.

McGlynn, Frank, and Seymour Drescher, eds. *The Meaning of Freedom: Economics, Politics, and Culture after Slavery*. Pittsburgh: Pittsburgh University Press, 1992.

Moore, Brian. *Race, Power and Social Segmentation in Colonial Society: Guyana after Slavery, 1838–1891*. New York: Gordon and Breach, 1987.

Mordecai, John. *The West Indies: The Federal Negotiations*. London: Allen and Unwin, 1968.

The Moyne Report: Report of the West India Royal Commission. Introduction by Denis Benn. Reprint, Kingston: Ian Randle, 2011.

Newton, Velma. *The Silver Men: West Indian Labour Migration to Panama, 1850–1914*. Kingston: Institute of Social and Economic Research, University of the West Indies, 1984.

Nicholls, David. *From Dessalines to Duvalier: Race, Colour and National Independence in Haiti*. New York: Cambridge University Press, 1979.

Noel, Baptist. *The Case of George William Gordon, Esq., of Jamaica*. London: Nisbet, 1866.

O'Malley, L.S.S. ed. *Modern India and the West*. London: Oxford University Press, 1941.

Olivier, Margaret, ed. *Sydney Olivier: Letters and Selected Writings*. London: Allen and Unwin, 1948.

Olivier, Sydney. *The League of Nations and Primitive Peoples*. London: Oxford University Press, 1918.

———. *White Capital and Coloured Labour*. 1906. Reprint, New York: Russell and Russell, 1971.

Palmer, Colin. *Eric Williams and the Making of the Modern Caribbean*. Chapel Hill: University of North Carolina Press, 2009.

———, ed. *The Legacy of Eric Williams: Caribbean Scholar and Statesman*. Kingston: University of the West Indies Press, 2015.

Patterson, Orlando. *The Confounding Island: Jamaica and the Postcolonial Predicament*. Cambridge, MA: Harvard University Press, 2019.

Petras, Elizabeth. *Jamaican Labor Migration: White Capital and Black Labour, 1850–1930*. Boulder: Westview, 1988.

Post, Ken. *Arise Ye Starvelings: The Jamaican Labour Rebellion and Its Aftermath*. The Hague: Martinus Nijhoff, 1978.

Prichard, H. Hesketh. *Where Black Rules White: As Reported by the First White Man to Traverse Haiti in Nearly 100 Years*. New York: Scribner's, 1900.

Richardson, Bonham C. *Economy and Environment in the Caribbean: Barbados and the Windwards in the Late 1880s*. Kingston: University of the West Indies Press, 1997.

Robinson, Arthur N.R. *The Mechanics of Independence: Patterns of Political and Economic Transformation in Trinidad and Tobago*. 1971. Reprint, Kingston: University of the West Indies Press, 2001.

Robotham, Don. *The Notorious Riot: The Socio-Economic and Political Bases of Paul Bogle's Revolt.* Working Paper no. 28. Kingston: Institute of Social and Economic Research, University of the West Indies, 1981.

Rodney, Walter. *A History of the Guyanese Working People, 1881–1905.* Baltimore: Johns Hopkins University Press, 1981.

———. *How Europe Underdeveloped Africa.* 1974. Reprint, Baltimore: Black Classic Press, 2011

Root, J.W. *The British West Indies and the Sugar Industry.* Liverpool: J.W. Root, 1899.

Rose, James. *The Strike of 1848.* Georgetown: History Society, University of Guyana, 1989.

Roundell, Charles. *England and Her Subject-Races, with Special Reference to Jamaica.* London: Macmillan, 1866.

Salmon, Charles S. *The Caribbean Confederation: A Plan for the Union of the Fifteen British West Indian Colonies.* London: Cassell, 1888.

———. *Depression in the West Indies: Free Trade the Only Remedy.* London: Cassell, 1884.

Schwartz, Stuart, ed. *Tropical Babylons: Sugar and the Making of the Atlantic World, 1450–1680.* Chapel Hill: University of North Carolina Press, 2004.

Semmel, Bernard. *Jamaican Blood and Victorian Conscience.* Cambridge: Cambridge University Press, 1963.

Sewell, William. *The Ordeal of Free Labor in the British West Indies.* New York: Harper and Brothers, 1861.

Shepherd, Verene, Bridget Brereton and Barbara Bailey, eds. *Engendering History: Caribbean Women in Historical Perspective.* Kingston: Ian Randle, 1995.

Simey, T.S. *Welfare and Planning in the West Indies.* Oxford: Clarendon, 1946.

Smith, Adam. *The Wealth of Nations.* 1776. New York: Canna, 1937.

Stark, James. *History and Guide to Barbados and the Caribbee Islands.* Boston: Photo-Electrotype, 1893.

Thomas, J.J. *Froudacity: West Indian Fables Explained.* London: T. Fisher Unwin, 1889. Reprinted with an introduction by C.L.R. James and biographical note by Donald Wood, London: New Beacon Books, 1969.

Thompson, R.W. *Black Caribbean.* London: Macdonald, London, 1946.

Trollope, Anthony. *The West Indies and the Spanish Main.* London: Good Press, 1859.

Wallace, Elisabeth. *The British Caribbean: From the Decline of Colonialism to the End of the Federation.* Toronto: University of Toronto Press, 1977.

Walvin, James. *Black Ivory: Slavery in the British Empire.* Malden, MA: Blackwell, 2001.

Ward, J.R. *British West Indian Slavery: The Process of Amelioration, 1750–1834.* Oxford: Clarendon, 1988.

Will, H.A. *Constitutional Change in the British West Indies, 1880–1903.* Oxford: Clarendon, 1970.

Williams, Eric. *British Historians and the West Indies*. Port of Spain: PNM, 1964.

———. *Capitalism and Slavery*. Chapel Hill: University of North Carolina Press, 1944.

———. *From Columbus to Castro: The History of the Caribbean, 1492–1969*. London: Andre Deutsch, 1970.

Williams, Ralph. *How I Became a Governor*. London: John Murray, 1913.

Zondi, Siphamandla, and Philani Mthembu. *From MDGs to Sustainable Development Goals: The Travails of International Development*. Cape Town: Institute of Global Dialogue and UNISA, 2017.

Articles

Archibald, Charles H. "The Failure of the West Indies Federation". *World Today* 18, no. 6 (1962): 233–42.

Austin-Broos, Diane. "Redefining the Moral Order: Interpretations of Christianity in Post Emancipation Jamaica". In *The Meaning of Freedom: Economics, Politics, and Culture after Slavery*, edited by Frank McGlynn and Seymour Drescher, 221–43. Pittsburgh: Pittsburgh University Press, 1992.

Beckles, Hilary McD. "Property Rights in Pleasure: The Marketing of Enslaved Women's Sexuality". In *West Indies Accounts: Essays on the History of the British Caribbean and the Atlantic*, edited by Roderick McDonald, 169–87. Kingston: University of the West Indies Press, 1996.

———. "The 200 Years War: Slave Resistance in the British West Indies: An Overview of the Historiography". *Jamaican Historical Review* 13 (1982): 1–10.

———. "The Wilberforce Song: How Enslaved Caribbean Blacks Heard British Abolitionists". In *The British Slave Trade: Abolition, Parliament and People*, edited by Stephen Farrell, Melanie Unwin and James Walvin, 113–26. Edinburgh: Edinburgh University Press, 2007.

Belle, George. "The Struggle for Political Democracy: The 1937 Riots". In *Emancipation III: Aspects of the Post-Slavery Experience of Barbados*, edited by Woodville Marshall, 56–91. Bridgetown: National Cultural Foundation, 1988.

Bernal, Richard L. "The Great Depression, Colonial Policy, and Industrialisation in Jamaica". *Social and Economic Studies* 37, nos. 1–2 (1988): 33–64.

Best, Lloyd. "Outlines of a Model of Pure Plantation Economy". *Social and Economic Studies* 17, no. 3 (September 1968): 283–326.

Biddiss, Michael. "The Universal Races Congress of 1911". *Race* 13, no. 1 (1971): 37–46.

Blackton, Charles S. "The Colombo Plan". *Far Eastern Survey* 20, no. 3 (1951): 27–31.

Bolland, Nigel O. "Systems of Domination after Slavery: The Control of Land and

Labour in the British West Indies after 1838". *Comparative Studies in Society and History* 23 (1981): 591–619.

Borra, Ranjan. "Subhas Bose, the Indian National Army, and The War of India's Liberation". *Journal of Historical Review* 20, no. 1 (2001).

Brereton, Bridget. "Post-Emancipation Protest in the Caribbean: The 'Belmana Riots' in Tobago, 1876". *Caribbean Quarterly* 30, nos. 3–4 (1984): 110–23.

Bryant, G.M. "The Colombo Plan: A Decade of Cooperation". *Australian Quarterly* 33, no. 2 (1961): 7–17.

Butler, Mary. " 'Fair and Equitable Consideration': The Distribution of Slave Compensation in Jamaica and Barbados". *Journal of Caribbean History* 22, nos: 1–2 (1988): 138–52.

Carlyle, Thomas. "Occasional Discourse on the Negro Question". *Fraser's Magazine for Town and Country* 40 (December 1849): 670–79.

Chan, V.O. "The Riots of 1856 in British Guiana". *Caribbean Quarterly* 16, no. 1 (1970): 39–50.

Checkland, S.G. "Finance for the West Indies, 1780–1815". *Economic History Review*, n.s., 10, no. 3 (1958): 461–69.

———. "John Gladstone as Trader and Planter". *Economic History Review*, n.s., 7, no. 2 (1954): 216–29.

Craton, Michael. "Continuity not Change: The Incidence of Unrest among Ex-Slaves in the British West Indies, 1838–1876". *Slavery and Abolition* 9, no. 2 (1988): 144–71.

———. "Reshuffling the Pack: The Transition from Slavery to other Forms of Labor in the British Caribbean, ca. 1790–1890". *New West Indian Guide* 68, nos. 1–2 (1994): 23–75.

———. "The Transition from Slavery to Free Wage Labour in the Caribbean, 1780–1890: A Survey with Particular Reference to Recent Scholarship". *Slavery and Abolition* 13, no. 2 (1992): 37–67.

Curtin, Philip. "Scientific Racism and British Theory of Empire". *Journal of the Historical Society of Nigeria* 2, no. 1 (1969): 40–51

Davidson, J.H. "Anthony Trollope and the Colonies". *Victorian Studies* 12 (1968–69): 305–30.

Elkins, F.W. "Black Power in the British West Indies: The Trinidad Longshoremen's Strike of 1919". *Science and Society* 33, no. 1 (1969): 71–75.

Eltis, David. "The Slave Economies of the Caribbean: Structure, Performance, Evolution and Significance". in *General History of the Caribbean*, vol. 3, *The Slave Societies of the Caribbean*, edited by Franklin Knight, 105–37. Paris: UNESCO, 1997.

Engerman, Stanley. "Economic Change and Contract Labour in the British Caribbean: The End of Slavery and the Adjustment to Emancipation". *Explorations in Economic History* 21 (1984): 133–50.

Farrell, Trevor. "The Caribbean State and Its Role in Economic Management". In *Caribbean Economic Development: The First Generation*, edited by Stanley Lalta and Marie Freckleton, 200–214. Kingston: Ian Randle, 1993.

———. "Decolonization in the English-Speaking Caribbean: Myth or Reality?" In *The Newer Caribbean: Decolonization, Democracy and Development*, edited by Paget Henry and Carl Stone. Philadelphia: ISHI, 1983.

Figueroa, Mark. "Peasants, Plantations, and People: Continuities in the Analysis of George Beckford and W. Arthur Lewis". In *The Critical Tradition of Caribbean Political Economy: The Legacy of George Beckford*, edited by Kari Levitt and Michael Witter, 36–56. Kingston: Ian Randle, 1996.

Fraser, Peter. "The Fictive Peasantry: Caribbean Rural Groups in the 19th Century". In *Contemporary Caribbean*, vol. 1, edited by Susan Craig, 319–47. Port of Spain: Susan Craig, 1981.

Froude, James Anthony. "England and Her Colonies". *Fraser's Magazine for Town and Country,* n.s., 1, no. 1 (January 1870): 1–16.

Green, Cecilia. "Caribbean Politics and the 1930s Revolt". *Against the Current* 70 (September–October 1997), https://www.marxists.org/history/etol/newspape /atc/1992.html.

Heuman, Gad. " 'Is This What You Call Free?' Riots and Resistance in the Anglophone Caribbean". In *Contesting Freedom: Control and Resistance in the Post-Emancipation Caribbean*, edited by Gad Heuman and David Trotman, 104–18. Oxford: Macmillan, 2005.

Higman, B.W. "The West Indian Interest in Parliament, 1807–33". *Historical Studies* 13, no. 49 (October 1967): 1–19.

Hurwitz, Samuel. "The Federation of the West Indies: A Study in Nationalisms". *Journal of British Studies* 6, no. 1 (1966): 139–68.

Hyman, Ronald. 'The Colonial Office Mind, 1900–1914". *Journal of Imperial and Commonwealth History* 8, no. 1 (1979): 30–55.

Johnson, Howard. "The Political Uses of Commissions of Enquiry (1): The Imperial-Colonial West Indian Context; the Forster and Moyne Commissions". *Social and Economic Studies* 27, no. 3 (1979): 256–83.

———. "The West Indies and the Conversion of the British Official Classes to the Development Idea". *Journal of Commonwealth and Comparative Politics* 15, no. 1 (1977): 55–83.

Lawrence, K.O. "The Evolution of Long Term Labour Contracts in British Guiana and Trinidad, 1834–1863". *Jamaica Historical Review* 5, no. 1 (1965): 9–27.

Levy, Claude. "Barbados: The Last Years of Slavery, 1823–1833". *Journal of Negro History* 44 (1959): 308–45.

Lewis, Andrew. "'An Incendiary Press': British West Indian Newspapers during the

Struggle for Abolition". *Slavery and Abolition* 16, no. 3 (December 1995): 346–62.

Lewis, W. Arthur. "Economic Development with Unlimited Supplies of Labour". *Manchester School of Economic and Social Studies* 22, no. 2 (May 1954): 139–91.

Lowenthal, David. "The West Indies Chooses a Capital". *Geographical Review* 48 (1958): 336–64.

Macmillan, Mona. "The Making of Warning from the West Indies". *Journal of Commonwealth and Comparative Politics* 18, no. 2 (1980): 207–19.

Marshall, W.K. "Notes on Peasant Development in the West Indies since 1938". *Social and Economic Studies* 17, no. 3 (1968): 252–63.

———. " 'Vox Populi': The St Vincent Riots and Disturbances of 1862". In *Trade, Government, and Society in Caribbean History*, edited by B.W. Higman, 85–115. Kingston, Heinemann Caribbean, 1983.

McIntyre, Alister. "Caribbean Economic Community". In *Readings in the Political Economy of the Caribbean*, edited by Norman Girvan and Owen Jefferson, 165–86. Kingston: New World, 1971.

Mill, John Stuart. "The Negro Question". *Fraser's Magazine for Town and Country* 41 (January 1850): 25–31.

Olivier, Sydney. "The Scandal of West Indian Labour Conditions". *Contemporary Review* 43 (March 1938): 282–89.

Ormsby-Gore, W. "British West Indies". *United Empire* 13, no. 7 (July 1922): 460–63.

Padmore, George. "England's West Indian Slums". *Crisis* 47, no. 10 (October 1940): 317.

Phelps, O.W. "The Rise of the Labour Movement in Jamaica". *Social and Economic Studies* 9, no. 4 (1960): 417–68.

Pierce, David. "Deolonisation and the Collapse of the British Empire". *Inquiries Journal/Student Pulse* 1, no. 10 (2009), http://www.inquiriesjournal.com/articles/5 /decolonization-and-the-collapse-of-the-british-empire.

Post, Ken "The Politics of Protest in Jamaica, 1938". *Social and Economic Studies* 18, no. 4 (1969): 374–90.

Proctor, Jesse. "British West Indian Society and Government in Transition, 1920–1960". *Social and Economic Studies* 2, no. 4 (1962): 273–304.

Reubens, Edwin. "Economic Aid to Asia". *Far Eastern Survey*, 10 January 1951, 6–12.

Rich, Paul. "The Baptism of a New Era: The 1911 Universal Races Congress and the Liberal Ideology of Race". *Ethnic and Racial Studies* 7, no. 4 (1984): 534–50.

———. "Sydney Olivier, Jamaica and the Debate on British Colonial Policy in the West Indies". In *Labour in the Caribbean: From Emancipation to Independence*, edited by Malcolm Cross and Gad Heuman, 208–33. London: Macmillan, 1988.

Richards, Glen. "Collective Violence in Plantation Societies: The Case of the St Kitts Labour Protests of 1896 and 1935". Unpublished paper, Institute of Commonwealth Studies, University of London, October 1987.

———. "The Maddened Rabble: Labour Protest in St Kitts, 1896 and 1935". Unpublished paper, 1987.

———. "Order and Disorder in Colonial St Kitts: The Role of the Armed Forces in Maintaining Labour Discipline, 1896–1935". Unpublished paper, 1993.

Richardson, Bonham C. "A 'Respectable Riot': Guy Fawkes Night in St George's, Grenada, 1885". *Journal of Caribbean History* 27, no. 1 (1993): 21–35.

———. "Depression Riots and the Calling of the 1897 West India Royal Commission". *New West Indian Guide* 66, nos. 3–4 (1992): 169–91.

Sambon, L. Westenra. "Acclimatization of Europeans in Tropical Lands". *Geographical Journal* 12, no. 6 (December 1898): 589–99.

Seers, Dudley. "Federation of the British West Indies: The Economic and Financial Aspects". *Social and Economic Studies* 6 (1957): 199–214.

———. "Federation in the British West Indies: An Exercise in Colonial Administration". *Economist*, 11 April 1960, 17–19.

Shelton, Robert. "A Modified Crime: The Apprenticeship System in St Kitts". *Slavery and Abolition* 16, no. 3 (1995): 331–46.

Shepherd, C. "Peasant Agriculture in the Leeward and Windward Islands". *Tropical Agriculture* 24 (1947): 61–71.

Sheridan, Richard B. "The Condition of Slaves on the Sugar Plantations of Sir John Gladstone in the Colony of Demerara, 1812–1849". *New West Indian Guide* 76, nos. 3–4 (2002): 243–69.

Stammer, D.W. "British Colonial Public Finance". *Social and Economic Studies* 16, no. 2 (1967): 191–205.

Thomas, C.Y. "Monetary and Financial Arrangements in a Development Monetary Economy". *New World Quarterly*. Kingston: Institute of Social and Economic Research, University of the West Indies, 1965.

Trouillot, Michel-Rolph. "Discourses of Rule and the Acknowledgment of the Peasantry in Dominica, 1838–1928". *American Ethnologist* 16, no. 4 (1989): 704–18.

Turner, Mary. "Chattel Slaves into Wage Slaves: A Jamaican Case Study". In *Labour in the Caribbean: From Emancipation to Independence*, edited by Malcolm Cross and Gad Heuman, 14–32. London: Macmillan, 1988.

Tyrell, Alex. "A House Divided against Itself: The British Abolitionists Revisited". *Journal of Caribbean History* 22, nos. 1–2 (1988): 42–67.

Wallace, Elisabeth. "The West Indies: Improbable Federation". *Canadian Journal of Economics and Political Science* 27, no. 4 (1961): 444–59.

Will, H.A. "Colonial Policy and Economic Development in the West Indies, 1895–1903". *Economic History Review* 23 (1970): 129–47.

Williams, Eric. "The British West Indian Slave Trade after Its Abolition in 1807". *Journal of Negro History* 27, no. 2 (1942): 17–91.

Wilmot, Swithin. " 'Females of Abandoned Character'? Women and Protest in Jamaica, 1838–65". In *Engendering History: Caribbean Women in Historical Perspective*, edited by Verene Shepherd, Bridget Brereton and Barbara Bailey, 279–95. Kingston: Ian Randle, 1995.

———. "Emancipation in Action: Workers and Wage Conflicts in Jamaica, 1838–1848". Paper presented at the Sixteenth Annual Conference of Caribbean Historians, Barbados, 1984.

———. "Emancipation in Action: Workers and Wage Conflict in Jamaica, 1838–1840". *Jamaica Journal* 19 (1986): 55–62.

———. "The Growth of Political Activity in Post-Emancipation Jamaica". In *Garvey: His Work and Impact*, edited by Rupert Lewis and Patrick Bryan, 39–46. Trenton, NJ: Africa World Press, 1991.

———. "From Falmouth to Morant Bay: Religion and Politics in Jamaica, 1838–1865". Paper presented at the Association of Caribbean Historians conference, Havana, Cuba, April 1985.

Witter, Michael. "Some Reflections on the Economic Development of Jamaica".In *Rethinking Development*, edited by Judith Wedderburn, 101–19. Kingston: Department of Economics, University of the West Indies, 1991.

Wright, G. "Economic Conditions in St Vincent, BWI". *Economic Geography* 5, no. 3 (1929): 236–59.

Illustration Credits

Grantley Adams: https://twitter.com/wcchen/status/1387322630173302784?lang=en

Jean-Bertrand Aristide: From LIBERIASTORY, CC BY-SA 4.0, via Wikimedia Commons, https://commons.wikimedia.org/wiki/File:President,_Jean-Bertrand _Aristide,_speaking_at_New_York%27s_John_F._Kennedy_airport,_says_he _remains_hopeful_of_returning_to_Haiti.jpg

George Beckford: https://www.stabroeknews.com/2011/06/26/features/%E2%80%98a -field-of-ideas%E2%80%99-the-new-world-group-the-caribbean-and-guyana-of-the -1960s/

Lloyd Best: https://lloydbest.institute/lloyd-best/

Maurice Bishop: http://caribbeanelections.com/knowledge/biography/bios/bishop _maurice.asp

Tony Blair: © European Union, 2010 / EU, photo: Pavel Golovkin, https://commons .wikimedia.org/wiki/File:Tony_Blair_2010_(cropped).jpg

Paul Bogle: leader of the 1865 freedom struggle in Jamaica, https://en.wikipedia.org /wiki/File:PaulBogleImage.jpg

Robert Bradshaw, first premier of St Kitts and Nevis: https://peace-post.com/saint -kitts-navis/

Gaston Browne: http://caribbeanelections.com/knowledge/biography/bios/browne _gaston.asp

Alexander Bustamante: http://caribbeanelections.com/knowledge/biography/bios /bustamante_alexander.asp

Thomas Buxton: Unknown, public domain, https://commons.wikimedia.org/wiki /File:Thomas_Fowell_Buxton_portrait.jpg

David Cameron: Tom Evans, OGL 3 (http://www.nationalarchives.gov.uk/doc /open-government-licence/version/3), via Wikimedia Commons, https://commons .wikimedia.org/wiki/File:David_cameron_announces_resignation_(cropped).jpg

Thomas Carlyle: Friedrich Bruckmann, public domain, via Wikimedia Commons, https://commons.wikimedia.org/wiki/File:Portrait_of_Thomas_Carlyle_(4674330) .jpg

Fidel Castro: Unknown [Mondadori Publishers], public domain, via Wikimedia Commons, https://commons.wikimedia.org/wiki/File:Fidel_Castro_1950s.jpg

Winston Churchill: Yousuf Karsh, Public domain, via Wikimedia Commons, https://commons.wikimedia.org/wiki/File:Sir_Winston_Churchill_-_19086236948.jpg

Thomas Clarkson: Carl Frederik von Breda, public domain, via Wikimedia Commons, https://commons.wikimedia.org/wiki/File:Thomas_Clarkson_by_Carl_Frederik_von_Breda.jpg

David Comissiong: http://caribbeanelections.com/knowledge/biography/bios/comissiong_david.asp

Jean Jacques Dessalines: Pôlehistoire, CC BY-SA 4.0 via Wikimedia Commons, https://commons.wikimedia.org/wiki/File:Dessalines_emperor_haiti.jpg

James Anthony Froude: National Portrait Gallery, public domain, via Wikimedia Commons, https://commons.wikimedia.org/wiki/File:James_Anthony_Froude_by_Sir_George_Reid.jpg

Mahatma Gandhi: http://philogalichet.fr/wp-content/uploads/2019/01/Gandhi_Photo-Alamy.jpg

Marcus Garvey: George Grantham Bain Collection, Library of Congress, digital iD cph.3a03567

Lloyd George: Bain News Service, public domain, via Wikimedia Commons, https://commons.wikimedia.org/wiki/File:LloydGeorge_(cropped).jpg

Lord Anthony Gifford: https://www.thejusticegap.com/justice-is-for-all-there-are-simple-truths-they-should-be-self-evident/

Norman Girvan: https://sta.uwi.edu/iir/normangirvanlibrary/who-norman-girvan

Ralph Gonsalves: Fernanda LeMarie – Cancillería del Ecuador, CC BY-SA 2.0 (https://creativecommons.org/licenses/by-sa/2.0), via Wikimedia Commons, https://commons.wikimedia.org/wiki/File:Ralph_Gonsalves_2013.jpg

Olivia Grange: https://jis.gov.jm/government/ministers/olivia-grange/

Walter Guinness (Lord Moyne): Bassano Ltd, public domain, via Wikimedia Commons, https://commons.wikimedia.org/wiki/File:Walter_Guinness,_1st_Baron_Moyne.png

Cheddi Jagan: Unknown, via Wikimedia Commons, https://commons.wikimedia.org/wiki/File:Cheddi_Jagan_Anefo.jpg

C.L.R. James: Unknown, public domain, via Wikimedia Commons, https://commons.wikimedia.org/wiki/File:CLR_James,_1938.jpg

W. Arthur Lewis: Courtesy of the Sir Arthur Lewis Institute for Social and Economic Research, University of the West Indies, Mona, Jamaica

Toussaint L'Ouverture: Langlays, CC BY-SA 4.0 via Wikimedia Commons, https://commons.wikimedia.org/wiki/File:Toussaint_Louverture_jpg.jpg

Kari Levitt: Aneel Karim, https://www.flickr.com/photos/theuwi/4398364892

Harold Macmillan: Cecil W. Stoughton, public domain, via Wikimedia Commons, https://commons.wikimedia.org/wiki/File:Harold_Macmillan_in_1961.jpg

Norman Manley: http://www.caribbeanelections.com/knowledge/biography/bios/manley_norman.asp

Michael Manley: https://jamaica.loopnews.com/content/phillips-accuses-holness-political-bad-mind-manley-criticism

Mia Mottley: UNCTAD, CC BY-SA 2.0 (https://creativecommons.org/licenses/by-sa/2.0), via Wikimedia Commons, https://commons.wikimedia.org/wiki/File:2019_Mia_Mottley_(cropped).jpg

Kwame Nkrumah: The National Archives UK, OGL v1.0 (http://NationalArchives.gov.uk/doc/open-government-licence/version/1/), via Wikimedia Commons, https://commons.wikimedia.org/wiki/File:The_National_Archives_UK_-_CO_1069-50-1.jpg

Lord Sydney Olivier: George Grantham Bain Collection (Library of Congress), public domain, via Wikimedia Commons, https://commons.wikimedia.org/wiki/File:Lord_Olivier_GGBain.jpg

Clement Payne: https://medium.com/@junior.griffiths/sir-grantley-herbert-adams-4f24093735ef

Queen Victoria: Alexander Bassano, public domain, via Wikimedia Commons, https://commons.wikimedia.org/wiki/File:Queen_Victoria_by_Bassano.jpg

Walter Rodney: https://www.walterrodneyfoundation.org/biography/

Verene Shepherd: Photograph by Aston Spaulding

Portia Simpson-Miller: http://www.caribbeanelections.com/knowledge/biography/bios/simpson_miller_portia.asp

Adam Smith: Scottish National Gallery, public domain, via Wikimedia Commons, https://commons.wikimedia.org/wiki/File:Adam_Smith_The_Muir_portrait.jpg

Clive Thomas: https://www.stabroeknews.com/2010/12/18/news/guyana/professor-thomas-honoured-at-annual-conference-of-monetary-studies/

Dudley Thompson: http://africansuntimes.com/2011/10/a-smashingly-successful-stratospheric-meeting-of-african-diaspora-leaders-in-new-york/

Eric Williams: Joop van Bilsen / Anefo, CC0 via Wikimedia Commons, https://commons.wikimedia.org/wiki/File:Eric_Williams_(cropped).jpg

Henry Sylvester Williams: Ernest Herbert Mills, Public domain, via Wikimedia Commons, https://commons.wikimedia.org/wiki/File:S._Williams_1905.png

Index

Pages in *italics* represent tables

CPSIA information can be obtained
at www.ICGtesting.com
Printed in the USA
LVHW030113020322
712334LV00004B/386